Developing a Learning Culture in
Professional Education

SRHE and Open University Press Imprint
General Editor: Heather Eggins

Developing Learning in Professional Education

Partnerships for Practice

Imogen Taylor

The Society for Research into Higher Education
& Open University Press

Published by SRHE and
Open University Press
Celtic Court
22 Ballmoor
Buckingham
MK18 1XW

and 1900 Frost Road, Suite 101
Bristol, PA 19007, USA

First published 1997

A catalogue record of this book is available from the British Library

ISBN 0 335 19497 4 (pb)   0 335 19498 2 (hb)

Library of Congress Cataloging-in-Publication Data
Taylor, Imogen.
    Developing learning in professional education : partnerships for practice /
Imogen Taylor.
        p.   cm.
    Includes bibliographical references (p.) and index.
    ISBN 0-335-19498-2 (hc). — ISBN 0-335-19497-4 (pbk.)
    1. Professional education—Great Britain. 2. Independent study—
Great Britain. 3. Open learning—Great Britain. I. Title.
LC1059. T34 1997
378'.013—dc21

                                                        97–12125
                                                        CIP

Typeset by Graphicraft Typesetters Limited. Hong Kong
Printed and bound in Great Britain by
Marston Lindsay Ross International Ltd,
Oxfordshire

For Roger, Ben and Nick

Contents

Acknowledgements

My thanks go first and foremost to my husband, Roger and my sons, Ben and Nick, for their unfailing support in writing this book. Without their love and understanding, and their practical help on all those occasions when I was unavailable, this book could not have been completed.

I would also like to thank two people who have mentored me in recent years. First, Phyllida Parsloe for her wisdom, and for her belief in me which sustained me through the research on which much of this book is based, and then through all the stages of writing. Second, David Boud for his leadership in adult learning, and his infinite capacity to give direct, specific and sensitive feedback, of the kind he advocates in his work.

I also want to acknowledge my social work colleagues in the School for Policy Studies at Bristol University. It is their interest in professional education, their implementation of an innovative approach to teaching and learning, and their enthusiasm for evaluating the process and outcome which initially led me to Bristol University, and then engaged me in very productive collegial relationships. In particular, I am grateful to Hilary Burgess as this book has benefited greatly from our friendship, collaboration and many discussions about adult learning. I am also grateful to Bristol colleagues from other professions, notably Patricia Broadfoot in Education, and Max Bachmann in Social Medicine, for their invaluable feedback on an early draft of this book.

It is important to thank the Halley-Stewart Trust for funding the research which informs much of my thinking in this book.

Finally, I want to thank the Bristol students who participated in the research and whose voices are heard throughout this book. Without them, it would not have been possible.

Part 1

Setting the Scene

1

Introduction

We are experiencing rapid and far-reaching change in higher education today, which presents both a challenge and an opportunity to educators to rethink approaches to teaching and learning. Professional educators in particular are 'presented with a complex pattern of pressures of demand, supply and quality in designing, delivering and managing professional education' (Watson, 1992: 7). This picture is in part the result of a massive expansion of claimants to professionalism with an associated increase in professional education and training courses, and in the number of students and staff, trainers and trainees, this represents. Shifting professional boundaries and the resulting emergence of non-traditional professions further contribute to the expansion of claimants to professionalism, and to the development of new kinds of professional education courses. Finally, the range and number of voices attempting to influence and control the quality and direction of professional education from both inside and outside the profession is increasing. This situation can be conceptualized as a crisis in professional education, with educators having to make difficult choices about competing priorities, and to resist being buffeted in a storm of conflicting demands.

Surprisingly, the literature about professional education has not kept abreast of these developments. We now have a considerable literature about the nature of the professions and professionalization. There is also a great deal written about education and training for specific professions. Furthermore, the fields of adult and higher education have become a subject for study in themselves to the point that, as Barnett (1990) suggests, the professionalization of the higher education curriculum probably represents the biggest, and largely unrecognized, shift in British higher education over the past thirty years. Yet, with a few exceptions (Jarvis, 1983; Eraut, 1992, 1994), there has been comparatively little written about professional education as a field of study distinct from higher education.

Professional education is distinctively different than higher education primarily because of its dynamic relationship with the professions, and more recently with employers and government. These forces both shape course structures and management, as well as curriculum content and delivery. Historically, education and training have played a central role in the professionalizing process and in controlling entry to the professions (Hugman, 1991). Today, as will be seen in the next chapter, the range of stakeholders in professional education has expanded, and the development, validation and accreditation of professional courses are subject to diverse and powerful influences. Professional education is also distinctively different because the curriculum addresses knowledge for and about practice and is delivered both in the context of the university and the field of professional practice. Furthermore, compared to many other students in higher education, students in professional education are distinguished by their motivation to study for a very specific purpose which will have a direct influence on the rest of their working lives. This feature, combined with the fact that professional education often attracts mature students, means that the latter are more likely to give voice as 'consumers' than the young undergraduate straight from school.

It is intriguing to speculate about why professional education has not significantly developed as a distinct focus of study, and why some of the key differences between professional and higher education have not been adequately explored in the literature. Is it possible that there has been a mutual benefit in focusing on similarity rather than recognising difference? Traditionally, as fields of 'applied' rather than 'pure' knowledge, professional courses are accorded secondary status in the old universities. Furthermore, within the framework of the wider university, the differences between professional and higher education undoubtedly generate organizational tensions. Has professional education been too aware of the sensibilities of the host setting to assert its difference? Certainly with the development of a knowledge base as a pre-condition to becoming a profession, the attention of each field of professional education has tended to be exclusively based on the development of its specific field of knowledge. One result of these dynamics is that the distinctive art and science of professional education has largely been ignored.

As professional educators we share common interests and dilemmas, regardless of our particular profession. In particular, educators for the 'interpersonal professions', defined by Ellis (1992) as those professions such as health care, teaching, social work, law, theology and management, who work predominantly through face-to-face interaction with service users, clients, patients, pupils or students, are all concerned with a number of crucial questions. How can students prepare for practice in a rapidly changing postmodern world where little is certain or predictable and where the knowledge of today is likely to be defunct tomorrow? How can students prepare to meet increasing requirements for interprofessional practice and a trend towards shifting professional boundaries (Walby *et al.*, 1994)? How can courses balance the predominantly outcome-focused interests of employers and government, with an emphasis on reflective learning and practice (Schön, 1983)? How can courses proactively respond to market pressures rather than react to the loudest or most powerful voice? Given the picture of all encompassing change, how can students prepare for lifelong learning?

The purpose of this book is to examine the development of learning in professional education and to suggest that if as educators and trainers we share a coherent philosophy and purpose, not only will we more effectively prepare professionals for practice in the next century, we will also be better able to respond to the pressures on us.

The first certainty about the world students will be practising in is that it will be characterized by rapid change and unpredictability. It is therefore essential that students learn to be independent, self-directed or autonomous learners:

> In a static, unchanging society there may be less need for an emphasis on autonomous approaches than there is in one in which learners need to adapt to frequent change and need to learn new forms of knowledge and how to use that knowledge.
>
> (Boud, 1988: 25)

In this book, I plan to explore those adult learning concepts which support the development of independent learners and practitioners.

The second predictable feature of future practice and focus for this book is that it will require partnership by practitioners within or between professions, and students must learn to learn and practise collaboratively and interdependently. The complexity of postmodern society means that problems presented to practitioners and structures to respond to them require responses which go far beyond those traditional, rigid professional boundaries which led Becher to coin his very effective metaphor of 'tribes and territories' (1989). To quote from the General Medical Council:

> There is also a redistribution of the tasks undertaken by members of the various caring professions. The overlapping of skills and responsibilities, whilst not diminishing the distinctive role of the doctor, calls for mutual respect and understanding of roles and a capacity for teamwork.
>
> (1993: 4)

Sue Dowling and her colleagues (1996) take this a step further and suggest in their study of the changing division of labour between the professions of medicine and nursing, that specific strategies must be put into place to manage appropriately new roles emerging between professions, including strategies to reduce risk.

The increasing emphasis on partnership with 'consumers' of professional services requires another kind of collaboration. We can see today that tomorrow's consumers of professional practice are likely to be actively contributing to the planning, delivery and evaluation of professional education, and professionals must learn to move beyond making decisions in the interests of consumers, to working with them and for them. The theme of partnerships will be addressed throughout this book, and partnership with users of professional services is focused on in Chapter 11.

Boud (1988) suggests that self-directed learning includes elements of independence, dependence and interdependence and conceptualizes these positions as being on a continuum with the student beginning from a position of being dependent on the teacher and moving through independence to interdependence. However, this continuum is too linear for professional education or practice. A student of the professions must learn to operate effectively as a practitioner from all three positions as required, and this will in turn involve learning to recognize which position is required at any one time. Certainly an essential pre-condition of operating effectively inter-dependently and in partnership is first developing the ability to learn and practise independently and before going any further, it is important to examine the concept of independent learning.

What is independent learning?

Various terms are used interchangeably in the literature, including inde-pendent, autonomous or self-directed learning. The term used predomin-antly in this book is 'independent learning' because it is possible to operate with a degree of independence within a proscribed framework of profes-sional practice, whereas it is generally not possible to be fully self-directed or autonomous. Furthermore, neither of the latter terms satisfactorily link with the concept of interdependent learning. In this next section, I briefly highlight key themes from the literature about independent learning which will be developed further in later discussion in this book, and in doing so I use the term predominantly used by the theorists referred to.

Theory about independent learning emerges directly from the humanist tradition which became prominent initially in the USA with growth of the 'human potential' movement of the 1960s and early 1970s. Notable in the development of this tradition is the work of Carl Rogers and particularly his book, *Freedom to Learn* (1969). Rogers' thesis was that learners innately know what they need to know and given an appropriate environment will learn and grow. Although Rogers' work is probably more frequently recognized today for its influence on counselling and therapy than education, the links between learning and personal growth continue to be strong.

One of the most influential early adult learning theorists linked with the humanist tradition is Malcolm Knowles (1980; Knowles and associates, 1984). Of central relevance to professional education and this book is that Knowles proposed that adults learn best when they have responsibility for their learn-ing, when they use their initiative and insight and discover for themselves what they need to learn. In relation to teaching, Knowles and associates (1984) attributed the term 'andragogy' to describe the art and science of helping adults learn, as opposed to the traditional notion of 'pedagogy'. Knowles (1980) also emphasized the importance of the climate for adult learning, a point taken up more recently by Hammond and Collins (1991).

Another important theme which also developed in the 1980s, and is related to independence and interdependence, is that of empowerment education and practice. This theme initially emerged from the work of Paulo Freire (1981) on critical pedagogy and literacy. Freire's work was focused on the development of literacy as a means to social action, but is relevant to the discussion of independent learning in this book in its analysis of the respective power of teachers and learners. Freire derided the traditional banking system of education where the student is a blank slate waiting to be filled up by the expert teacher. He emphasized the importance to learning of the empowerment of learners and their liberation from the oppression of teachers. The notion of empowerment may also be linked with that of interdependence in that working collaboratively can result in empowerment of a group or collective (Mullender and Ward, 1991).

Linked with notions of learning as growth and development is the theme of student developmental readiness for independent learning. A number of theorists and researchers have explored this issue and propose explanatory frameworks for the development of self-directedness (Perry, 1970; Taylor, 1986). The work of Mary Belenky and her associates (1986) is significant because of their attempt to identify differences in developmental readiness for independent learning between men and women learners.

Some of the early work on independent learning is criticized by later theorists for its absence of discussion about critical reflection and analysis. The work of Jack Mezirow (1983, 1990) has been significant in emphasizing the importance of fostering critical reflection in learning. Similarly, Stephen Brookfield (1983; 1986) has contributed to the development of theory about critical reflection, in particular theory about facilitating critical self-directed learning.

The recent literature on independent learning has attempted to become more specific about a concept which in the early literature is quite vague and general. Phil Candy (1991) and David Boud (1988) clarify that self-directed learning refers both to a goal to which learners aspire and where teachers assist; and to an approach to educational practice, a way of conducting courses. Candy warns that it cannot be assumed that studying using self-directed methods results in the learner being self-directed. However, Boud suggests that if students have the opportunity to learn to be independent learners this is likely to be carried into practice:

> It is not likely that students who are dependent on their teachers are going to be as effective in the world of learning or subsequent employment as those who have developed strategies which enable them to find and use their own resources for learning. Similarly, if students are denied opportunities to participate in decision-making about their learning, they are less likely to develop the skills they need in order to plan and organise for life-long learning which depend on their decisions about their learning needs and activities.
>
> (Boud, 1988: 21–2)

Whereas, this point contains an irrefutable logic, there are few examples of it being empirically tested. In Chapter 10, a small exploratory study is described which indicates that professional education students who develop the ability to learn independently and interdependently do transfer these skills into practice.

When self-directed learning is defined as an approach to educational practice, Boud (1988) identifies the student taking responsibility for her/ his learning as its main characteristic. He suggests taking responsibility for learning might involve any or all of the following: identifying learning needs, setting goals, planning learning activities, finding resources for learning, using teachers as facilitators, engaging in self-assessment, deciding when learning is complete and reflecting on the learning process (Boud, 1988: 23). The development of process knowledge of this kind is one essential element of the development of professional knowledge, together with personal and process knowledge (Eraut, 1992).

Finally, a very pragmatic but influential argument has crept into the literature about independent learning. We are being forced to consider new learning strategies because of economic realities. Yet, as Gibbs and Jenkins (1992) point out, staff in higher education continue to teach and assess in ways compatible with high staff–student ratios, low course enrolment, a highly selected student group, and a high level of resources. 'If the traditional pattern had ever worked, it had done so only through being oiled by easy and frequent individual exchanges between teacher and student' (Gibbs and Jenkins, 1992: 38). Now that this tradition is breaking down, its inherent weaknesses are being exposed. Adult learning, and in particular independent learning strategies are looked to as a solution to the problem of shrinking resources. As such, independent learning risks becoming an 'unwitting accomplice' of educational change (Candy, 1991: 411). If it is introduced simply as a cost-cutting measure it seems likely that the strategies to develop and support the independent learner will not be fully conceptualized and integrated into professional education, they are instead an outcome of a political struggle rather than a positive choice for change in the interest of the learner and professional education.

What this book will cover

My focus in this book is an exploration of learning in professional education, looking particularly at developing the skills of independent and interdependent learning and practice. Such a discussion will also inevitably include discussion of dependent learning, or being directed by experts, a beginning point for all students and one to which they are temporarily likely to return in response to a new situation. Specifically, I will focus on the student experience of these dimensions of learning and, from the basis of this analysis, I will identify the features of the learning milieu which promote independent and interdependent learning and the barriers which inhibit it.

To illuminate my discussion, I draw on data from three years of research into student learning on a professional education course designed to encourage independent and interdependent learning. The course is known as 'Enquiry and Action Learning' (EAL) and is described in detail in Appendix 1. My research was an in-depth longitudinal study, beginning in 1990, of a cohort of students undertaking a two-year professional social work education course at Bristol University and their first year of newly qualified practice. For the sake of simplicity in ensuing discussion and to distinguish my research from that of other studies I will be referring to, the research subjects will be identified as the 'Bristol students' and the 'Bristol staff'.

The research strategy I adopted (Taylor, 1993) was that of illuminative evaluation, developed to evaluate educational innovation where the 'primary concern is with description and interpretation rather than measurement and prediction' (Parlett and Hamilton, 1972: 8). I adopted an action research role where respondents become 'both subjects and researchers' (Argyris and Schön, 1991: 6) and which led me initially to work collaboratively with course staff, the primary and immediate users of the research findings (Patton, 1986). Action research has learning value to participants who are encouraged to reflect and raise their consciousness (Reitsma-Street and Arnold, 1984: 230), and as an approach it was well suited to provide information usable for a course which was in a formative stage (Dehar *et al.*, 1993: 212). I also adopted a participant observer role which enables me in this book to draw on rich ethnographic examples of students and staff experience. My later appointment on the same course as a 'lecturer' enables me to engage actively in making the changes suggested by the research and by more recent developments.

In this book, I also draw on existing research into adult learning in a range of 'interpersonal professions', defined earlier as those professions such as health care, teaching, law, management, theology and social work who primarily work through face-to-face interactions (Ellis, 1992). It will be noted that practising interdependently is increasingly required by these professions. It is anticipated that discussion in this book will also be relevant to other professions, such as the built environment, where interestingly some of the earliest innovative methods of teaching and learning using adult learning principles were introduced in engineering courses in the United Kingdom (Cowan, 1988; Stephenson, 1988).

My focus here will be primarily on initial professional education, which I conceptualize as being on a continuum with continuing professional development (CPD). Jarvis suggests that one characteristic of being a professional is that s/he is 'one who continually seeks the mastery of the branch of learning upon which his (her) occupation is based, so that he (she) may offer a service to his (her) client' (1983: 27). This makes an assumption that graduates from professional courses are equipped by initial professional education for lifelong learning. Usher and Bryant identify the initial professional education stage as crucial to the development of lifelong learning:

If we want practitioners to be reflective, critical and self-directing in the world of practice then we must create conditions, through teaching, for them to be reflective, critical and self-directing in the world of the classroom.

(Usher and Bryant, 1987: 211)

In this book I will identify the patterns and behaviours established at the initial stage of professional education which appear to be positive indicators for lifelong learning.

In Chapter 2, on the basis that the social and political context is crucial to the shape and direction of professional education and practice, I begin by examining significant features of the context and climate of professional and higher education today. I introduce the framework of an uneasy partnership between the providers, sponsors and clients of professional education (Watson, 1992). I then introduce the notion of partnership between different elements of the professional education curriculum and discuss Eraut's framework for professional knowledge of personal, process and propositional knowledge (1992).

The following chapters are then divided into three broad sections which explore different aspects of professional education: beginning learning; the learning infrastructure; and, promising outcomes. In 'Beginning Learning', I examine in Chapter 3 the transitions involved in becoming a student on a professional education course, and discuss the importance of creating a climate for adult learning and preparing students for independent and interdependent learning. In Chapter 4, I discuss the significance in professional education of building on students pre-course experience and suggest that in professional education, personal and process knowledge must be given as much attention as propositional knowledge (Eraut, 1994).

In the following four chapters which comprise, 'The Learning Infrastructure', I discuss selected aspects of professional education and their relationship to supporting or inhibiting student-led learning. These include: learning with and from peers; the teacher as facilitator; problem-based learning as an approach which enhances students independence and interdependence; and, assessment in professional education.

In 'Promising Outcomes', I focus on three quite different outcomes of an approach to learning which enables independent and interdependent learning, all of which have significant implications for professional education in the future. I begin in Chapter 9 by discussing the experience of students who are often disadvantaged in traditional educational approaches by virtue of gender, race and class. In Chapter 10, I examine the experience of students in field placements and in their first year of newly qualified practice. Finally, in Chapter 11, I anticipate the future and look at partnership in professional education with the users of professional services, a group of stakeholders who I suggest in the next chapter will have an increasingly significant role to play in the delivery of both professional education and practice.

2
Uneasy Partnerships?

The adult learning literature is noteworthy for its tendency to omit discussion of the social, political and economic context. This gives it limited applicability to professional education. Whereas professional education has traditionally had a more permeable boundary than higher education and has had to be more responsive to the macro context, in recent years the latter has become particularly significant to the shape and direction of professional education. At best, the external influences of the context can be negotiated and take the form of a partnership between professional education and various agencies or stakeholders. At worst, professional education can be colonized and become the province of stakeholders whose agendas are dominated by short-term objectives and political considerations.

The theme of this chapter is partnerships. For partnerships to work effectively there needs to be clarity and agreement about who the partners are and what they bring. There also needs to be a balance of power in the relationship which is not to suggest that there must be equal power, but there must be clear and negotiated agreement about who holds what power and related responsibility. Partnership practice may seek to change power relationships where it is possible to have influence.

I begin the chapter by examining influences on higher and professional education at the macro level and explore the differing, and to some extent competing, models of education and the ideologies each espouse. I then identify the various stakeholders seeking a voice in professional education and discuss the possibilities for partnership each group presents. Finally, at a micro level, I look at a model of professional education (Eraut, 1992) which requires partnership between three distinct elements of a curriculum.

Facing a common challenge

One of the most significant challenges we are facing today are competing ideologies of the purpose of higher education. Jarvis (1993) is one of the few adult learning theorists who addresses in depth the influence of the social, political and economic context on education. He analyses the relationship between social policy and education and identifies four existing models of education which govern how it is approached. The market model with an emphasis on competition, efficiency and education as a commodity. The progressive liberalism model where education is viewed as enriching individuals. The welfare model where education is viewed as putting right structural injustices. And the social control model where education has become part of the political agenda of the New Right and policies redirect education away from individual needs to the demands of an industrial and commercial society.

The balance in western society today has shifted towards the merging of market and social control mechanisms, driven by the ideology of the New Right and producing an extremely powerful force for change in professional education and practice. Historically, the professions have been self-regulating but increasingly this is being challenged, particularly by governments concerned to reduce the power of professionals. In addition, employers are demanding responsiveness to market mechanisms and accountability to structures led by managers increasingly unlikely to come from the profession they manage. Employers, managers and professionals do not necessarily share the same values or priorities and this can result in difficult dilemmas. In the UK, one field of practice where this has become evident is in the relationship between Trust Hospital Executives and clinical staff. Here a central priority for the professional manager is balancing a budget with the inescapable consequence of having to ration treatment, which at times inevitably conflicts with the ethics of the clinician whose responsibility is to treat those in need. 'Public interest' further contributes to the tensions inherent in these different perspectives with an ever watchful media, adept at recognizing what is alleged to be incompetent, inefficient or unethical practice. One of the most worrying and retrogressive outcomes of a scenario of this kind is a trend towards defensive practice which may not be in the best interests of the patient.

Another factor which has contributed to the emphasis on education as a commodity to be delivered efficiently is the impact of years of economic restraint and cutback, experienced by educators and professionals as 'doing more for less'. Whereas this may have a longer history in education in the UK than some other countries, significant resource cutbacks have become a feature of professional and higher education throughout the developed western world. One result of this is the evolution of new approaches to teaching and learning reflected in the recent spate of publications for educators on topics such as how to maintain quality with reduced resources (Gibbs and Jenkins, 1992). The scenario of reduced resources is portrayed as certainly long term, if not permanent, with the golden days of small staff/ student ratios and infinite resources gone forever. 'Academics who have experienced the last two decades as a period of rapidly worsening staff-student ratios, are faced with the nigh certainty of that increase significantly accelerating' (Gibbs and Jenkins, 1992: 13). The problem of shrinking resources is compounded in professional education which relies on qualified practitioners to supervise field practice, yet these resources are similarly being squeezed and are increasingly unavailable for student learning.

The trend towards standardization is another outcome of the emphasis on education as a marketable commodity. This has spawned developments such as modularization, credit accumulation and transfer (CATs), accreditation of prior experience and learning (APEL), and, perhaps most significantly for professional education, the competence approach. Barnett suggests that 'operationalism' may be becoming a new unifying principle in education which is effectively being 'colonized by the state, with unifying agendas being urged onto the academic community' (1992: 7). In this scenario, an effective curriculum is one where individuals learn to act in an instrumental way on their environment. Whereas in professional education the 'technical rationality' model of knowledge (Schön, 1983) has always been pervasive, today it is being given a significant boost by government schemes such as National Vocational Qualifications (NVQs). The challenge for professional education is to be technically good enough and at the same time safeguard process skills and knowledge.

Linked with the moves towards competence and increasing specialization are the shifting boundaries of the professions (Walby *et al.*, 1994; Dowling *et al.*, 1996), and what appears to be a trend towards interprofessionalism, at least in the developing discourse of centres and courses. This is reflected in the development in universities of interprofessional or interdisciplinary centres such as a 'Centre for Health and Social Care' or 'Socio-Legal Centre' which imply a shift away from the traditional knowledge and occupational demarcation. Similarly, the development of new modularized degrees often cut across disciplinary boundaries. These changes reflect a response to the pressures from employers that traditional specialized knowledge and expertise, and professional demarcations must 'be deconstructed and recast in new frameworks and forms of knowledge and action' (Bines, 1992:127) to respond to changes in the wider society.

Another challenge common to both professional and higher education and one which at first sight appears to be in direct contrast to the discourse of competence, is the shift away from the conservative ideology of knowledge as being in the hands of the expert technocrat towards the development of the political ideological view of education as empowerment of the individual (Jarvis, 1993). Linked with this development, the discourse in relation to the concept of the client or patient, user or consumer is significantly changing, albeit more quickly in some professions than others. Such changes are enshrined in documents such as the Citizen's Charters and in recent far reaching legislative changes in the UK such as the Children Act (1989), the National Health Service and Community Care Act (1990), and the Education Act (1993). The discourse used in this legislation, and the accompanying guidelines which lay down practice and management principles for a range of professionals involved in implementation of the legislation, is permeated with a philosophy of partnership, consumerism and empowerment.

Finally, in ways we can only yet imagine, there is the impact on higher and professional education of the breaking down of European boundaries. It is increasingly apparent how professions across Europe have different traditions, for example some professions are more highly trained than their counterparts in other countries. Cross-country recognition of qualifications is central to the development of Europe as a community, and as a result the knowledge base of the professions is falling under close scrutiny (Eraut, 1992: 114). Staff and student exchange schemes in higher education, such as 'Erasmus', 'Socrates' and 'Tempus', are rapidly developing and one eventual result will surely be intra-European professional education.

Sponsors, providers and clients

There are a number of different stakeholders or interest groups seeking a voice in professional education and the extent of the influence of each group varies for different professions. Watson (1992) suggests the interest groups include sponsors (professions, government, employing agencies), providers (higher education institutions) and clients (students, consumers of professional services). If this triangular model of sponsors, providers and clients is closely examined for its usefulness as a concept, it emerges as appealing in its simplicity but deceptive in that it masks the existence of sub-groups who cannot be assumed to share common interests. There may indeed be more differences between some sub-groups who share a profession than between professions (Bines, 1992).

Included among sponsors are the professions represented by associations who establish entry and exit requirements and codes of practice, employers who are seeking suitably qualified entrants and are wielding increasing influence, and government in its financial support for professional education and training, and in its role as legislator and policy maker. Views of professional education by sub-groups may be quite different. For example, employers and government keen to promote NVQs may be seeking to train newly qualified practitioners ready to implement quite instrumental knowledge and skills, whereas professional bodies may assign more value to the knowledge and skills of reflective learning and critical analysis. This dichotomy is reflected in debates about the relative merits of education or training. Newly qualified workers have to learn to manage these contradictions.

Important differences also exist between professional bodies, as clearly identified for example in a comparative study of pharmacy, nursing and teacher education in the UK where the various professional bodies exercise quite different controls on the academic community (Barnett *et al.*, 1987). Pharmacy education is the most independent of external control as the Pharmaceutical Society exercises only moderate control and courses remain broadly within academic control. Degree courses in nursing are subject to relevant National Board control. In teacher education there is no professional regulating body as such, but in the absence of such a body it is more vulnerable to external influence by government who in 1996 announced plans for a National Curriculum for teacher training. Likewise, undergraduate medical education has been left to the medical schools but there are signs of change as reflected in recommendations by the General Medical Council about undergraduate medical education:

> We do not think it would be right to recommend the development of a 'national core curriculum' since this might promote undesirable rigidity and resistance to change. However, our recommendations presuppose a much greater degree of consensus on core content and required attainment than has been customary in the past.
>
> (1993: 9)

General Medical Council recommendations are significant because of the priority given to students taking greater responsibility for their own learning.

Within the provider group are deep-rooted differences between higher and professional education, an issue introduced in Chapter 1. Both have traditionally maintained an uneasy partnership, reflected in the paradigm of higher education being the 'host site' to professional education. Furthermore, the significance of a degree qualification varies across the professions (Barnett *et al.*, 1987), although this gap appears to be closing in the UK, most recently with nursing acquiring degree status. Professional education implies learning with an operational objective, whereas higher education emphasizes the intrinsic value of learning (Birch, 1988). Higher education gives priority to propositional knowledge, professional education also emphasizes the importance of personal and process knowledge (Eraut, 1992). These differences to some extent echo the education and training split between sponsors referred to earlier. Here, however, the perception by higher education providers is that the training shoe is on the professional educator's foot. These distinctions are closely linked to power and status, as knowledge is assigned high status, and skills assigned low status (Young, 1971).

Jarvis (1983) identifies some additional tensions in the relationship between professional and higher education in his analysis of how the teacher in the professions is confronted with a number of problems not shared by higher education teachers. Most notably, professional educators work within a contractual relationship with their higher education institution as well as with the professional accrediting body, and are accountable to both. This results in professional educators experiencing a constant dilemma about the competing priorities of teaching, research or practice.

An offshoot of the tensions between higher and professional education is the relationship of the contributory academic disciplines to those professional education courses which are broad based and select from a wide range of disciplines. The disciplines are concerned with propositional knowledge rather than personal or process knowledge, and negotiations for territory within the structure of a professional course are often hard fought for. Becher's (1989) enduring metaphor of the disciplines as 'academic tribes' each with their own set of intellectual values and their own patch of cognitive territory was mentioned in Chapter 1. Innovations such as problem-based learning increase the pressure on disciplines to move away from an exclusive departmentally based focus.

In some fields, practice is challenging established interprofessional bound-aries and a 'quiet revolution is occurring in the division of labour between the professions of medicine and nursing' (Dowling *et al.*, 1996: 121) with the scope of new roles and standards of practice which apply to them being unclear. Similarly, in the field of health and community care, 'care man-agement' may be a role filled by a range of professionals including social workers, nurses, occupational or physiotherapists. The focus may increas-ingly be on interprofessional learning between professions, which again challenges the department based contribution of traditional disciplines.

There are, however, significant mutual benefits which contribute to a part-nership between professional and higher education providers (Eraut, 1992). First, for professional education there is the benefit that the claim for a specialist knowledge base and establishing a degree entry route is validated by university recognition. Secondly, recruitment to professional education through the university system sustains the quality of the profession's intake. Higher education in turn benefits by the presence of professional depart-ments who support the institution's claim that they are preparing students for employment and contributing to society. Professional education students also contribute to the expansion of student numbers and to the strength of those individual disciplines who contribute to professional teaching. Last, but by no means least, students on professional courses generate a sub-stantial income for universities.

Finally, there are some fascinating and potentially far-reaching changes within the diverse group defined as 'clients'. Watson (1992) only includes students in this group, yet even this term is under challenge by the adult learning literature which uses the term 'learner' as opposed to 'student'. The implications are that both learners and educators are open to learning, and the term 'learner' allows for the possibility that professionals continue learning once qualified. In professional education it is suggested that the 'client' must include the recipient of a professional service, who is increas-ingly seen as having a direct role to play, not only in supervised field prac-tice but in the design and delivery of professional education in the classroom (Beresford and Croft, 1993; Beresford, 1994; Beresford and Trevillion, 1995; Hopton, 1994/95).

Discourse on the topic of 'clients' is varied, reflecting the confused and confusing perspectives on the issue of the receivers of service, and the power they hold. Whether a recipient of a professional service is a patient, client, purchaser, user, or consumer, tends to vary not only with the pro-fession being discussed and whether a fee changes hands, but also within different professions. Each term carries its own connotation. For example, a person who has been treated by mental health professionals may view her or himself as a 'patient' or a 'user', or perhaps as a 'psychiatric survivor'. The different discourse conveys an immediate message about the self-concept of the person concerned relative to mental health services, as well as the political perspective of the professional.

In this book, although the term 'learner' is preferred, for the sake of clarity it is used interchangeably with 'student', reflecting the reality that much of this book is written based on research into the experience of students who self-identify as such, and are perceived as students by the system. The term 'consumer' has come recently to higher education and reflects the influence of the market model rather than any substantive change in student status. The term 'consumer' or 'user' of a professional service is used in preference to 'client', while recognizing that there are problems with the terms. In the UK, the term 'user' more closely fits those who use a service where no money changes hands, but in North America it has connotations with drug user. Both 'consumer' and 'user' imply choice and power of a kind which may in reality not be present. However, I use the terms here as they have common currency across professions and, perhaps most important, are ones which the consumer her/himself may readily identify with.

As has been seen, different sub-groups inevitably have different interests and this presents a major challenge to partnership. Abrams and Bulmer (1984) suggest that there are four possible different forms of relationship between interest groups: colonization, conflict, confusion, and integration or partnership. 'Colonization' means one group invades or subordinates another; an approach illustrated earlier in relation to competences and professional education. It may be achieved by domination, such as the government ordering a review of a field of professional education with a view to introducing far-reaching change. Or, colonization may come about by appropriation. This is a somewhat more subtle strategy illustrated in the UK by the redrawing of employment boundaries currently being carried out in relation to NVQs.

'Conflict' may result from colonization. For example, the current attempt by the government to move teacher education out of higher education and into schools has resulted in conflict between the profession, the government, and higher and professional education. It is important in professional practice to view conflict as inevitable within and between professions and to address ways of approaching and resolving conflict rather than deny its existence.

'Confusion' may be the result of the coexistence of different values and organizational structures. The earlier discussion of the discourse of consumers, users, clients and patients is an example of this. Abrams and Bulmer suggest that 'given the nature of most of the alternatives, perhaps a more or less chronic entanglement with confusion is the best we can hope for?' (1984: 428).

There is, however, a fourth and preferable option of 'integration' or partnership where the different sectors can power share and deal on equal terms. The concept of 'partnership' is increasingly referred to in different professional contexts. It is a complex and intriguing notion which merits in depth discussion in its own right. For our purposes here, I suggest that as providers and professional educators we will be stronger and less vulnerable to 'colonization' if we collaborate and form alliances. Partnership collaboration can be viewed as value capture, where one organization takes resources from another, or value creation, where collaboration results in increased value produced (Haspelagh and Jemison, 1991). Our business is the education and training of professionals and the immediate challenge for professional educators is to create value by developing the profession of professional education to respond to the context and climate of change described earlier.

The nature of professional education

So far in this chapter the focus has been on partnerships in education at the macro level, setting the scene for later discussion which is primarily focused on the learning of the individual student in professional education. Before going further, it is essential to examine the nature of professional education which requires partnerships at another level, between students, between students and staff, between staff, and between different elements of the curriculum. Michael Eraut's (1992) analysis of the elements of professional education is described in some detail in this section as it provides a useful framework for later discussion. Building on the work of Schön (1983), who defines professional knowledge as including personal knowledge, tacit and process knowledge, and propositional knowledge, Eraut proposes a map of three different kinds of knowledge essential for professional education.

First, there is propositional knowledge which includes discipline based concepts, generalizations and practice principles which can be applied in professional action, and specific propositions about particular cases. Most discipline based knowledge is public, although some case material may be private. Propositional knowledge is the traditional focus of higher education, as it has also been in specific fields of professional education where the concern has been to develop the knowledge base seen as crucial to acceptance as a profession. However, the pace of change in postmodern society means that knowledge quickly becomes obsolete and new knowledge is developing all the time making the management of propositional knowledge increasingly difficult for both students and staff. Eraut also warns of the risk of providing the learner with propositional knowledge and encouraging her/him to uncritically accept ideas, as well as deny the learner the opportunity to gain practice in the appropriate selection of relevant knowledge.

The second kind of professional knowledge identified by Eraut is personal knowledge and the interpretation of experience. Much of this knowledge remains prepropositional at the impression level and the challenge of professional education is to bring the assumptions to the surface so they can be examined for their impact on professional practice. It is this area of knowledge which is likely to distinguish those professional education courses which are preparing students for interpersonal work, with students from other kinds of professional courses such as engineering where personal knowledge may have less direct bearing on practice.

Thirdly, Eraut identifies process knowledge, 'knowing how to conduct the various processes that contribute to professional action' (1992: 105). Eraut suggests that process knowledge of all kinds should be given high priority, while recognizing the contribution that propositional knowledge can make to learning. He identifies process knowledge as including five types of process and because of their relevance to professional education they are described in detail:

1. *Acquiring information*: the ability to select and implement appropriate methods of enquiry. Eraut refers here to the typology of Parker and Rubin (1966) who define three processes associated with enquiry: processes such as formulating questions and collecting evidence which lead to a particular body of knowledge; processes such as analysing, reorganizing and integrating, which allow the student to derive meaning from the body of knowledge; and, processes such as testing for useability and generalizing which enable the learner to make meaning from the knowledge;
2. *Skilled behaviour*: 'the complex sequence of actions which has become so routinised through practice and experience that it is performed almost automatically' (p. 109);
3. *Deliberative processes*: those activities such as 'planning, problem-solving, analysing, evaluating, and decision making' (p. 110) which require combinations of propositional knowledge, situational knowledge and professional judgement;
4. *Giving information*: the ability to ascertain what is needed, and be able to communicate in a way which can be clearly understood;
5. *Controlling one's own behaviour*: the evaluation of what the professional is thinking and doing and includes self-knowledge and self-management. This type of process knowledge clearly links with personal knowledge and a crucial feature is the ability to seek and receive feedback.

The interweaving of propositional, process and personal knowledge is one of the ongoing themes of this book, examining how each area of knowledge may complement or contradict each other, and what the implications are for students and staff. Different professions will vary in the respective balance accorded to propositional, personal and process knowledge. The comparative study of nursing, pharmacy and teaching courses mentioned earlier illustrates some of these differences (Barnett *et al.*, 1987). For example, it was found that pharmacy focused predominantly on the acquisition of formal knowledge and theoretical understanding (propositional knowledge), whereas teaching and nursing education saw it as crucial that theoretical understanding should critically inform practice (process knowledge). In turn, the different emphases have a number of related outcomes. For example, there were differences in the kinds of journal to which staff contributed and subscribed. Pharmacy staff favoured journals focused on the sciences rather than the profession, whereas nursing and teaching staff focused on professional journals, as well as those which were more academic.

Eraut does not specifically develop concepts of independent or inter-dependent learning but obvious links can be inferred from his analysis. His discussion of personal and process knowledge includes concepts such as 'self-knowledge' and 'self-management'. His discussion of process know-ledge implies collaboration and interdependence and echoes some of the processes identified by Boud (1988) in his description of what students taking responsibility for their learning might involve. These links will be explored further in later chapters. The links between Eraut's framework of professional knowledge and the processes of enabling independent and interdependent learning will be discussed in more detail in the following chapters.

Setting the scene

I have suggested that professional education is in crisis as educators are having to make difficult choices about priorities and withstand a multitude of conflicting and competing pressures. I have also suggested that if we agree that our priorities are to develop approaches to teaching and learn-ing which prepare students for independent and interdependent practice, this not only provides us with a coherent philosophy and purpose, it also equips us to respond collaboratively and collectively to the pressures which we are facing from stakeholders.

As educators we are not independent and we must work interdependently and in partnership with various stakeholders who have interests in the design, delivery and outcome of professional education. For partnership to be effect-ive such participation must be active and negotiated. As mentioned earlier, students are also stakeholders in education and this brings me to a crucial aspect of partnership which is listening to the various voices concerned. In Part 2 of this book, I move from a focus on the macro context to the micro level of student learning, listening to students' experience of an approach to active learning which is designed to encourage independence and interdependence. Active participation is an essential element in part-nership practice.

Part 2

Beginning Learning

3

Transitions: Traditional Expectations and Non-traditional Courses

All of us working in professional education will be aware of the major life transition which entering professional education represents for students, regardless of their education, their experience prior to the course, or the nature of the course they are embarking on. Many of us will vividly remember the shock of this transition in our own professional education with all the related feelings of excitement and anxiety. For some students, moving into professional education is also concurrent with leaving home and moving into higher education, a major transition from dependence on the family unit into independence and adulthood (Erikson, 1968).

If Eraut's (1994) framework for professional knowledge is accepted, instead of the predominant focus of traditional courses on propositional knowledge, entry into education for the interpersonal professions carries additional expectations. As seen in the last chapter, Eraut proposes that learning is required at the levels of personal and process knowledge, as well as propositional knowledge. Students are required to become aware of the way they see themselves and others, and be open to revising those assumptions and perceptions if they are not consistent with professional knowledge and values. For students socialized only to propositional learning, integrating process and personal knowledge can be disconcertingly unpredictable and difficult, and they may put considerable energy into remaining focused on the propositional level.

Entry into a professional education course which expects independent and interdependent learning, adds a further dimension to the transition. Marilyn Taylor's research is illuminating on the 'discontinuity and disconfirmation' (1986: 70) of this transition,

Learning to be self-directed in the classroom involves reorientation of an entire set of assumptions about the reality and ways of relating to others, including the instructor. There is a change in how self, others, authority and knowledge are understood.

(Taylor, 1986: 69)

The revision of assumptions about learning in relation to 'self, others, authority and knowledge' (Taylor, 1986: 69) can be an overwhelming experience.

This chapter explores the impact on students of entering such a professional education course and identifies some strategies which appear to be effective in helping students manage the transition. The focus is on the initial transition into professional education, which is not to deny that other later transition points are undoubtedly also significant, including the transitions into supervised field placement and then back into the university based course, and finally the transition into qualified practice. This latter transition will be discussed in Chapter 10.

Why should educators be concerned about student transitions?

As educators we have an ethical if not a contractual obligation to help students learn effectively. There is at times a tendency to think our role ends once we have provided students with what we, and/or the governing professional bodies, think they should know. The risk is that the didactic approach may become more pervasive as class sizes increase, curriculums become overloaded and dominated by rapidly expanding propositional knowledge or lists of competences students are expected to learn, and educators become distracted by demands other than those of teaching. Educators on a course which expects independent and interdependent learning have a responsibility to help students make a particular kind of transition, 'to force learners into a self-directed or learner controlled mode for which they may feel unprepared seems, to me, every bit as unethical as denying freedom when it is demanded' (Candy, 1987: 163).

A pragmatic reason to help students manage the transition is that the degree of student anxiety about change may interfere with or block learning, for the individual student and for others in the group. One of Carl Rogers' (1969) principles of learning is that when the threat to the self is low, learning can proceed. Perry (1970) found that when students felt their ideas were under threat they reverted to an earlier stage of intellectual development. Research has demonstrated that when anxiety is high, students approach study in a surface-processing way (Fransson, 1977; cited in Gibbs, 1981: 89).

Anderson *et al.* (1996) in their discussion of learning contracts suggest that although students may know about the course and be excited about it, they may still have difficulties as they begin to apply their ideas to formal work. Many of the Bristol students were at best uncomfortable and at worst acutely anxious early in the first term. As a student said as she reflected back at the end of the first term,

If I'm anxious I'm not putting much effort into it because I'm tied up with my own anxiety. If I'm comfortable, I can thrash out a difference of opinion. I can't do this if I'm uncomfortable.

Some students emotionally withdraw full of self-doubt and anxiety, while others become angry and attacking. Feeling overwhelmed by the perceived expectations of the system can provoke very strong reactions without students fully understanding what is causing them (Salzberger-Wittenberg *et al.*, 1983).

If steps are taken to address such anxiety early in the course, as suggested by the student quoted earlier, this may alleviate future difficulties. There is a particular pressure to manage this in the limited and fixed time typically available on professional education courses, when the timetable for completion of a course is often determined by external criteria which do not take into consideration individual differences in student learning pace. Generally, allowances are not made for blocks to learning, unless under the aegis of illness and medical certificates.

The final argument in favour of helping students manage transitions is that on entering professional education, student motivation to succeed is high. Students have often made a considerable economic, social, intellectual and emotional investment in order to begin a professional course. They are likely to have been working towards this point for a long time, often over many years. It is important for educators to maximize the potential of building on such motivation and not allow it to become undermined and demoralized by a process which can become overwhelming if not contained and managed.

The orientation of students to self-directed learning

It was the Bristol students who first drew my attention to the need for a process of 'orientation'. In a focus group discussion held for research purposes at the end of the course there was consensus with this student's view, 'I see it (orientation) as being given the tools to do the job . . . a good induction would help save time and eliminate some of the pressure in the first term.' The term 'orientation' is used here to denote a process in which the student engages, facilitated by planned learning opportunities, which 'prepares the learner for an approach to learning which may be new to her/him and which may involve changes to established habits and expectations of learning' (Taylor and Burgess, 1995: 87). The term 'orientation' is used because it implies a dynamic process, rather than 'induction' which denotes a fixed, time-limited experience and a process which is 'done to' the student by the expert.

In an earlier paper written with my colleague Hilary Burgess (Taylor and Burgess, 1995), we noted that surprisingly little attention has been paid in the adult learning literature to specifically helping students manage the transition from a conventional approach to teaching and learning, to an approach which is designed to build independence. (Since then Anderson *et al.* (1996) have addressed the issue of orienting students to learning contracts.) We speculated that the relative omission of discussion of orientation is because the notions of independence and growth may be viewed as antithetical to that of 'orientation' which involves an 'expert' leading and guiding the process of student learning.

The literature on self-directed learning which focuses on the growth and development of the learner appears to preclude guidance by others in the process of learning. Humanists, such as Carl Rogers, have been central in the development of self-directed learning and their philosophy is that learners will realize their own potential, given appropriate opportunities. There is a further suggestion in this literature that self-directed learning is a 'natural way of learning' (Knowles and associates, 1984: 420), with the implication that any process introduced to change this would be unnatural and therefore unnecessary.

More recently, adult learning literature has focused on what the student needs to learn to become an independent learner. Engel proposes that,

> Adapting to, and participating in change and self-directed learning are composite competences. Each will require the development of a number of component competences, such as the skills of communication, critical reasoning, a logical and analytical approach to problems, reasoned decision-making and self-evaluation.
>
> (Engel, 1991: 24)

However, Engel is not explicit about whether or how students should be helped to develop these competences, some of which may be quite unfamiliar to students socialized in traditional education.

The studies which have most meaning and relevance for orientation and the Bristol students are those which focus on student readiness for learning and stages of development in learning, and which address the implications for teaching staff. I will briefly describe the studies here as I will refer back to them in my discussion of the Bristol findings.

Based on experience at Harvard in running study skills courses and in student counselling, Perry (1970) constructed a framework for understanding students' stages of readiness for self-directed learning. In total he identified nine stages of development which fall into three broad areas. Student A listens for the lecturer to state what theory must be learnt and waits for the correct answer, assuming there is only one answer to a problem. Student B makes the same general assumptions but with an elaboration that lecturers do not always provide answers and may present problems and procedures. Student C assumes that an answer can only be right in light of its context or frame of reference, and that different theories and perspectives may be legitimate. The important implication of this study is that students will be at very different stages of readiness for independent learning. Perry initially responded to these differences by offering study skills courses, and then later moved towards individual study counselling based on the student's stage of development. These responses assume a highly resourced environment of a kind which is not available to most educators today.

Perry's study was based on male students only. An interesting study, also in the United States, of the developmental readiness of women for self-directed learning was undertaken by Belenky and her colleagues (1986). They proposed five categories of epistemological development, and the first two categories are relevant for this chapter. The first category is 'silence, a position where women experience themselves as mindless and voiceless and subject to the external whims of authority'. The second category is 'received knowledge, a perspective from which women conceive of themselves as capable of receiving, even reproducing, knowledge from the all-knowing external authorities but not capable of creating knowledge on their own' (p. 15). Clearly for women students in these two categories, a professional education course which does not address these stages of development, and assumes students all have the same starting point is highly problematic.

Marilyn Taylor's research in Canada specifically focused on the readiness for self-directed learning of a group of mature students who had extensive training, experience and education in the professions prior to entering a graduate course which was designed to promote capability and understanding in helping other adults learn (1986: 56). Taylor found that the learners moved through four distinct phases. The first phase was 'disconfirmation' where there was a major discrepancy between expectations and experience, characterized by a process of 'disorientation' accompanied by a crisis of confidence and withdrawal from persons associated with the confusion. The second phase was 'naming the problem' without blaming self or others, characterized by a process of individual and collaborative exploration. The third phase was 'reflection', characterized by a process of reorientation and a new approach to the learning task. The final phase was 'sharing the discovery', testing out the new understanding and acquiring a new perspective. Taylor suggests that her findings imply a greater level of demand on the educational environment as well as the learner than is implied by the literature on self-direction. She goes on to suggest that 'the capabilities of instructors promoting self-direction include special social and psychological understanding and expertise' (1986: 70). However, Taylor is not specific about the kinds of strategies which might be employed by instructors.

The other research which has explanatory value in examining the transition of Bristol students and the impact of expectations of interdependent learning is the literature about learning in groups and the more general literature about group work. This literature (Abercrombie, 1983; Heron, 1989; Brown, 1992; Jaques, 1992) discusses the theme of stages of group development. In particular, these authors identify the central role of the facilitator early in the development of the group. Initially, the facilitator helps members form a group, learn how to work together, and use the group and each other as resources. As the group develops the facilitator moves towards a more peripheral role.

In those professional education courses which have set out to encourage independent and interdependent learning, two broadly different practices have emerged to help students acquire the necessary skills. The different practices reflect a debate about whether students can learn to develop skills of independent and interdependent learning separately from the actual curriculum content of the course. For example, in medical education, Health Sciences at McMaster University adopted a 'learn by doing approach' (Neufeld and Barrows, 1974). Whereas at Newcastle University in Australia, a large part of their first term is allocated to introducing students to the educational approach (Engel and Clarke, 1979). The Bristol course, as will be seen, initially began closer to the McMaster end of the continuum but, based on findings from the research, subsequently has focused more attention on helping students become familiar with the expectations of the approach and acquire initial competence with the tools for learning early in the first term.

The need for orientation and the Bristol students

As mentioned earlier, one of the first areas actively drawn to my attention by students was the need to help them begin to learn how to learn independently and interdependently. To provide a framework for discussion I am building on the work of Marilyn Taylor (1986) who found that learning for self-direction required change in four particular areas: a change in students' views of their own responsibility for learning; a change in their views of knowledge; a change in the role of others in learning; and a change in the views of experts. This framework is useful because, although I did not set out to replicate Taylor's study, her findings are very similar to my own.

Initial view of their own responsibility for learning

There was a major discrepancy between the expectations of students about the course, what it would be like, how they envisaged learning, and their actual experience when they arrived. The realization of this in the first days and weeks of the course resulted in considerable disorientation and confusion, particularly for some students. This comment by a woman student as she looked back at the beginning of the course typified that of many of her peers:

> I think the thing that shocked me most was that I knew that EAL meant you got out and did things yourself, but I was expecting a lot more even so, than happened. Not being a very structured person . . . I

actually wanted someone to point me in the right direction rather than say go out and find out for yourself . . . I felt as if I was in the sea really and the people around me were also floating in the sea and no-one really knew what we were doing.

Even though this student had some intellectual understanding that independent learning meant 'you got out and did things yourself', the reality of the process came as a 'shock', confirming the view of Anderson and his colleagues (1996) that intellectual preparation, or telling students what to expect is not enough. The use of a metaphor involving water was also used by other students describing their experience early in the course. This may be linked to what Taylor talks about as 'the absence of an adequate conceptual map for what one is experiencing' (1986: 60), which results in a feeling of being directionless and lost, drifting or being buffeted around by external forces.

Another student focused on the intense feelings of anxiety associated with taking responsibility for learning:

All the decisions you have to make yourself as a student. Whereas in another model of learning the staff would make it for you, it's taking responsibility which is a good thing but it's a bit frightening at times.

In the context of a small group approach to learning, such fears are likely to be communicated to other students and there is a risk of escalation unless the facilitator actively intervenes and helps group members contain their anxieties.

The process of disorientation and anxiety took different forms for different students. For some the crucial issue was the fear of not knowing what direction to take. For others, an immediate anxiety was managing unscheduled time available on the timetable for independent and group study. As this woman student said,

When you haven't got a meeting or a lecture, to actually say, right well I'm going off to the library or I'm off to the Resource Room, that's my struggle. I have to write my own timetable and stick to it.

For students where the demands of their caring responsibilities or the effects of student poverty are ever present, having the 'freedom' to determine their own priorities in these circumstances was very difficult. The temptation to opt for the short-term relief of allocating time designated for study to deal with immediate practical problems was too much for some students to withstand, in spite of anxieties about long-term consequences.

Initial student view of the expert

Students expectations of dependence on the expert were also challenged in the first few days and weeks of the course. Students were not only asked to confront their view of the expert as having the answers, but additionally to see themselves and each other as having expertise. For some students this came as another kind of shock:

> She [the facilitator] was asked a question and she didn't give the answer although I'm sure she knew it. She threw it back to us. It was frightening – we might go off on the wrong track and waste time.

The risk of going 'off on the wrong track' reflects the lack of self-confidence in identifying the right track, a dynamic also identified by Taylor (1986).

Some students were particularly insistent that answers must be provided by the experts. One student talked about the experience early in the course of 'clutching at straws' provided by staff, and went on to talk about the anxiety of, 'I don't know when I've made mistakes and I don't know when I've got it wrong.' This is alarming for students used to the certainty of right and wrong answers identified by experts. Such students would fall into the category of an early stage of learning development (Belenky *et al.*, 1986; Perry, 1970). One response was to make angry accusations that staff were playing games with them, withholding information which they could share. As Taylor reports, at this stage 'aggravation and hostility are expressed towards others particularly the instructor' (1986: 61). This is powerful pressure for the facilitator to withstand. Not only is it difficult to be on the receiving end of student anger and to risk further hostility by not providing answers and direction, it is also tempting to be seduced into the role of expert.

Initial view of others

Being placed immediately in a structure which expects students to learn interdependently was also very anxiety provoking. Students met in the groups they would be working with for the first term on the first day of the course and inevitably had questions or concerns about working together:

> It was difficult and it was quite frightening . . . I wasn't used to being in groups and at the time I found it very difficult to speak out in groups and although I knew that was what we were going to be doing the reality is different. And I think there was also the feeling that you don't know other people yet you are relying on them to do the work with you.

Once again, this student voices the theme that although she 'knew' they were going to be learning in groups, 'the reality was different'. It was frightening to realize that in this course on which so much depended, the student was going to be reliant on unknown entities of fellow students. Anxieties were about whether other students were reliable enough, and whether they were a valid source of knowledge.

Linked with concern about others, there was also considerable reluctance to view themselves as being good enough providers of knowledge to other students. As this student said early in the first term during a discussion of her concerns about her perceived 'Lack of confidence and ability to give that feedback. I can look at a piece of work and say "that's very good", but what else can I say?'

One resulting pattern, also identified by Taylor (1986), was that of psychological withdrawal in the group. A number of women students at Bristol reflected back on their tendency early in the course to adopt a passive observer stance rather than risk actively participating. This response echoes the finding of Belenky and her colleagues (1986) that women students in the early stages of development as learners see themselves only as capable of receiving knowledge, not of creating it.

The degree of anxiety or enthusiasm about learning with others appeared at least in part to be related to having a pre-course positive experience of working or learning groups. Women students were more likely than men to have had pre-course experience of formal and informal groups. In contrast to those women students who assumed a passive observer role, there were others who took a leadership role from early in the course, and for whom their skills in leading the group appeared to give them confidence in finding their voice.

Initial view of knowledge

There were two identifiable areas of anxiety for students in their initial view of knowledge. First, there was the shift in understanding for many students about what constitutes knowledge. The curriculum required students to move away from viewing knowledge as solely propositional, to including process and personal knowledge (Eraut, 1994). A woman student reflected on her surprise when she fully realized the emphasis on personal and process learning and appreciated the risks involved:

> I hadn't realized how much of myself I was actually going to have to reveal being in a group all the time and I think you have to reveal something for the group to actually work.

Concerns were regularly raised about there being too much emphasis on process learning: 'Too much time is spent on process rather than getting down to the nitty gritty of what you need to know.' There was some evidence that male students particularly were concerned to focus on propositional knowledge and were impatient with time being spent on process and personal knowledge. The pressure on staff builds to provide pre-packaged propositional knowledge in the form of handouts.

The other source of anxiety in relation to knowledge was in learning to view knowledge as different perspectives on an issue, rather than viewing it as the right answer to a question. This links to the importance of students developing a critically reflective approach to knowledge. It was apparent that the skill of critical reflection tended to be more developed among those students with undergraduate training, whereas non-graduates tended early in the course to view knowledge delivered by experts as a given which one did not question. The encouragement in the first term of learning activities such as debates enabled students to begin to deconstruct knowledge and view it as different perspectives on an issue.

Orientation in the early stages of EAL

When EAL was initially implemented, course planners had integrated some attempts to help students familiarize themselves with the approach to learning and with each other. These were primarily built into the first few days of the course when the focus was on building a cooperative learning climate (Knowles and associates, 1984; Hammond and Collins, 1991). At this time a central objective was for students to acquire a sense of the total group of 80 students, in addition to the small study group they would be working in for the term. Students participated in collaborative 'games' and activities designed to help them begin to get to know each other.

In study groups, the focus of activity in the first study unit was on getting to know the social work department, the university and the city. Equally important to the group at this early stage of development (Jaques, 1992) was the process of building trust to enable students to begin to address their anxieties about learning from others (Taylor, 1986). The facilitator took a central guiding role and a key strategy was the early drawing up of 'ground rules' by each group. These rules were in effect an initial contract for working together and typically ranged from agreement about practical issues such as the timing of a coffee break, to complex issues such as confidentiality and guidelines about giving each other feedback.

The other important process to occur at an early stage was to enable students to begin to identify and share with each other the knowledge, skills and values which they brought to the course. This directly addressed students' traditional view of knowledge as external, and encouraged them to begin to view themselves and each other as having expertise, and to challenge their view of expertise being held only by staff (Taylor, 1986). This was a powerful exercise as inevitably among a group of mature students, where having some social work related experience, either paid or voluntary, was essential to being accepted on the course, there emerged a considerable range of relevant personal and professional expertise. One effect of this activity was to ensure that all group members gave voice to their experience (Belenky *et al.*, 1986), albeit for some students this was brief and tentative, and followed by withdrawal.

Another key feature of the first term, specifically designed to increase students feelings of safety, was that there was no requirement for summative assessed work. The intent was for students to be able to engage in the process of learning, without learning being driven by assessment requirements (Heron, 1988). In contrast, there was considerable emphasis on formative assessment, including self-assessment, feedback from peers and from the facilitator.

However, as described above through student voices, these strategies designed to encourage students to begin to develop the skills for independent and interdependent learning were not enough. The first cohort of students were vocal about the need for more attention to helping them develop such skills early in the course. They prioritized three areas for orientation: the specific skills of independent learning; knowing how to learn interdependently; and knowing how to use the facilitator.

Additional orientation strategies

The request from students for more attention early in the course to helping them develop their skills as independent and interdependent learners made eminent sense to a staff group who were also engaged in their own process of orientation (see Chapter 6). Staff readily agreed to devote more time in the first unit to introducing students to these skills. The alternative option adopted by Perry (1970) of offering individual study counselling was clearly unrealistic in the existing economic climate, and arguably unnecessary anyway. The other option of developing learning skills manuals for use by individual students has been developed by distance learning courses, but was not appropriate to a course which also emphasized interdependent learning.

At the propositional level, one strategy was to attempt to increase students knowledge and understanding of independent and interdependent learning. This strategy is based on the premise that it is important for students to understand the purpose of what they are doing (Gibbs, 1981) and that for some, their 'willingness to accept increased control will depend on whether or not, in any particular case, they judge it to be a valid strategy and a situation from which they can learn' (Candy, 1987: 174). Having the chance to discuss a process they are embarking on can also demystify the experience and help normalize any disorientation which results from change (Anderson *et al.*, 1996).

Almost paradoxically, on a course which emphasizes the value of active independent learning, a lecture was introduced about EAL which included showing a video about the approach and providing additional information about its philosophy and structure, including initial findings from the research. It is clearly important to limit the expectations of how much effect a lecture such as this can have, particularly bearing students comments in mind about 'knowing' they were going to participate in a self-directed learning course when they arrived, yet experiencing the reality as different. However, initial feedback from students is that the timing of such a lecture soon after they have arrived is crucial, their anxiety is palpable, the realities of what they are embarking on are evident, and their commitment to making a success of their chosen profession is high. Also there are indications that acceptance of the rationale for the approach to learning is an important element in helping sustain students through initial difficulties. For example, students accept that in professional practice they will have to make decisions on their own, without direction, and that learning these skills on the course is crucial. Having the opportunity in small groups to discuss the lecture and share their concerns was also important to students understanding they were not alone in their anxiety.

Another related strategy was to try to increase students' knowledge and understanding of the approach to learning prior to their beginning the course. Applicants must be clearly informed about the nature of the course they were considering. Particular evidence for this was provided by the experience of one student in the initial intake who was angry for the entire course about the approach to learning which she felt she had not contracted for. She had been accepted into the course the previous year when she would have studied within a more conventional approach, but for personal reasons she had deferred taking up a place. Even students who had been 'told' about the course prior to beginning were surprisingly unprepared about the nature of the course they were enrolling in. As one student said, 'I read it [pre-course material] but it didn't prepare me for what this was going to be like at all.' The theme of lack of prior knowledge about the course recurred in research interviews.

Indications were that information provided at the selection stage had to become much more 'user friendly' for students to be clear about what they were choosing. An example was provided by Health Sciences at McMaster who had developed for their admissions material a strongly worded letter from current students highlighting the differences in learning methods at McMaster compared to conventional approaches (Ferrier *et al.*, 1978). Specific efforts are made at Bristol to be very clear about the nature of the course. One particular strategy is to show the video about EAL to prospective students at the Information Day, clearly contrasting the approach with that of more conventional courses. Prospective students are asked to think specifically about whether they want and are suited for active and independent learning, how they will feel about learning from and with each other, and how they will view working with staff who will not be central in providing knowledge and direction to students.

A different kind of orientation strategy was the introduction of a 'Frameworks' lecture at the beginning of each study unit. This was designed to address student and staff concerns about students not having an adequate initial conceptual map to guide their work in the study unit, with the result that they often experienced feeling directionless and lost valuable time pursuing unproductive options. The purpose of the lecture is to provide a 'map' of theoretical perspectives which students can use as a starting point for their study unit work. This innovation was very positively received by many students, although inevitably in common with any lecture it is difficult if not impossible to pitch it to the level appropriate for all students.

Orientation strategies were also introduced to help students develop the range and depth of their process knowledge, particularly in relation to independent learning. Specifically, the range of 'learning activities' available early in the course was increased. Each learning activity is designed in part to enable interdependent learning and increase safety in the group (Gibbs, 1981). Typically a learning activity begins with participants reflecting on their own experiences and ideas, and progressively opening up and working with other group members, moving from working alone, to pairs, small groups and then the large group. Additional structured learning activities were introduced to develop process skills which contribute to interdependent learning, including: giving and receiving feedback; using each others experience; and chairing group meetings. These areas were selected based on feedback from students about what they were experiencing particular difficulty with.

It is apparent that the learning activities described above essentially ask students to anticipate what they will be doing, and to practise in preparation for future requirements. For example, in the activity about chairing meetings, students are asked to discuss how they would respond as chairperson to various eventualities such as a student dominating discussion, withdrawing from active participation, or frequently arriving late for meetings. Although such eventualities may still only be in the realm of possibility, the chances are that even in the first two weeks of term they will already have been experienced within the group and they quickly assume real proportions. Learning activities of this kind provided at the right time can take on the quality and intensity of a dress rehearsal.

The activities have been well received by students and staff who experience them as useful and also report returning to the exercises later in the first term to refresh or renew skills. One proposal made by students to further enhance their orientation which it has not yet been possible to fully implement is to use 'experienced' students as mentors for each group. Regrettably, due to the structure of the course, the 'experienced' students are not readily accessible as they are all in field placements, often at some distance from the university.

Finally, there is another factor which appears likely to have been unintentionally significant in the increased confidence of students in the early stages of the course. Staff are also more oriented and confident in their role than they were in the first year of implementation when there was at times some considerable confusion. As this member of staff said reflecting on the first year:

> Lack of experience and understanding of what we were supposed to be doing some of the time makes any academic feel uncomfortable. It's a bit like giving your first lecture when you don't really know what was expected and that feeling of I don't actually know what was expected of me in a situation is extremely difficult to live with.

This uncertainty and anxiety was undoubtedly conveyed to the students. One student commented as he looked back on the first term that it did not matter how active or directive staff were, as long as they were confident in what they were doing. This point will be explored further in Chapter 6.

The resistant student

It is apparent that a very small minority of students reject attempts to orient them to independent or interdependent learning. An analysis of the experience of two women students who continued to be angry and dissatisfied with the course may provide important clues about students for whom such an approach to learning is an inappropriate choice. There were indications that these students entered the course in the early stages of learning development, in particular they assumed that answers would be provided by staff (Perry, 1970) and did not view their own expertise or that of others as having value (Belenky *et al.*, 1986). As one student angrily said to the facilitator and group in the first term, 'You're [the facilitator] the only person who can give feedback . . . I don't trust people in this group, I don't know why.' This student felt unable to relinquish viewing the facilitator as expert and to learn from others, and she tenaciously held to this position throughout the course.

The second student focused her anger on the lack of external structure and direction. Early in the first term she reported,

> I find it incredibly hard to push myself, motivate myself . . . should I be a good girl and do what I am meant to do, or should I say, 'No, I don't want this, I want to learn that way'?

At times she 'played the game' and at other times she rebelled. As she looked back on the first year she continued to express anger and disappointment with the lack of structure: 'I don't like airy-fairiness with no organization.' Interestingly, this student's placement provided a significant degree of structure but this too became a focus for some resistance.

Neither woman fitted into the passive modes of the early stages of the Belenky *et al.* (1986) framework. Both students openly expressed their anger and disappointment. The most significant commonality in their experience appeared to be a deep ambivalence about authority and expertise, more complex than a wish for the expert to take the lead. At the same time as seeking direction, they also rejected it in a counter-dependent way. Both students also experienced intense interpersonal conflict with other students, perhaps not surprisingly given their explicit rejection of working collaboratively and their tendency to be angrily critical.

It would be illuminating to further research those students for whom an approach to learning which expects independent and interdependent learning does not work, and to explore whether their difficulties on the course continue to be experienced in professional practice.

Later transitions

There is evidence that at key points in the course, initial anxiety and uncertainty recurs and there is a need to help students prepare for the forthcoming transition. Taylor aptly describes 'the orchestration of emotional states and the web of relationships with other persons which are precisely timed with these phases and phase transition points' (1986: 69). Students revert back to earlier stages of intellectual development when they feel under threat (Perry, 1970). This is particularly true of the transition to field learning which is a time of high anxiety for students.

Gradually, bridging mechanisms have been introduced which are designed to help students deal with the field-classroom transition. For example, a unit has been designed to orient students to placement and another to help students debrief placement experiences and make the transition back to the university based part of the course. It is clear that such transitions are very important, particularly in a learning context where time is of the essence and a course cannot be geared to the pace of each individual student. The timing of transitional activities and the linking of these activities to the past and future events are important as they can quickly lose their relevance. It is the balance of looking back and letting go in order to move forward which is crucial.

Moving forward

It is not possible to remove student anxiety about independent and inter-dependent learning. As this student commented, 'I don't know how you can start a course gently.' Indeed, a certain amount of tension and anxiety may be productive for learning. Orientation in the initial stage of the course can be deemed to be successful if students have gained confidence in their ability to learn independently and interdependently, enough that they develop a commitment to continue to learn this way. Timing is important. Not only is the student early in the course more open to orientation when anxiety is high and commitment to learning is at a peak, the development of early confidence and commitment will help withstand setbacks or later transition points when there is a tendency to seek increased external direction.

As this student, who had enjoyed the conventional lecture based approach of her first degree and began EAL quite sceptical about the approach, reflected at the end of the first term:

> I've got used to the EAL method now and I've got more faith in it. One thing it's done for me is give me more confidence in my own resources and that's been good. I don't feel I've been a passive creature who has just been fed a whole load of information. I've actually had quite an active role in my learning.

This increase in confidence and readiness to use their own resources was noticeable in many students. Some students clearly reached this point earlier than others, but if there is a big enough critical mass of readiness in the learning group, individuals who continue to have doubts, or to become disoriented in face of a particular hurdle, can be supported by the group or the facilitator to continue to move forward.

4

The Personal is Professional: Using Pre-course Experience for Learning

Personal knowledge is as important as process and propositional knowledge in education for the interpersonal professions. Each sphere of knowledge inevitably influences the other. Propositional knowledge cannot be characterized independently of how it is learned and used, it is constructed through experience and its nature depends on the selection and interpretation of the learner. This has been described as 'the personal meaning of a public idea' (Eraut, 1994: 106). In the previous chapter, I explored the theme of transitions into independent and interdependent learning and discussed the challenge of orienting students to a course which views professional knowledge as personal, process and propositional. In this chapter, I explore the use of personal knowledge, particularly pre-course experience, in professional education.

Personal knowledge is about understanding and interpretation (Usher and Bryant, 1989; Eraut, 1992), whereas propositional knowledge is directed towards representation and explanation. Personal knowledge includes assumptions and impressions gained from experience which may not be immediately accessible to the student on a conscious level. One purpose of professional education is to enable these assumptions to be brought to the surface so that their implications for professional practice can be explored. In doing so they can be examined and brought under 'critical control' (Eraut, 1994: 106). Eraut identifies the activity of bringing the assumptions to the surface as an element of process knowledge. This process includes professional self-management or 'the thinking involved in directing one's own behaviour and controlling one's engagement' in learning (Eraut, 1994: 115). Discussion of personal knowledge in this chapter will include the process of accessing personal knowledge.

Personal, process and propositional knowledge are not equally valued by higher education and rather than partnership there are tensions between the different areas of knowledge. 'Higher education has been bewitched by a sense that real knowledge is scientific knowledge' (Barnett, 1994: 14). Propositional knowledge is overvalued (Eraut, 1994), as is the 'technical rationality' approach (Schön, 1983). Professional education has tended to assume the same perspective, in part because the growth of a profession has depended to a significant extent on the development of a knowledge base. Propositional knowledge brings with it an aura of certainty, and this in turn signifies the profession is sufficiently erudite to justify a long period of training and defines the profession as different from others (Eraut, 1994: 14).

Yet, it is crucial for professional education to enable the development of personal knowledge and to recognize and address its impact on propositional knowledge. It is the understanding, interpretation and application of propositional knowledge which is important to professional practice. Argyris and Schön (1989) drew our attention to the difference between 'espoused theories' or the explicit theories which explain professional behaviour, and 'theories in use' or the implicit theories which actually determine behaviour. Implicit theories are governed by attitudes, values and beliefs which in turn influence the interpretation of propositional knowledge. Research has consistently shown, for example, that teacher education programmes have had little effect on encouraging students to challenge existing assumptions (Tann, 1993); and that teachers pre-existing views of teaching and learning are so pervasive that unless directly challenged, any attempt to alter teaching styles is ineffectual (Johnson, 1988).

One explanation for the gap between espoused theories and theories in use is the lack of attention in professional education to the dynamic relationship between propositional knowledge and personal knowledge, and the undervaluing of the influence of personal knowledge and the contribution it makes. It is also important not to view personal knowledge as an unwelcome influence which taints propositional knowledge or professional practice, or as there simply to be brought under control by the student or practitioner. Personal knowledge is potentially enriching and stimulating for the individual student as well as providing a learning resource for other students.

In this chapter I outline some key theoretical concepts in relation to using experience for learning. I then locate my discussion in my own experience as a learner. I go on to discuss using personal knowledge in professional education. Then, based on research into students using experience for learning on a professional social work course, I examine the gains to be made for students from using experience in learning, and the barriers which may they may encounter or erect. Finally, I suggest some general principles which emerge as essential to underpinning strategies and structures for developing the potential for using experience in learning in professional education.

What is using experience for learning?

The discourse about experience and learning is confusing. A term such as 'experiential learning' is unsatisfactory, and Barnett suggests 'it is a weasel term being unclear, susceptible to different meanings, and attractive to groups with markedly different agendas' (1994: 108). This point was underlined for me at an international conference on experiential learning, held in Cape Town (1996) where there was a wide variation in interpretation placed on experiential learning by different participants. Industry based trainers from the developed world were concerned with recognizing and building on the work experience of employees, whereas adult educators from rural Africa were concerned with acknowledging the value of the experience of a largely illiterate population. It is a particularly unsatisfactory term in the context of this discussion because of the implication that the learning process itself is entirely experiential, whereas in professional education the most crucial aspect may be the reflection which occurs during or after the experience and the bringing into full consciousness what has already been learnt.

In this chapter I am adopting the term 'using experience in learning', selected by Boud and his colleagues for their recent book on the topic (1993), because this term conveys the notion of a deliberative activity. They suggest that using experience in learning involves perception, consciousness and meaning, and that experience is a meaningful encounter. It is not just an observation, a passive undergoing of something but an active engagement with the environment of which the learner is an important part (1993: 6). In addition, the individual learner is part of a learning milieu, 'enriching it with his or her personal contribution and creating an interaction which becomes part of the individual as well as the shared learning experience' (Boud and Walker, 1990: 18). Thus the opportunities for using experience are multi-layered and multi-faceted, affect the individual and others in the learning milieu and include both enabling and disabling features.

I am also suggesting that experience is the primary constituent of personal knowledge, and that process knowledge enables us to use experience constructively. It will be argued that if experience, or personal knowledge, is not consciously processed and remains at the impression level, it may not be in the 'critical control' of the learner (Eraut, 1994: 106) with possible negative consequences for practice. Mezirow emphasized the importance of becoming critically aware of how and why our assumptions shape the way we see ourselves and others, and only by reconstituting this framework is it possible 'to permit a more inclusive and discriminating integration of experience and acting upon those understandings' (Mezirow, 1983: 125). This process is essential for professional practice.

Boud and his colleagues (1993: 8–17) identify five propositions about learning from experience. The first is that experience is the foundation of, and stimulus for, learning. Every experience is potentially an opportunity for learning, although experience does not inevitably lead to learning. 'Experience may be the raw material but it has to be processed through reflection before it can emerge as learning' (Usher, 1985: 60–61). Reflection is an active process of exploration and discovery, it involves both feeling and thinking, and can take place during or after the experience (Boud and Walker, 1990). Reflection may be done by oneself or with others, 'they can often see what may be obvious but which is too close for us to notice. By supportively drawing it to our attention, they can help us learn from experience' (Boud *et al.*, 1993: 85). Reflection may be viewed as a private event, yet it can also play a central role in interdependent learning.

The second proposition is that learners actively construct and deconstruct their experience. The major influence on how experience is constructed is the learner's 'personal foundation of experience' (Boud and Walker, 1990), or the cumulative effect of their experience. The effect of the learner's history will vary according to the individual and his or her world. The world of professional education should have a significant effect on the construction and deconstruction of experience, although as mentioned earlier it is perhaps often not the case because of the undue emphasis on propositional knowledge.

The third proposition is that learning is a holistic process. All learning involves thinking, feeling and doing, although one aspect of learning may be prominent at any particular time. As stated earlier, in professional education in the context of higher education, the high value assigned to intellectual or propositional knowledge may have implications for the learning aspired to and achieved, and the degree to which it is, or is not, holistic.

Fourthly, all learning is socially and culturally constructed. This links very closely with the second proposition because the construction learners place on their experience is inevitably influenced by their social and cultural norms and values. This is particularly crucial in education for the interpersonal professions as practitioners ultimately will be working with people who also have norms and values shaped by the context, and assumptions about these may directly influence a specific judgement made, or a course of action taken.

The final proposition is that learning is influenced by the socio-emotional context in which it occurs. Boud (1993) suggests there are two key sources of influence. First, there is the influence of past experience which sets expectations for the present and future about what can and cannot be achieved. Secondly, there is the influence of the current context which will mediate the effect of past experience and may either support or inhibit the learner from moving forward. By its very nature, using experience in learning means being open to the discovery of phenomena and information which are unexpected, unpredictable and perhaps uninvited, presenting a risk and a challenge to the learner and the facilitator. In professional education, the mediating role played by staff and other students will be discussed both in terms of opportunities and barriers to using experience for learning.

Using my experience

'Our experiences as learners provide us with a powerful lens through which we can view our own practices as educators' (Brookfield, 1993: 21). As an educator, my views are influenced by my own initial professional education. It is important to locate our own position as educators, cautious of the fact that there cannot be 'a set identity or position, for both of these are relational, contested and shifting. But it is a beginning to recognize that we each come from a particular position, no matter how reluctantly or conditionally we occupy them' (Pettman, 1991: 164). I will be saying much more on the issue of being clear about our positions in Chapter 6 in my discussion of educators as facilitators.

As I reflect now on my initial professional education of over 20 years ago, my memories of classroom learning are vague. The only clear memories are of the experience of learning activities. One particularly vivid memory is of using paints and materials to create a collage in a class where the focus was using non-verbal methods for working with groups. I had not been looking forward to this class and secretly viewed it as likely to be a waste of time and irrelevant to my practice as a social worker. Working with art materials also had negative connotations for me as I came from an actively artistic family and I had dealt with their perceived high expectations by opting out and denying my own artistic impulses, instead over-valuing the verbal and cognitive. However, to my surprise the activity gave me enormous enjoyment and satisfaction. The classroom provided the opportunity to learn from experience that 'doing' art was very rewarding and boosted my self-esteem, in addition to giving me the opportunity to work in a new and productive way with peers.

My memories of field placements, in contrast to classroom based learning, are vivid and numerous. While on field placement, I had the opportunity to transfer the experience of using non-verbal methods for working with groups into practice with a group of Eastern European Jewish women, all over 80, living in residential care, most of whom were survivors of the Holocaust. They were somewhat isolated from each other even though they shared many common experiences and communal facilities. They were both unable by virtue of language differences, and unwilling by virtue of cultural beliefs to use a group to talk about their experience of living in residential care. Yet, the women came together very powerfully in the context of an activity based around aerobics in water. The activity generated a range of experiences including interactions on the journey in the mini-bus, in the changing rooms, and in the water, on themes such as ageing, its impact on physical abilities, and on appearance; and on the advantages and risks of temporarily leaving the safety of the care facility. Although I realized on one level when I was working with the group that I was participating in an important and empowering experience for the women concerned as well as an important learning experience for myself, it was not until I was required to write a paper about the experience that I fully reflected on its meaning.

The other distinct memory of using experience in learning is of the importance of learning from and with others. The learning experiences I remember always include a significant other, either another student or a teacher, who I was interacting with and learning from. In the situation of learning non-verbal methods of working with groups, it was significant that the teacher who I respected for her theoretical knowledge of practice explicitly valued my well-developed propositional knowledge and verbal skills and supported me to develop an area which for me was fraught and completely undeveloped. Using experience for learning was not a process which as a student I knew how to do by myself and interaction with others was crucial.

Finally, a central aspect of my professional development relevant to discussion in this chapter is learning the skill of containment (Bion, 1970). I essentially learnt this skill after I had qualified as a social worker and was working in supervised practice in a psychiatric setting using a pschyodynamic approach. Containment allows me to address difficult developmental issues even when the material is painful. It allows me to be calmly receptive, enough to encourage the expression of conflicted, value laden material by students and to be able to help them reflect on it and gain control of it themselves. Pietroni (1995) in her discussion of professional education suggests that a central aim of professional education must be to provide a 'containing environment' where students can reflect on their experiences. In dealing with personal knowledge, containment is an important skill for facilitators which I will discuss further in Chapter 6.

The relevance of using experience in professional education

I suggested earlier that personal knowledge is as crucial as propositional knowledge to education for the interpersonal professions. There are a number of reasons for this.

First, as discussed in Chapter 1, in professional practice in a rapidly changing society new and unpredictable experiences are inevitable and learning to use these experiences is essential for continuing professional development and lifelong learning:

> Where nothing can be taken for granted and where there are no self-evident truths available or waiting to be found the reflexive, self-monitoring individual becomes crucial to making sense of the world and trying to impose a degree of consistency and control upon it.
>
> (Parton, 1994: 106)

The characteristics of the student entering the interpersonal professions suggests personal knowledge is particularly important. The learner's intent in selecting a particular profession can act as a filter or a magnifier and determine how much a student invests and what outcomes are sought (Boud and Walker, 1990). Also, students entering professional education are often mature and as a result, their life experiences are likely to influence the nature and quality of their learning. Merriam and Caffarella (1991: 321) summarize some of the possibilities mentioned by earlier writers about how life experience might influence the nature and quality of learning of mature students. In particular they note that the need to make sense of one's own life experiences and transitions may be a major incentive for engaging in a particular learning activity. This is an issue I will return to later.

As discussed earlier, the personal values and assumptions of an individual have an impact on the understanding and interpretation of propositional knowledge and ultimately on professional practice. In the newly revised Diploma of Social Work (CCETSW, 1995) 'core values' have attained a pre-eminence not specified in former statements of learning outcomes to be achieved by qualifying social workers. There are six values requirements and students must demonstrate evidence that these have been met as part of the requirements for qualification. Particularly pertinent to this chapter is the first requirement, that students must 'identify and question their own values and prejudices, and their implications for practice' (CCETSW, 1995: 18).

Using experience for learning is a means of bringing values and assumptions to the surface for critical appraisal and control. Often this is done retrospectively, using a strategy to retrieve an experience, then reflecting on the experience, perhaps at this point linking it with propositional knowledge, and considering the implications for practice (Bogo and Vayda, 1986). There are other situations in the classroom where the process of reflection is concurrent with experience and examples of this will be discussed later in this chapter in the context of the Bristol course.

There are increasing moves towards the formal recognition of pre-course experience. The initiation of government led schemes such as APL (Accreditation of Prior Learning) formally value and assign credit to prior experience. Butler (1993) discusses APL as a means particularly for women to gain recognition for what they have learned outside formal education and training. She identifies that although APL has wide appeal as an education and training concept, it has been practised in the UK from about the second half of the 1980s and has so far achieved little more than marginal status, particularly in the 'old' universities. Butler identifies seven barriers to APL:

1. Women themselves may not realize that their life experiences outside formal education and training, particularly unpaid work in the home, provide opportunities to learn.
2. Women may not be able to see and articulate the value of their experience.
3. Educators and trainers have difficulty in assessing prior learning, particularly in respect of unpaid work.
4. The embedding of APL within the higher education requires the development of programmes such as modularization which offer 'top-up' education and these have been slow to emerge.
5. APL is an expensive process which educators and trainers are reluctant to spend time and money on unless there is a benefit such as more students.
6. Awarding bodies may have regulations or policies which discourage the award of credit through APL.

7. Finally, there is a concern by some educators and trainers that APL will mean lowering standards, particularly where it leads to the accreditation of competence or knowledge acquired in unpaid work.

The marginalization of APL mirrors the low priority given to personal knowledge in higher education. Yet as we will see in the next section of this chapter, analysis of the experience of students on a professional course underlines the value of using experience in professional education.

The value of using experience for professional education

Social work students on the Bristol course were mature students, their average age was 35 with a range of 23 to 53, and many students had considerable paid and unpaid experience prior to entering the course, some of it already within the social work or probation field. The nature and degree of their experience was one of the factors central to their being successful in the admissions process.

Once on the course, a significant emphasis was given in course philosophy and implemented in course structures and tools to students actively identifying their relevant pre-course experience and considering its implications for their learning on the course. This process was encouraged primarily within the context of small group learning as well as in group and individual tutorials. Students were expected to begin to identify and record their relevant experience and think of it in relation to the knowledge, skills and values they brought to the course and those they hoped to acquire during the course, with the ultimate objective of attaining the objectives set out by the professional accrediting body. They were encouraged to consider any experience which might be relevant to their chosen profession, not only paid or volunteer experience, but also personal experience of the kind they might expect to encounter in the work they would be doing with service users.

Inviting in pre-course experience in this way is in direct contrast to the blank slate approach to learning criticized by Freire (1981) which can be so deskilling for mature students. Recognizing experience clearly had the effect of validating what the students brought to the course and empowering the students themselves. As a woman student commented at the end of the first term, 'On this course I feel I do know things and I've got things to offer from my own experience and that experience has been valuable.' The validating impact of valuing pre-course experience was most evident in its impact on non-traditional learners who typically came from groups disadvantaged in society, including students from ethnic minorities, from the working class and women. By virtue of having spent much less time in education these students' pre-course experience was often varied and extensive, and they described how the valuing of this experience enabled them to feel equal to their peers who had prior academic degrees (see Chapter 9).

Another potent aspect of the validation for non-traditional students of using pre-course experience was that for some they began, perhaps for the first time, to give voice to their experience of being disadvantaged and oppressed. 'Where language and naming are power, silence is oppression, is violence' (Rich, 1977). Similar experiences are described in a study of black students where students are described as beginning to speak freely among themselves in an educational setting for the first time, 'they began to argue and discover their own powers. They perceived teachers prepared to listen to them and take their ideas separately' (Rosen, 1993: 179). Facilitators not only listen, they may also provide the public language to describe a private experience (Thompson, 1995). Facilitators help make the links with propositional knowledge about structural disadvantage and in some instances clearly help the students understand their experience as part of a wider whole, rather than feel isolated, different and somehow responsible for the oppression they experienced.

From early in the course, on the basis that 'adults are themselves the richest resource for one another' (Knowles, 1984: 10) students were also expected to contribute their experience to the learning of others, to see themselves as experts and consultants on certain topics, and to be able to access other students who held knowledge they were seeking. Not only did this enhance the feeling of being valued, viewing each other as resources for learning also opened up possibilities for learning which are not readily available in a traditional higher education context where propositional knowledge emphasizes the expert sharing with the novice. The range and variety of experience available was striking, and perhaps of most significance is that it was available in a synthesized form rather than being compartmentalized into disciplines or competences.

An example of the gains to be made from sharing experience occurred in a class working on the topic of child protection where a woman student shared her experience of being sexually abused as a child by a family member, and then of being revictimized by the 'helping' system. The experience of hearing an oral history had a powerful impact on group members and on the facilitator. The student described a number of different dimensions to her experience, including her feelings as a child, the impact of the abuse on her adult life, and her perceptions of the interventions and in many instances her 'revictimization' by the system. These aspects of experience are all in themselves subjects for extensive research and theorizing and can be read about or viewed on video, yet the multi-dimensional experience of the student telling her story had a powerful impact which propositional knowledge in itself is unlikely to achieve. It is also interactive and enables sharing to be tailored to the needs of the learner, in user-friendly language with associated affect, in a way not possible with even the most sophisticated computer software. This is an example of the interweaving of experience and reflection.

The sharing of experience described in the above example occurred spontaneously in response to the topic being studied. Another kind of learning activity which generated sharing experience was planned and constructed as part of the course. For example, while studying the topic of working with older people, students were asked to assume the roles of various members of an interprofessional team trying to reach a decision about the discharge from hospital to the community of a frail elderly person. This kind of learning activity clearly engaged the imagination and energy of the students, and enabled them to draw on their own experiences relevant to the scenario in addition to researching the topic by reading about it and by interviewing appropriate professionals. Re-enacting an experience in the classroom gives an immediacy to learning which, if the students view the issue as relevant to their learning, appears to engage their energy and motivation to learn and build on the experience.

Following from the proposition that learning from experience is socially and culturally constructed (Boud *et al.*, 1993), learning in groups allows the opportunity for students to examine their different construction of the same event. An example of this arose in a group working on the topic of child protection who chose to do an apparently simple exercise 'What is child abuse?' In this exercise students were asked to consider a number of trigger situations and rate them on a scale of 1–5 according to how abusive the act was considered to be. One situation which generated much heated discussion was that of 'a 7-year-old sent to a boarding school where he will only see his parents once a month'. A young middle-class woman student shared that she had been sent to boarding school at this age and was taken aback to consider it as abuse, whereas a working-class man student was surprised to be considering abuse in what he assumed to be a situation of privilege, and a third student felt this situation was clearly potentially abusive and gave it a high rating. As part of the exercise students were encouraged to explore together the differences in the rating assigned to the situations and what they meant. This learning activity helped students share different perspectives on the same issue and understand that they contribute to the construction of social realities.

There is evidence to suggest that reflecting on experience requires a supportive environment (Calderhead and Gates, 1993). In observing groups of students at work it was clear that the socio-emotional context was crucial to their learning (Boud *et al.*, 1993). Students in the well-functioning group working on the issue of child protection trusted each other and their facilitator enough to be able to constructively debate their differences and give each other good quality feedback. I have also observed a group of students studying mental health where the prevailing mood of the group was anti-psychiatry, particularly critical of approaches such as medication and electro-convulsive therapy and it later emerged that this was experienced negatively by a group member with a close relative who had been conventionally treated for mental illness. She did not feel safe enough at the time to present her point of view. It can be difficult for students in a group to share values which may not be politically correct, and this may require active intervention by the facilitator, an issue discussed further in Chapter 5.

In observing students share their experience with others, it is evident that doing so requires them to learn the process skills or competences of telling a story, deciding what to include and what to leave out, judging what is appropriate for the particular audience, linking the experience with existing theory or research, and evaluating the process. These quite often complex competences are part of process knowledge, knowing how to conduct various activities which contribute to professional practice (Eraut, 1994: 107). In the first term students often floundered regarding knowing what to select from their experience, how to give voice to it, and how to establish boundaries. As this student said at the end of her first term:

> It's knowing where to go into things in depth and where to skim over the surface and all the decisions you have to make yourself as a student. Whereas in another model of learning the staff would make it for you. It's taking responsibility which is a good thing but it is a bit frightening at times.

Students who graduated from the course identified process knowledge as one of the most valued aspects of their learning on the course.

One important category of processes include learning to manage the impact of experience and to gain a measure of control over something which may otherwise block or cloud learning or practice. The examples described earlier of students working on a topic of child protection challenged students to learn to manage affectively laden material within the context of learning, whether they were the students at the centre of the experience as it was being told, or other group members whose assumptions were being challenged. Learning to contain difficult material (Bion, 1970) is essential for practice in the interpersonal professions and the learning groups offered many possibilities for rehearsal, and for observing others model the skills involved. The essential difference between this process and that of group therapy is that the focus always returns to learning objectives, and to linking personal with process and propositional knowledge.

The boundary between group learning and group therapy may at times be unclear but it is always important to be conscious of it. Merriam and Caffarrela (1991) in their summary of research into mature students suggest that the need to make sense of one's own past experiences may be a reason to engage in a particular learning activity. Past experience may also be a factor in the choice of a particular profession. Recent United States studies (Black *et al.*, 1993; Russel *et al.*, 1993) have examined the incidence of family problems in the early life of students in professional education and suggest that 'working through' a background of personal difficulty may enable professionals to work more effectively in the interpersonal professions. Such working through may include personal therapy. However, my observation of students sharing experiences or listening to others share them suggests they develop confidence in managing and containing such experiences by being supported to give voice to them in the process of learning, to reflect on them, to set boundaries around them and to view them as resources potentially valuable to learning and to practice.

Inevitably because the Bristol course is largely group based, the discussion in this section has been about learning in groups. It is important to note that individual students can and do learn from their own experiences. Sharing experiences in groups is not an approach that suits all students all the time. Tools such as journal writing or learning logs provide an opportunity for individual reflection and learning (Boud and Knights, 1996). Another kind of opportunity may be in personal therapy.

Pettman (1991) points out in her paper about her work as a facilitator in anti-racist and anti-sexist education in Australia that we may be successful in eliciting the expression of values but the resulting discourse may be hurtful to other students. Pettman raises questions about the responsibility of the facilitator to deal with the effects of intervention and suggests that much more has been written about the politics and ethics of research than teaching. I suggest that the issues of responsibility are different for a facilitator on a professional education course than they are for Pettman, a consultant brought in for specific training. As facilitators in professional education we clearly have a responsibility to work towards change alongside the students. They are responsible for making any changes, indeed it is only within their control. We have a responsibility to support, advise, guide and monitor, and ultimately to determine whether the student is eligible to qualify. The ethics of facilitating are further discussed in Chapter 6.

The barriers to using experience for learning

The marginalization of APL in higher education was discussed earlier in this chapter. The premium placed on propositional knowledge may be held less strongly in some areas of professional education where there is an emphasis on the application of knowledge and understanding to practice. However, this cannot be assumed of all interpersonal professions. For example, Barnett *et al.* (1987) found that the value attributed to propositional knowledge by the three professions of pharmacy, nursing and teacher education varied significantly. In pharmacy training, the focus was on scientific knowledge with relatively little discussion of its practical application, whereas in teaching and nursing, theory was seen as generated from and informing practice. Furthermore, even if the relative value of propositional knowledge is diminishing, there is evidence that the dominant emerging ideology today is of operationalism with its pervasive discourse of competence (Barnett, 1994). The latter discourse values certain kinds of processes which result in very specific outcomes.

The barriers to using experience for learning may best be conceptualized as on a continuum. At one end is a small minority of students who actively challenge any diversion from propositional knowledge, questioning both the rationale and the process. At the other end are the students fully committed to personal knowledge and to using experience for learning. For some students their position on the continuum may be related to their familiarity with using experience for learning and, as discussed in the previous chapter, as the course progresses they become more accepting of its philosophy and structures.

The position of the student on the continuum may be linked to learning style (Kolb, 1984). For some students exploring experience is straightforward, they may be familiar with working in groups and/or their preferred way of learning may be experiential. Other students may be more comfortable working on an abstract conceptual level. Also, there are always students for whom being able to access the emotional aspect of their experience is difficult. One of the advantages of learning in groups is that there is the possibility of learning from each other about the value of experience and how to access it.

In the Bristol cohort there was a small but vociferous minority of students who expressed intense and ongoing frustration with the expectation of using experience for learning and who potentially had a powerful and undermining effect on the group as a whole. Student concerns fell into three main areas which are discussed separately here, although they are often inter-linked and reinforce each other.

First, there were students who were impatient with the process of reflecting on experience and viewed it as an unwelcome diversion from reaching their objective of qualifying for professional practice, and irrelevant to their professional needs. These students were very focused on objectives and they also viewed knowledge as external, occurring outside themselves. There appeared to be a gender bias towards men falling into this category which may be further evidence that women focus on understanding and define themselves in terms of their relationships with others and men define themselves in relation to their objectives (Miller, 1976; Chodorow, 1978; Gilligan, 1982). The number of students in this category diminished as the course progressed, a reflection of the increasing recognition of the value of personal and process knowledge.

Secondly, there were those students who objected to the sharing of personal experience and particularly to any associated painful or conflicted feelings. 'It's not a therapy group' was a phrase heard more than once. This barrier may be reinforced if experiences described are overwhelming and their relevance to professional education is lost, and there were occasions when an experience was recounted and the degree of feeling was temporarily overwhelming with the individual student choosing to leave the room. It is very important for the facilitator to manage this process, talk to the student individually, in addition to supporting the group in talking about the meaning of the student's leaving. An experience like this, if mismanaged and not resolved, can have an impact which influences the work of the student group for the rest of the term. Calderhead and Gates (1993) comment on the risk in teacher education of becoming too process oriented and it was interesting to note that as the course progressed students became more efficient at establishing boundaries and holding the different areas of knowledge in balance.

Thirdly, there were students who felt deprived and cheated of expert teaching and direction by the facilitator about what was right or wrong. As discussed in the previous chapter, students at an early stage of development in independent learning see knowledge in right or wrong terms, and expect external authority to teach knowledge (Perry, 1970). Yet, Usher (1993) suggests that for students to learn from experience they must view learning as dependent on perspective and experience, and view it as active and interactive and not as receiving information about what is right or wrong. Observation of the Bristol students suggests that the actual process of engaging in active learning and sharing experience helps them learn about the value and significance of learning from each other. The earlier example of students grappling with their own experience and resulting stereotypes about child abuse and boarding school is an example of this. Inevitably in a group there are students who have varied experience and perspectives and some are usually more ready to take the lead in sharing experience and to model its value.

There are other barriers to a focus on personal knowledge. In professional education, where passing or failing a course may be seen as crucial to the life chances of the individual student, it is difficult to establish a sufficient climate of trust to enable students to move beyond the internal pressure to say the 'right' thing or behave in the 'right' way. It is difficult to reconcile concerns about assessment with the need for reflection (Calderhead and Gates, 1993). For example, a student with a prior history of alcohol misuse carefully considered the implications of sharing this experience. On the one hand, it was an important aspect of his past experience and his decision to enter a caring profession. It was also potentially a very useful experience for him to share with other students, many of whom would encounter service users with alcohol problems in practice. However, the advantages of sharing had to be weighed against the inevitability of questions about whether the student was currently abstaining, and whether a past history of such a problem signalled 'weakness' on the part of the student and a lack of suitability for the profession. This student carefully weighed up the pros and cons of sharing experience before deciding to do so. Others feel moved to spontaneously share an experience as an immediate response to a stimulus, but then later regret having taken that step, feeling too much was risked in the heat of the moment. This dynamic again raises ethical issues not only for the facilitator but also for the group, and certainly is an indication of the importance of agreeing a set of 'ground rules' which are then regularly reviewed.

Related to the issue of trust is the reluctance of students to be critically reflective of assumptions expressed in the sharing of experience. It is undoubtedly easier to raise questions and challenge propositional knowledge than personal knowledge. It is difficult to challenge assumptions which appear to be part of an individual's identity. Classic guidance about giving feedback recommends differentiating between giving feedback about what a person says or does, rather than about the person. However, this is not always easy to distinguish in practice. As this student commented at the beginning of the course,

> I'm afraid of treading on people's toes. I'm afraid of other people's reactions and of course a lack of confidence and ability to give that feedback.

The relationship of group norms to giving feedback is further discussed in Chapter 5.

As with other kinds of knowledge, not all experience or personal knowledge is relevant to professional education, for the individual or other students. The experience may be anecdotal, as Usher (1985) described occurred when he asked student teachers to record and talk about critical incidents. This may be attributed to an experience being shared in a way which does not invite participation, and there is no effort to arrive at a new understanding. Belenky and her colleagues found evidence of this in their study where they differentiated between 'real talk' which requires careful listening and reaches into the experience of each participant, and 'didactic talk' which involves holding forth and reporting an experience. In real talk, domination is absent, the emphasis is on cooperation and reciprocity (1986: 145). Among the Bristol students there were occasions when didactic talk was predominant, and this often appeared to involve a bright articulate student, keen to make an impression, who is hard to challenge. Another factor which can make a difference between whether an experience is anecdotal or not is whether it is linked to propositional knowledge. A story takes on a more universal meaning if it is embedded in propositional knowledge. For example, an individual experience may confirm or challenge findings from a particular piece of research, linking the story with the research can add meaning to both propositional and personal knowledge.

An increasingly significant barrier to using personal knowledge is lack of time. The amount of time required to share and reflect on an experience is difficult to control and unpredictable and this can be a considerable disincentive to using experience for learning in an already full curriculum. Time is required to identify and reflect on the experience and to deal with any impact it may have on the individual student or other students in the group. As the course progressed Bristol students became increasingly proficient at managing time. They learnt how to set priorities for agreed activities and how to renegotiate these if the need arose, an important skill for practice.

Not all students have had the same opportunity to acquire a bank of personal knowledge. A question often asked of educators expecting experience to be used for learning is whether the age and stage of the student is significant. Certainly, for example, the difference in experience between the medical student straight from school who is likely to have excelled academically will be more narrow than that of the mature entrant who has been in employment prior to entering medical education. However, the latter may be less open to reflecting on experience than the former. Furthermore, all students share a commonality of experience of family life, albeit very different forms, structures, and cultures, and have been exposed to experience through friends, films, books, and so on. It is also possible to expand student experience. An innovative example of this is provided by St Bartholomew' and the Royal London School of Medicine and Dentistry which require first year students to go out and actively learn about a local community (Kelly and Wykurz, 1996). Alternatively, a rich array of video material is now available which documents diverse experiences and can be used to bring them into student consciousness.

Using experience for learning: some emerging principles

The classroom has been described as,

> A living context that becomes part of the text of people's experience, and therefore a character in the story. Above all the classroom is a site of interaction, of other responses and confirmations where meanings can be reassessed and learning redefined.
>
> (Usher, 1993: 179)

To develop the potential of the classroom, structures and strategies are required. The adult learning literature includes an increasing repertoire of strategies to encourage reflective use of experience. Boud and Knights (1996) give examples of strategies used in their teaching including learning journals, learning partners, use of learning contracts, and, self-assessment schedules.

However, if strategies are to be more than techniques which rattle like stones in a bucket, they must be located within a coherent framework which is underpinned by some general principles for using experience for learning in professional education. The principles which emerge from discussion in this chapter include the requirement, particularly initially, of providing guidance and support to students in using experience for learning; the importance of linking personal and process knowledge with propositional knowledge; respecting the significance of the socio-emotional context; and, the importance of allocating time for reflection. These principles link with the propositions made by Boud and his colleagues (1993) about using experience for learning.

Although experience is the foundation and stimulus for learning, students do not automatically know how to use it, either individually or in groups. Many students need guidance and support, particularly initially, to identify what is relevant, and how to talk about it and reflect on it. For example, Brookfield (1993) describes his efforts to evolve ground rules to guide discussion participation and to make explicit his ideas about what good discussion looks like. This includes identifying that it is as important to listen carefully and critically as it is to make contributions oneself, and that hard work is not equated with verbal contributions. He also broadens definitions of participation to include being group recorder or bringing a piece of research to the attention of the group. Experience on its own is of limited value unless the student has developed processes for using it.

As students actively construct and deconstruct their experience this must be linked with propositional knowledge. Brookfield emphasizes that if experiences are to be more than celebrating personal experience or 'experiential travellers tales from the front lines of practice' (1993: 30), they must be submitted to two forms of critical review. First, formal theory must be used as a resource against which the experience can be tested and viewed. Being encouraged, perhaps for the first time, to view their experience as valuable to learning can be engrossing and it is crucial that students also use theoretical and research material to help develop a critical analysis. Secondly, assumptions derived from experience must be submitted to collaborative scrutiny to determine their validity, to assess when there is agreement about the assumptions and where there is difference. It is by making links such as these that different kinds of knowledge complement each other and contribute to the holistic process referred to by Boud *et al.* (1993).

Student learning is undoubtedly influenced by the socio-emotional context in which it occurs, and attention must be paid to those factors which influence the quality of the context. For example, one important part of assuring the quality of the socio-emotional context is agreeing the ground rules for group participation. Typical ground rules for student groups must include rules about confidentiality; for example, not discussing what happens in the group meeting with other students on the course except in general terms. Another important feature of the context which enables or disables the use of experience is clarity about the use of power, particularly in relation to the facilitator and assessment. These themes are both discussed in later chapters.

One crucial element of the context which shapes the possibilities for using experience is the priority given to time for reflection. This seemingly simple requirement is very difficult to introduce into curricula which are typically full to overflowing. Furthermore, it is even more difficult to sustain the allocation of time for reflection in face of demands from stakeholders that students have more of what is thought to be good for them. On professional courses these demands often come from powerful sponsors including government, professional associations and employers, and their demands can be difficult to withstand. The General Medical Council comments that in spite of repeated exhortations,

> There remains gross overcrowding of most undergraduate curricula, acknowledged by teachers and deplored by students. The scarcely tolerable burden of information that is imposed taxes the memory but not

the intellect. The emphasis is on the passive acquisition of knowledge, much of it to become outdated or forgotten.

(1993: 5)

Pressure to overload the medical curriculum can be traced back as far as 1863.

These principles for using experience in learning require the facilitator to be active in operationalizing them, a theme which will be fully discussed in Chapter 6. In inviting or expecting students to share their experiences and subject them to critical analysis, Brookfield identifies the importance of the facilitator establishing authenticity and credibility by modelling this process:

> When I feel that someone has some valuable skill, knowledge, experi-
> ence and insight, and when I know that he or she is being open and
> honest with me, I am much more willing to try something which holds
> great threat for me, and to risk failure in the attempt.
>
> (Brookfield, 1993: 27)

However, it is also important for facilitators to be clear that they are not risking themselves in the same way as the students. Although facilitators may risk appearing foolish or incompetent, they hold considerable power and are not in a pass or fail situation. Secondly, for Brookfield's strategy of sharing his own experience to continue to be effective, it must be genuine and not take on a routinized or rehearsed quality.

The uncertainty of new experience

Emphasizing personal and process knowledge and using experience for learning is essential to education for the interpersonal professions but it is often difficult and daunting for students and staff, as well as challenging and exciting. It can be tempting to keep to the tried and tested path of equating student learning with being taught propositional knowledge. Amy Rossiter (1996) describes how teaching can make us feel successful when we achieve the imagined harmonious classroom community with the resulting feeling of having done the right thing. By its nature, using experience in learning is unpredictable and therefore less open to control and more demanding of both students and staff than the traditional focus on pro-positional knowledge.

When the dominant paradigms of certainty and control threaten to encroach, Rossiter reminds herself that the experienced person has become so not only because of prior experience but also by openness to new experiences,

> The experienced person . . . is radically undogmatic; who, because of
> the many experiences he has had and the knowledge he has drawn
> from them, is particularly well-equipped to have new experiences and

to learn from them. The dialectic of experience has its proper fulfilment not in definitive knowledge but in the openness to new experience that is made possible by experience itself.

(Gadamer, 1992, cited in Rossiter, 1996: 149)

Finally, professionals will be working with people who will also be shaped by their experiences. The experiences of service users, clients, patients, pupils or consumers will influence their approach to the professional concerned. A beginning point for practice in the interpersonal professions is identifying and working with that experience. Using experience for learning may model using experience for practice.

Part 3

The Learning Infrastructure

5

Learning for Teamwork

One central trend which characterizes practice today in the interpersonal professions is the increasing recognition of the importance of cooperation and collaboration between the professions. This is endorsed in the UK by recent major social legislation, notably the Children Act (1989), the National Health Service and Community Care Act (1990) and the Education Act (1993), where the prevailing ideology is reflected in the discourse of 'partnership', 'working together' and a 'seamless service'.

Recognition of the need for collaboration is not new. In the 1970s the need for interprofessional cooperation in the health care and social work professions began to be identified with the first government enquiries into child abuse tragedies, beginning with the 'Report on the Enquiry into the Death of Maria Colwell' in 1974. Challis *et al.* (1988; cited in Weinstein, 1994) describe how initiatives to improve coordination in the 1970s were overtaken in the 1980s by the move towards a market approach and increased emphasis on competition. However, then came a renewed impetus to the need for interprofessional collaboration with the deaths of children such as Jasmine Beckford (Blom-Cooper, 1985). This impetus was further reinforced by government policy on care in the community (Department of Health, 1989).

Barriers to collaboration have also been extensively discussed in government reports (Griffiths Report, 1987; Cleveland Report, 1988). Partnership and provision of a 'seamless service' are proving complex to implement. Barriers are both structural and cultural and include differences in 'political control and accountability; status, gender and pay; the nature and definition of the patient/client; and timescales for care and cure', conflicting occupational cultures, and ignorance of each others roles, skills and duties (Carpenter and Hewstone, 1996: 240).

Education is central to the development of interprofessional collaboration, 'education must now prepare professionals to work in organisations in collaboration with people from other professions' (Goodlad, 1984: 8). In particular, initial professional education is increasingly recognized as a site for developing interprofessional collaboration (Areskog, 1995; Carpenter and Hewstone, 1996; CCETSW, 1996). Carpenter and Hewstone (1996) describe a number of shared learning initiatives, including an in-depth study of shared learning for doctors and social workers at Bristol University. Areskog (1995) describes a multi-professional undergraduate education initiative in Sweden which includes six health care professions.

EAL course planners recognized the importance of education for co-operation and collaboration and designed a structure of small group learning, 'our aim then is to engender skills and habits of cooperation and collaboration that will go with the students into practice' (Burgess, 1992: 18). The assumption is that if professionals can learn to effectively collaborate with each other within a profession, this will contribute to the skills of interprofessional work. In this chapter, I examine student experience of learning from and with each other in groups in light of some of the literature about teamwork. I then identify issues which emerge from my research as particularly relevant to learning in groups but are less discussed in the teamwork literature, including the influence of differences in power between students, and the tensions between collaboration and competition, sanctions and support. Finally, I discuss the importance of interprofessional education.

Interdependent learning as a theme runs throughout this book. In Chapter 6, I focus on the issue of facilitating interdependent learning. In Chapter 10, I look at the experience of newly qualified workers and their views of learning in groups as preparation for practice. In Chapter 11, I take another perspective on interdependent learning when I suggest that some of the processes of interdependent learning mirror working collaboratively with service users.

My thinking about interdependent learning derives from having spent many fascinating research hours observing groups of students work together, both in sessions with a staff facilitator present and sessions which were student led. My analysis also reflects student comments about group learning as they talked in individual and in focus groups interviews. In addition, this chapter builds on my own experiences as a member of a learning group, of a social work child protection team, and of an interprofessional team in a health care setting.

Effective teamwork

For our purposes in this chapter, a useful definition of a team is provided by the World Health Organization:

> A health team is a group who share a common health goal and common objectives, determined by community needs, to the achievement of which each member of the team contributes, and in accordance

with his or her competence and skill in co-ordinating with the functions of the other.

(WHO, 1984: 13)

Although this definition is specific to health care, its discussion of shared goals and objectives, and coordination of role and function is directly transferable to other fields of practice such as teaching or social work.

The term 'team' can be used in a number of different ways. Brown and Bourne (1996) suggest there are two basic task dimensions to a team, the degree of interdependence of team members and the degree of difference in formal power between members. In this chapter, the focus is on the former because all members of single professional learning groups have equal status, there are no formal power differences between them. This is a crucial difference between a single professional and an interprofessional group. Brown and Bourne (1996) also identify three levels of interdependence in teams: the integrated level where team members work together on a common task and where the effectiveness of one member is dependent on the others; the collaborative level where part of a workload may be shared; and the independent level where team members work individually with little collaboration between them. The learning groups which provide the data for this analysis move back and forth between the integrated and the collaborative levels. Interdependent learning may be defined as working together on a common learning task where the learning of one member is in part dependent on the learning of others.

A review of the literature on teamwork (Hallett and Birchall, 1992; Øvretveit, 1993, 1995; Leathard, 1994; Soothill *et al.*, 1995) identifies a number of factors as important to a well-functioning and effective team. These include: a supportive organizational context; common and achievable goals and objectives; shared values; the ability to make decisions and handle conflict; role clarity and complementarity; effective leadership; and shared patterns of communication. If these factors are crucial to a well-functioning team, what is their significance in a learning group? Are there process skills associated with interdependent learning and practice which can be developed in learning groups? In the next section of this chapter I examine these factors in relation to the Bristol students experience of learning in groups.

Organizational context

A team cannot exist in a vacuum and it is essential that the wider organizational context supports and sustains the learning group, as it must support the team in practice. Learning groups are directly influenced by the wider university in relation to several key structural features: a physical climate conducive to group learning; allocation of timetabled time for meetings and study unit work; the size of the group; resources to support group learning; and adequate staffing.

Provision of a physical climate to support group learning might reasonably be assumed to be a given in a university context. However, the reality of much teaching in a large institution is that space is designed for large groups or lectures and is not conducive to small group teaching (Hammond and Collins, 1991). Furthermore, furniture frequently conforms to a traditional classroom norm of institutional tables and chairs, which are often fixed either to each other or to the floor making it impossible to move them into the format of a circle for a small group session. The other prevailing reality is that access to accommodation is often not designed to enable inclusion of disabled people in learning groups.

Similarly, timetable provision for small group learning requires a number of rooms to be allocated for meetings at the same time, rather than a much more simple structure of one large space allocated for a sizeable group of students. This variation in provision challenges the norm and requires delicate negotiation with other courses in the university, all of whom are competing for the same accommodation.

The other crucial aspect of timetabling is that adequate time is allocated, over and above meeting time, for students independent and interdependent learning. Bristol students have several blocks of time for this, including one study day per week. It is essential that this time is protected and viewed as crucial to learning rather than as large chunks of 'free' time which are available to be filled by a system susceptible to external pressures to constantly add more to the curriculum.

In response to diminishing resources, learning group size in Bristol has increased since EAL was introduced. The original aim was to begin with a group of eight students, in between the norm of six students per group at McMaster Medical School and 12 students per group at the University of New South Wales Social Work course (Burgess, 1992). However, by the time EAL was implemented the number had increased to 10 students per group and more recently has increased to 12 students, the largest number seen by staff to be feasible. This reflects the literature which suggests that once group size increases beyond twelve members, the pattern of participation becomes uneven and may allow for the dominance of particular members or subgroups (Brown and Bourne, 1996).

For students, the organizational issue which far outweighs any other is the provision of written, audio-visual and computer resources to support independent and interdependent learning. In a small group approach to learning which is following a problem-based approach, resources are used far more intensively over a short period of time than on a traditional course. For example, a group will study mental health almost daily over a two-week period, rather than once a week for a term. This requires resources to be available when needed. Given that EAL was introduced at a time when resources, such as library holdings, were being cut back, there was intense frustration in the first year with lack of availability of resources. As a result, the structure of the curriculum was re-organized so that across the total year group, students would be working on different topics at the same time.

The unconventional use of resources also places unusual requirements on facilities such as the university library and it is essential to engage their support.

Learning groups are facilitated by staff for half their meetings, the other half are student led. To date the provision of staff resources has enabled this important balance to be held. Staff can maintain enough continuity to provide support and guidance and the group also has the opportunity to learn how to work independently. There are times when a group is experiencing tension and conflict, or losing its way and drifting, when students would prefer facilitators to be present more often. There is also an opportunity to use staff resources differentially, providing more staff time early in the course when students need more direction, in contrast to later in the course when they have developed the skills of working interdependently and independently.

Students tend to be somewhat unaware of the wider infrastructure which supports their learning, unless there is an area of tension or dissonance in the organization which directly affects their learning. If the latter occurs, the group has power as a collective to influence the wider organization in a way which is not feasible for the individual student on a traditional course (Mullender and Ward, 1991).

Common goals and objectives

One of the defining characteristics of a team is that members share common goals and objectives. By virtue of being on a professional course, students share the common goal of obtaining a professional qualification. However, beyond this broad area of commonality, there are significant areas of difference, many of which are also found in an interprofessional group. The purpose of a team is to bring these differences together and combine them (Øvretveit, 1995) so that in systems terms the totality is greater than the sum of the parts. The learning group offers the opportunity to explore barriers to defining and achieving common goals and strategies to overcome them.

Motivation for beginning a professional course varies, some students are committed to improving their knowledge and skills, others have been working in the field in an unqualified capacity and have reached the point where they cannot develop their career any further without obtaining a professional qualification. Furthermore, students entering a course have different images of practice which are significant in shaping how they behave. Research comparing student imagery of practice in social work and teacher education identifies how images 'can be considered as powerful frames which heavily influence their conceptualisation of their profession and their subsequent professional development' (Gould and Harris, 1996: 234). For example, some social work students see themselves as becoming counsellors, others are more interested in social action. Given that these frames are powerful determinants of practice, Gould and Harris suggest that students should be helped to articulate their initial frames so they become accessible to review and modification. The learning group provides a prime opportunity to explore these areas of difference.

Observation of learning groups suggests that it is important to locate a core of commonality in relation first to objectives, and secondly, to the ways the group is going to work together, particularly in relation to the balance between personal, process and propositional knowledge. On a professional education course it is crucial to establish clear links between student objectives and those of the accrediting body. This presents a challenge to a course which sets out to support independent learning, including ownership of educational goals. EAL planners attempt to resolve this tension by expecting students to begin by identifying what they want to learn about in relation to the selected topic. A list of learning objectives, linked to the course learning outcomes identified by the professional accrediting body, is provided with each unit and is used by students for reference purposes or as a check-list for reviewing what they have achieved at the end of each unit. As students identify what they want to find out about using their own discourse, and as they discuss their objectives, not only does this enhance ownership of learning objectives, the latter also take on a meaning which simply adopting an externally provided list is unlikely to achieve:

> Sifting out what's relevant and what isn't has been very crucial. In our Study Group when we decide what is relevant we use the board and we brainstorm and think about what we are going to have to know about.

If there are gaps or differences between the student list and that of the accrediting body, these are noted as areas for learning to be carried forward by the student and addressed elsewhere in the course. To date the outcomes defined by CCETSW, the accrediting body, have been written in vague enough language for this to be possible. The challenge of the recent revisions (CCETSW, 1995), is that they are more specific and detailed about the competences students must achieve, and linking student objectives with professional objectives will require creative strategies to ensure ownership by the student.

It is also important for the group to achieve a core of agreement in relation to the balance between personal, process and propositional knowledge. Group learning enables acknowledgement of personal as well as process and propositional knowledge, but inevitably individual members will allocate different priority to these elements. As one student commented in the first term:

> The goal is to develop personally and professionally and not just produce a piece of work at the end of two weeks. There is a danger of being too task oriented and losing sight of personal development or undervaluing it.

As seen in the previous chapter, other students may consider that too much emphasis is given to personal and process learning. It is difficult but essential to achieve a balance so that the needs of each group member are met, as well as the group as a whole.

Shared values

Shared norms and values are central to effective teamwork. A strength of learning in groups is the opportunity to experience the richness of diversity and confront the expression of different perspectives with the resultant opportunity to amend one's own. Considerable emphasis is given in the first term to helping students identify and agree the values which will govern the way they work together. One activity useful for beginning to do this is the process of agreeing 'ground rules' which regulate how the group will work together. There are typically four areas addressed in group rules, all of which are directly relevant to team practice.

The first area is that of confidentiality. As students realize they will be dealing with personal and process knowledge, the issue of confidentiality takes on a new significance. By discussing confidentiality they also come to appreciate its complexity. For example, the need to resolve confidentiality about what, with whom, and if there will be exceptions? Such a discussion of confidentiality is directly transferable to practice on teams, and to professional practice generally.

Secondly, ground rules address expectations about participation. These are an important area as students negotiate the right of all members to speak and be heard and consider what might be the barriers to managing this, particularly in a group of 12 students. Students take this issue very seriously and learn to negotiate the complex power issues involved in participation, particularly in relation to race, gender and class, a topic I will return to later. At a more pragmatic level in relation to participation, whereas course attendance is likely to be a requirement in professional education, students decide how they will handle keeping each other informed if they are unavoidably absent, or how they will deal with late arrival at meetings. Again issues of participation and attendance are key to the work of the team.

Thirdly, giving and receiving feedback is an area which causes students considerable anxiety, as discussed in the previous chapter. Agreement about some basic rules for managing this contributes to development of shared trust, particularly as students realize through the process of discussion that it is a shared concern. Whereas giving and receiving feedback about learning has different objectives than feedback about practice, the key issues about the process are very similar.

Finally, group rules will include practical matters such as the timing of coffee and tea breaks, and how they will manage a small budget allocated to each group for purposes such as photocopying. Agreement about how the group will manage activities such as chairing meetings, establishing agendas, keeping notes and so on, all provide students with some measure of control over their learning.

In the first term the process of developing group rules is taken very seriously and considered at some length. It is noticeable as the course develops that less time is spent on them, to the point that frequently by the second year group norms are accepted as understood and not explicitly addressed by groups, unless in relation to a specific issue which has arisen. The strategy of groups each determining their own rules appears to be important not only to their ownership of the rules and the values they represent, but also to their sense of self or group directedness.

Ability to make decisions and handle conflict

A clear and agreed decision-making process, and strategies for dealing with conflict and difference are essential to effective team practice (Øvretveit, 1995). However, my research indicates that probably the most difficult aspect of learning groups is negotiating diversity. There is often a pressure to minimize or deny difference and avoid conflict. Øvretveit (1995) identifies a number of reasons for the minimization of differences in interprofessional teams. These include fear that expression of differences will destroy the group and that competition and conflict will undermine cooperation, and a fear of losing autonomy. I will discuss these fears separately as they both appear to be significant to student experience in the learning groups.

Students work very hard to ensure that differences do not undermine cooperation. Certainly in an approach to learning which relies extensively on interdependence, the investment in achieving a well-functioning group is significant and students are likely to be afraid of destroying the group and undermining their learning if cooperation is not achieved. Students devise creative and often quite complex decision making procedures, guided by their strong sense of natural justice. One first term group developed a system of taking turns in relation to making choices. Their intent was to recognize that different students have different priorities. This same group also adopted a weighting system for decision-making so that for example, if a particular student was doing a piece of assessed work on the theme in question, her or his preference for selecting a particular focus would have priority. The significance of these strategies is that students devised and agreed a system which to them seemed equitable, protecting both the rights of the individual, as well as enabling the group to make decisions and work together. Learning about the process of decision-making is quite as important as learning to make decisions.

Øvretveit (1995) also suggests that differences are minimized in teams as members endeavour to preserve autonomy, afraid of losing their independence. Certainly in learning groups, one of the most difficult areas is negotiating a balance between individual and group needs, maintaining some independence yet balancing this with the interests of other members. As this student said, 'I feel torn. I feel very responsible for the group and very responsible for my own thing.' This was a very common feeling among students. Some students respond by always putting their own learning needs second and giving priority to the needs of others. Reviews of how the group is working and the experience of individual students in it can be useful for identifying this kind of pattern and developing strategies for new behaviours.

Students learn over the course how to advocate on their own behalf. This student commented at the end of the two years about how she had gained confidence to raise those issues which concerned her, 'I'm more prepared to ask, come forward and see what's going on. I've got more confidence in confronting things.' This kind of confidence is essential to full participation in an interprofessional team.

Conflict may be difficult but it can also be creative. The expression of difference can stimulate group learning:

> It's better when people challenge. It stimulates the whole group and feeds the excitement . . . It's not taking it personally . . . Now I'm realizing you can have a discussion and it really does help to challenge and confront.

This student had begun the course fearful about tension and conflict, doing her best to avoid it, but over the period of one term had come to understand the value of the expression of difference.

For conflict to be allowed to emerge to generate learning, it is important that the group learns how to contain conflict and understands that it need not have a devastating effect. Conflict appears more likely to come to the surface when the facilitator is not present, which initially seemed surprising as I had assumed students would seek the safety of the facilitator's presence. However, the unspoken 'rule' is that students do not criticize each other in the facilitator's presence. I have observed students try with reasonable success to resolve conflict in a session where the facilitator was not present. I have also observed situations where resolution was not reached and there is an often implicit agreement to try to get on with the task and set the conflict aside. Students occasionally approach the facilitator individually outside group meetings, or seek advice from their tutor about intra-group conflict. In either eventuality, they are likely to be supported to take the matter back into the group. An important skill for the facilitator, discussed further in the next chapter, is the skill of containing conflict. Perhaps most important for teamwork is that students learn about the inevitability of conflict and processes of conflict management, even if the outcome is not always comfortable.

Students learn a great deal in groups about how to make decisions and handle conflict. As one student commented in a focus group discussion at the end of the course,

> We've learnt to get to know each other, learnt how to make decisions . . . I've learnt how to negotiate, how to pass on information without offending others . . . how to be aware of what other people are feeling.

These seemingly simple achievements may be very significant to the students future practice in teams.

Role clarity and complementarity

The literature on teams gives considerable emphasis to role clarity and complementarity, particularly in relation to interprofessional work. Much can be learnt about role clarity and complementarity in a single profession learning group as interdependent learning is based on the notion that each member of the group contributes to the whole and the result is greater than the sum of the parts. The outcome is that more information is available to the individual student than he/she could have achieved individually and in isolation. Clarity and complementarity are achieved in the process of students deciding who is going to do what, how and when, and they are quite rigorous about this work at the planning stage. As this student described,

> There are various processes: some personal interest, some people seeing something needs to be done on this issue for the group. If you can identify a clear area to work on you're half way there. And there's little bits left that people sort of mop up. And then hopefully the next time you meet up you've got the right bits of the jigsaw puzzle so that at the end you've got the whole one. But quite often you haven't.

An essential aspect of complementarity is for the group to identify where the gaps are in the puzzle at the end of the unit, so that they can be addressed later in the course. However, time is always short, and there is a tendency to move on before an adequate review had been undertaken.

Another aspect of the importance of roles in groups is the influence of informal roles, equally significant in a single profession as interprofessional group. Students assume various informal roles and frequent among these are the roles of mediator and entertainer. Less frequently the role of scapegoat occurs, where one person becomes a repository into which others can project bad feelings. One advantage of such roles emerging and being identified is that this may enable students to learn something valuable about the roles they tend to play in groups and to think about how they might disengage themselves from a dysfunctional role which is detrimental to their development (Brown, 1992). An example of this was provided by an older woman student who reflected on how she held back from identifying her learning priorities until other students had decided what they wanted to work on, and then she picked up what was left, compromising her own needs, 'I tend to be a bit of a mopper up.' She partly attributed this to feeling responsible for other students, and partly to not having very strong feelings about what she wanted to do. She had become aware of this role as a result of group discussion about how effectively the group was working.

She discussed the pattern of her behaviour with her tutor and with the group, and as a result was determined to be more assertive about her needs. The group had also discussed how they might avoid depending on her to be in this role.

The informal role of 'internal leader' commonly occurs where one person is regarded by the others as their leader and representative. This can be a real asset to a group and to a facilitator (Brown and Bourne, 1996). One important element of informal roles which is likely to influence the adoption of the internal leader role, is the influence of race, gender, class, age and sexuality. The impact of personal roles is discussed later in this chapter in a discussion of power in groups.

Leadership

Øvretveit's (1993) review of research into teamwork suggests that more problems are caused by leadership than any other single issue. Øvretveit suggests this is not, as often believed, because the team manager is inadequate but because her/his role is unclear and not right for the team. The role of staff facilitator as leader is discussed in the next chapter. The other important formal leadership role in the learning group is that of student chairperson.

The value of the role of chairperson both for individual student learning and the functioning of the group has become apparent with the development of EAL. This role was not initially construed as significant but emerged as important particularly to those sessions not attended by the facilitator when it was apparent that students needed to learn how to manage the group. Regardless of whether the facilitator is present or not, the main tasks of the chairperson are to establish an agenda for the group session, keep the attention of the group focused on agreed objectives, hold the group to a timetable, and negotiate any diversions from the agenda. The chairperson may also play an important supporting role by, for example, chairing a 'go-round' at the beginning of the meeting to see how each person is feeling, and an end of session review where students briefly evaluate the work of the group that day. As discussed in Chapter 3, students are introduced early in the course to the skills of chairing meetings and they are expected to take turns in this role. Students take the role very seriously and often go to some lengths to prepare for it.

As might be expected, the range of competence of student chairpersons early in the course is varied. Some students perform the role very competently early on and model the role for others in the group for whom the role is unfamiliar and daunting. Chairpersons are given feedback by group members and the facilitator about their skills and as the course progresses almost all students demonstrate visibly increasing competence in the chairperson role. They are not only performing an important group function, they are also rehearsing skills which will be useful in team practice.

Communication

Communication, both formal and informal, is essential to teamwork and particularly to interprofessional teams where team members may be speaking almost a different language, reflecting differences in professional education and culture. There are two key learning group tasks which provide students an opportunity to practice communication skills: giving and receiving feedback; and presenting the contribution of individual student learning to the group. These communication skills are also central to team practice and the group provides a forum for sustained rehearsal.

Early in the course a common worry is about giving feedback, in part related to the fears discussed earlier in this chapter about the expression of difference. Students are unsure what feedback to give, and how to give it in a way which is acceptable. In the group discussion about how they were going to manage a review and feedback session at the end of Term 1, two members shared their concerns:

'I worry about getting the language right, so people don't get me wrong'.

'I worry about what I'll say. It's too hard to speak from the heart'.

Sharing such concerns is in itself supportive and helps group members understand they are not alone in having anxieties of this kind.

As discussed in Chapter 3, the level of concern about giving feedback resulted in more attention being paid to orienting students to feedback skills early in the course. Students make significant progress with this skill. In part this is a result of providing them with the opportunity to practice simple 'rules' about commenting on behaviour rather than the person, and making 'I' rather than 'you' statements. It is also a process of familiarizing students with the language of feedback.

The other important aspect of communication is the development of confidence and competence in presenting the outcome of independent or sub-group learning to other group members. Students are expected to take responsibility for complementary tasks, either individually or in sub-groups, and then come together to share their findings. Early in the course they tend to begin by sharing information in didactic ways associated with their image of teaching, using for example mini-lectures and providing each other with written handouts. They then reach a point when they begin to find this approach boring and unproductive and have also developed enough confidence to try out different approaches. One student described the benefits experienced of having a discussion rather than a presentation, 'We've been able to discuss rather than present. This allows for an interchange of ideas rather than presenting one point of view.' If they opt for a discussion or debate, some groups decide to provide briefing notes for students to keep. Group members demonstrate a significant increase in presentation skills over the course. They increase their repertoire about how to present effectively, using a range of aids. They also learn to consider their use of language to ensure they present in a user friendly way. Regrettably, because they are a one-profession group they are not regularly challenged to think about presenting across professional barriers. However, there are learning activities specifically designed to encourage students to role-play membership of another occupational group and explore related communication issues.

Further learning group issues

Three themes emerged from my research as significant to the student experience of learning groups, but which are not generally much discussed in the literature on teamwork. These themes include: the influence of personal power; the tensions between collaboration and competition; and the group as provider of sanctions and support.

The influence of personal power

> I don't feel very positive so far. I'm not sure why . . . How we define who does what is unsatisfactory. There is a danger of people taking over and frantically grabbing at things.

This woman student was expressing concern about other people in the group 'taking over'. In his study of power in the caring professions, Hugman comments that power is socially constructed, it 'is not an isolated element of social life, but one which interweaves occupational and organisational structures with the actions of professionals individually and collectively' (1991: 38). Power interweaves teams, whether they are interprofessional or single professional, and similarly learning groups. Brown and Mistry (1994) identify in their work on issues of race and gender in 'mixed membership' groups (the term 'mixed membership' refers to groups which include black and white people, men and women), that the small group is a microcosm of society and patterns of social oppression will be replicated here, unless steps are actively taken to counteract these tendencies.

In this chapter I focus on oppressions in relation to race, gender and class because of their centrality to the learning group. This is not to deny that other oppressions are equally important, including age, disability and sexual orientation (Mullender and Ward, 1991), all of which require further research into their impact on learning groups. There is an increasing literature about the extensive influence of race, gender and class on group behaviour and process (Davis and Proctor, 1989; Brown and Mistry, 1994). As a result, considerable attention is paid in the first term to structuring the mix of membership of the Bristol groups. The primary rule which governs membership is that no member of an oppressed group will be knowingly placed in an isolated position in a group. This is particularly pertinent to black students who are in a numerical minority on the Bristol course and who are placed in groups so there are at least three black members in a group to counteract the tendency for singleton members to be prone to marginalization (Brown and Mistry, 1994). One regrettable outcome of this decision is that some groups are all white, although because membership of groups changes over the course there will be an opportunity for all students to work alongside students of another racial origin. As consciousness has increased about oppression in learning groups, the same basis for structuring membership of first term groups is also used for disabled students and gay and lesbian students. As the course progresses, students may give priority to choices which may result in being a singleton member from an oppressed group. This then becomes an issue for the group, and particularly the facilitator, to be aware of and respond to as necessary.

The other factor which is taken into consideration in group membership is the graduate or non-graduate status of the student, with the intent being also to mix these in groups. Initially, course planners were concerned that a hierarchy of graduates and non-graduates might develop. As is fully discussed in Chapter 9 this has not occurred, in part because of the value attributed by students and staff to the often extensive experience relevant to social work which non-graduates bring to the course. The other factor which counterbalances the power of the graduate is that academic achievement on a traditional course does not necessarily mean a student assumes a dominant role in groups. The personal factors of race, gender and class, although they may of course be directly correlated with educational status, appear to be more significant than prior educational experience.

The position of students from oppressed groups changes over the course. This white woman graduate began the course feeling very lacking in power in her group, and talked in an individual interview about an issue she wanted to address in the group but did not feel able to do so:

> Did I have the courage to say what I want or would I go meekly along? I didn't have the courage to do it on my own. I got the courage when someone else said it.

By the end of the first term the change in her perspective was dramatic:

> I've enjoyed working with groups very much ... I've been able to develop certain qualities that were perhaps there but I didn't know I had. One of these is being able to lead and work with people.

Working in a learning group had provided this student with opportunities she had not had in formal education before.

Power associated with personal roles is also a factor in teamwork. In interprofessional teams particularly it is often overshadowed by expert power associated with different professions. Expert power and personal power may reinforce each other (Hugman, 1991). For example, a hospital consultant is likely to be a white male and to hold considerable power in relation to nurses, occupational therapists and physiotherapists and social workers, all of whom are more likely to be female. Although in a single profession group, students do not gain experience of dealing with differences in formal power, they do experience and learn to negotiate differences in informal power. For example, men are more likely to dominate verbally in groups (Garvin and Reed, 1983; Davis and Proctor, 1989). Student experience of negotiating informal power is considerable by the end of the course and should provide a sound basis for negotiating the formal power which is so often a feature of interprofessional work.

Collaboration or competition?

Working collaboratively in groups is a new experience for many students whose earlier experiences of education have been characterized by individualized competition. As this student said in the first term, 'We're all fighting against our formalized education of the past when it's everyone for themselves.' The following excerpt is from a focus group interview with students at the end of the first term:

> *Student one (white)*: 'EAL reduces competitiveness.'
> *Student two (white)*: 'It encourages sharing.'
> *Student three (black)*: 'It takes away inequalities as well.'
> *Interviewer*: 'And after here?'
> *Student one*: 'I'll be more ready to share my knowledge.'
> *Interviewer*: 'You'll feel you have something to offer?'
> *Student one*: 'I'll be willing to admit I don't know things.'

This sequence illustrates student experience of sharing and its implications for competitiveness. The final student comment also illustrates a point made by several students about being confident to admit not knowing, rather than to pretend to know, which is so often part of a competitive educational environment.

Collaboration takes the tangible form of sharing material resources as well as knowledge and experience. However, early positive experiences with collaboration are to some extent diminished by later pressure towards obtaining 'good' marks in individual assessed work, as will be discussed further in Chapter 8. Strong competitive feelings can also be generated within groups, particularly in relation to the facilitator. However fair and even-handed the facilitator is, it is inevitable that she or he will be more closely identified with some group members than others, or have stronger feelings about some members than others (Brown and Bourne, 1996).

Competition also occurs between groups. Although the groups work in parallel and share the same curriculum, inevitably differences develop. Such comparisons can contribute to rational and irrational feelings and competitiveness (Brown, 1992). This again is likely to occur early in the course when some students are not clear about whether there is a right or wrong way (Perry, 1970), as this piece of dialogue demonstrates:

> *Student one*: 'I'm anxious because of what other groups are doing.'
> *Student two*: 'That's their problem.'

Student three: 'There's not a right and a wrong way of doing this.'
Student one: 'There's a right way for our group.'

The process of students comparing notes about their different group experiences also at times is an advantage in that a useful idea or strategy generated in one group may then be adopted in another.

Learning groups offer a means of fostering cooperation rather than competition, and they increase the learners commitment, enjoyment, support and participation (Jaques, 1992). As this student said,

> I'm happy with the way the group works. We've got people who are keen and good at using their own initiative. There's a lot of group support. We are a unit, not just individuals doing the same task. We're overlapping and conferring. We're using different people's abilities so if we've got a good organizer we use that, and that's not to put someone down who's a supporter, they enable things to happen. The group is embryonic but it's there.

The recognition of individual strengths and ability to bring these together cooperatively is crucial to the effective working of a learning group or a team.

Support or sanction?

The literature on teams generally does not deal with issues of team members' accountability to each other and the sanctions they might use. The expectation is that members work in a line management structure, often accountable to the team leader or manager. An exception is Øvretveit (1993) who identifies teams as experiencing lack of clarity about who members are accountable to and for what, and whether they are accountable in any way for the actions of fellow members.

In learning groups there is an expectation that students hold each other accountable for interdependent learning, but their success in achieving this is variable. In the first year when students are very energized by group learning there is typically a culture of high productivity and a corresponding pressure to contribute. As this student commented,

> I felt a huge sort of pressure to be there which is what makes me more anxious I think. I actually want to learn something . . . I don't want to sit around and chat about it, I actually want to learn.

She travelled a total of four hours daily to attend the course, group productivity was crucial to her and she expected the same degree of commitment from other group members.

However, agreements about what each student will do are not always followed through with the same degree of productivity, or the same level of skill. Student commitment may be diverted by other demands such as those of caring responsibilities. Groups work for at least half the time without facilitators present, and student attendance may drop unknown to the facilitator.

As this student said, 'Some people in the group have disappeared. I pay for child care and I can't afford it . . . If you come on this course you must have a commitment to it'. It is demoralizing to students who make an effort when others do not and the latter are perceived to 'get away with it'.

Sanctions may be imposed by the system for non-attendance, for failing assessed work, or for unethical or illegal behaviour. The facilitator may put the wheels in motion to begin a process of instituting sanctions, although these will be implemented by other staff members who carry specific roles. For staff in an approach to learning which is designed to foster independence and interdependence, there is a reluctance to invoke sanctions and, for example, to use tools such as attendance registers. For students, the only viable sanction available is peer pressure. As a group they will rarely 'tell' on a fellow student. Issues of this kind have professional implications. Not contributing to a clear requirement for interdependent learning is a professional matter, similar to a team member not contributing to team practice. There must be course structures in place to manage a situation of this kind, even if used as a last resort.

Not contributing to interdependent learning may be a result of the student experiencing personal problems. Mutual aid is identified by Papell and Rothman (1980) as a 'core element' in educational group work. The learning group is frequently a significant source of support for students as 'people with similar needs can be a source of mutual support and problem solving' (Brown, 1992). Often, the first group remains central to the support of the members throughout the course. Groups may introduce mechanisms which enable them to routinely check whether members are okay. Typical of this is a 'go round' where students begin each session briefly checking in about how each member is feeling that day. Often this is handled in a very routine way, but it is an opportunity for a student to raise a problem if she or he chooses. The mutual support provided by the learning groups is reported by staff to have had the effect of diminishing individual student demands on tutors, although this outcome is very difficult to quantify. It also models a source of support available to professionals in practice where, as will be seen in Chapter 10, the traditional support role of a supervisor is increasingly unavailable.

Interprofessional learning

So far the discussion has focused on single profession learning groups, although I have suggested that many issues relevant to effective learning group functioning are transferable to interprofessional groups. There is increasing interest in interprofessional education, also known as 'shared learning' and 'multidisciplinary education'. Interprofessional education or training still tends to be *ad hoc*, unresearched and has not been systematically introduced into mainstream professional education. The only significant investigation into the nature and extent of interprofessional education and training was undertaken in 1987/6 by the Centre for Interprofessional Education which showed that most of the activities were at the post-qualifying level (Weinstein, 1994: 22). Weinstein recommends in her survey of interprofessional education and training that 'participative training methods and a problem-solving approach work better than didactic input' (1994: 32).

Carpenter and Hewstone (1996) analyse a 'shared learning' project for final year medical and social work students which emphasized participative working and collaborative problem solving. They found that overall attitudes towards the other profession improved (although in 19 per cent of the cases attitudes actually worsened) and that each saw the other as more professionally competent at the end of the programme. Participants also reported increased knowledge of the attitudes, skills, roles and duties of the other professions and of how to work together more effectively.

Another example of interprofessional education is provided by Areskog (1995) who describes an undergraduate problem-based learning programme in Sweden which includes students from six different health care professions. Initiatives of this kind are important because they enable professionals who will be working together in practice to begin in their initial professional education to deal with some of the differences between them which are less accessible in a single profession learning group.

Interprofessional education does not remove all barriers to collaboration, many such barriers are structural (Carpenter and Hewstone, 1996). There are examples of collaborative initiatives designed to deal with some of the structural barriers to shared learning. For example, in the field of learning disability there are joint initiatives by the English National Board for Nursing, Midwifery and Health Visiting (ENB) and the Central Council for Education and Training in Social Work (CCETSW) (Elliott-Cannon and Harbinson, 1995).

Interprofessional education enables the recognition at an early stage in professional development of differences in values and attitudes, as well as differences in role, status and function. As has been seen in this chapter interdependent learning enables some learning to take place in these areas. Interprofessional education takes interdependent learning a step further and – very importantly – it enables the breaking down of 'myths, misunderstandings and inappropriate expectations between professions' (Barr and Waterton, 1996). The combination of interprofessional learning in groups appears to offer a promising way forward to the interprofessional collaboration which will undoubtedly be a feature of professional practice in the next century.

6

Facilitating Independent and Interdependent Learning

The facilitator is of central importance to students learning to work independently and interdependently, particularly early in the course. The responsibility of the facilitator is to facilitate students' independence in learning what the content is, as well as learning how to learn it and whether they have learnt it (Heron, 1989: 14). The responsibility of the facilitator in a group based programme is to help students learn to work interdependently. While the responsibility of the facilitator is to help students learn, and to monitor and evaluate student learning, the primary responsibility for learning rests with the student. In professional education this must occur within the context of proscribed requirements for practice, and ultimately this means students must meet externally set criteria before qualifying for practice.

The extensive literature about independent learning focuses primarily on the student, perhaps on the assumption that if the student takes responsibility for learning, the facilitator is peripheral. Surprisingly little has been written specifically about the role of facilitator in the context of professional education. Heron (1989) discusses facilitating learning in some detail, although not in the context of professional education. Nevertheless, a key concept from his work, which is particularly useful for an analysis of facilitating professional education, is his framework of three modes of learning. The hierarchical, cooperative and autonomous modes define the different ways that the facilitator can handle decision making. In the hierarchical mode, the facilitator takes full responsibility, thinks and acts on behalf of the group and directs the learning process. In the cooperative mode, the facilitator shares power over the learning process and negotiates outcomes, collaborating in managing the learning process. The view of the facilitator, although influential is not final. In the autonomous mode, the total autonomy of the group is respected and the facilitator gives the group members freedom to exercise their own judgement, 'This does not mean abdication of responsibility. It is the subtle art of creating conditions within which people can exercise full self-determination in their learning,' (Heron, 1989: 17).

The modes are useful to a discussion of professional education because they address the crucial question of who decides what students learn and how they will go about it,

> These three modes deal with the politics of learning, with the exercise of power in the management of different dimensions of experience. They are about who controls and influences such management. *Who makes the decisions* [author's italics] about what people learn and how they learn it?
>
> (Heron, 1989: 17)

Heron only goes so far as to suggest that that the decision-maker might include the facilitator alone, the facilitator and students, or the students alone. However, in professional education the decision makers who hold ultimate power are the university and the profession, although as discussed in Chapter 2, the respective roles vary according to profession. The facilitator is at the interface of the student, the profession and the university and in this position performs important linkage and mediating functions, which I will say more about later.

One feature of the facilitator role which has been identified in the literature and which appears centrally relevant to facilitating professional education is its relational aspect. From this position, she or he is responsible for helping students negotiate a complex set of relationships characterized by potentially conflicting philosophies of independent and interdependent learning and professional requirements.

Jaques in his study of learning in groups identifies the relational element of facilitating as staff and students sharing responsibility for student learning,

> It should not be supposed that the facilitator role represents a laissez-faire style of leadership; rather there is a sense of shared or developed responsibility for learning. It usually requires that the tutor be learner centred, helping students express what they understand by respecting them for what they know rather than for what they should be.
>
> (Jaques, 1984: 147)

This description of the facilitator role is appropriate to professional education in its discussion of shared responsibility, although the student and facilitator share different roles. However, Jaques does not deal with the question of where ultimate responsibility lies. Moreover, whereas respecting students for what they know is important, this potentially conflicts in professional education with knowing that students require more or different knowledge, values and skills to qualify for professional practice.

Taylor also identifies the significance of 'learning as a relational phenomenon' (1986: 70) where learning for self-direction is not brought about solely by the initiatives of the individual learners, but by the relationship between environmental events and learners. The facilitator is viewed as one aspect of the students learning environment where, 'relational events between the learner and other persons (authority figures and peers) are critical in the movement towards the new perspective' (1986: 70). Taylor suggests that in self-directed learning, the demands on 'socio-emotional resources' are greater than might be anticipated, and in particular facilitators need 'special social and psychological understanding and expertise' (1986: 70). Taylor does not expand further on the kinds of challenge self-directed learning presents to the facilitator, or what the requisite special expertise might entail.

Brookfield (1986) introduces the concept of facilitation as a 'transactional dialogue' between students, and between staff and students, who 'each bring experiences, attitudinal sets, and alternative ways of looking at their personal, professional, political and recreational worlds' (1986: 23). He defines the role of facilitator as being to 'challenge learners with alternative ways of interpreting their experiences and to present them with ideas and behaviours that cause them to examine critically their values, ways of acting and assumptions' (1986: 23). This goes further than Jaques' learner-centred emphasis of accepting what students know, but in common with Jaques (1992) and Taylor (1986), Brookfield does not examine the complexities of facilitating in a professional education context where exploration of alternate views is necessary but not sufficient. If, for example, the student adopts a view which is inconsistent with professional values, the facilitator must not only present an alternative view but must monitor requisite change in the student.

Boud (1987) focuses on the tasks for the facilitator, identifying the facilitator as planner and evaluator, resource person, and an instrument of social action and change. These tasks are all important as will be seen in this chapter. The concept of the facilitator as an 'instrument' of change is particularly helpful in professional education. This can be extended to viewing the role of facilitator as a change agent, a catalyst in the transactions between students and learning events. The concept of a change agent emphasizes the notion, which I suggest is centrally relevant to professional education, of a planned and deliberative process of change towards externally defined goals and objectives. For example, for those students whose values are inconsistent with those of the profession, the facilitator may be a catalyst in the process of change.

My research suggests that the transactions between student and learning events cluster in a number of interwoven but discrete areas. I present them here as dilemmas because they potentially pull the student and facilitator in conflicting directions and by taking a central role in managing these tensions, the facilitator enables students to negotiate independent learning in professional education. The dilemmas include: facilitating student-led or profession-led learning; facilitating personal, process or propositional learning; the nature of facilitator expertise; the facilitator as supportive or critically reflective; facilitating formative assessment; and, facilitating in response to student change. Finally, I explore the question of who is responsible for student learning on a professional education course which is designed to encourage and develop independent and interdependent learning. Issues of responsibility lead to a discussion of the ethics of facilitating teaching and learning, an issue which is much discussed in relation to research but little discussed in relation to teaching and learning. However, before examining the dilemmas of facilitating it is important to identify key features of the learning context which influence the shape and direction of the role.

The context for facilitation

In an earlier paper co-authored with Hilary Burgess (Taylor and Burgess, 1995), we suggested that there are three central dimensions to the context for facilitation: the level of the political and economic context (fully discussed in Chapter 2); the level of the institutional context; and, the level of the intradepartmental context.

There are a range of institutional factors which directly affect the student and the facilitator. Notably, there are increasing pressures on facilitators to generate income for their departments by obtaining research grants or developing publications to enhance the department profile. These demands divert facilitator energies away from student concerns and from taking time to develop the skills of facilitating. In addition, changes such as modularization potentially have a fragmenting impact on courses built on an integrated structure and philosophy. At best, modularization may require the facilitator to select a more hierarchical mode and direct the experience of students who are likely to be entering from a variety of courses and following a curriculum which requires links to be made between different modules.

At the micro level, intradepartmental factors influence the operation of facilitators and study groups. As seen in the last chapter, students working in parallel in study groups are part of a wider course community, thus creating a multiplicity of role relationships and associated feelings (Brown, 1992), mirroring the experience of group workers in day or residential settings (Brown and Clough, 1989; Brown, 1992). Differing facilitator styles and group membership result in significant variation between groups, in spite of them following the same curriculum. This results at times in rivalry, comparison and competitiveness (Brown, 1992). Such tensions need to be recognized so that diversity is valued and inconsistencies managed. Regular facilitators meetings can be particularly helpful for sharing the experience of the impact of contextual factors and exploring how they might be negotiated.

The dilemmas of facilitating

Student-led or profession-led learning?

As we have seen, the central question on a professional education course where the objective is to facilitate independent and interdependent learning, is who defines what the student will learn, how they will learn and how learning is assessed (Heron, 1989)? As discussed in Chapter 2, there are an increasing number of stakeholders who insist on decision making power in relation to professional education. Their focus tends to be on what students learn, hence the tendency always for the curriculum to become overloaded as it suffers under the weight of agendas of different lobby groups.

One outcome of the influence of employers and government is the pressure to focus on short-term results and people being trained to do specific tasks in specific posts, typified by developments such as NVQ, or apprentice teacher schemes. In social work education this pressure is manifested in the increasing predominance of a particular approach to competence based learning. Social work competencies defined by CCETSW (1995) are 'highly technical, decontextualised practice skills which can be broken down into smaller and smaller constituent parts', which can then be assessed (Dominelli, 1996: 163). Everything from professional ethics to legal knowledge become competencies to be ticked off from a functional checklist (Gould, 1996). It is important to recognize that competences do not have to be conceived of as discrete behaviours associated with atomized tasks, they can focus much more on the general attributes of the practitioner which are crucial to performance (Gonczi, 1994), an approach largely adopted by the Australian professions.

For the purpose of discussion here, my primary concern with the checklist approach to competence is that it is highly prescriptive and risks dictating not only what is to be learnt, but also how it is to be learnt and how it is to be assessed. This renders negotiation increasingly difficult as systems become more rigid and hierarchical, and opportunities for independence decrease.

The task of the facilitator is to help the student negotiate the tension between learning which is externally prescribed and student-led learning. This also involves a linkage role for the facilitator in helping students interpret professional discourse and then enabling connections to be made between student and course objectives. As seen in Chapter 5, it is crucial for facilitators to encourage students to identify their learning objectives based on what they think is relevant. The facilitator may then propose objectives which appear to have been left out. This process establishes student ownership of the objectives. Blumberg and Michael (1991) found in their study of medical students, that if externally generated objectives are looked at after students have identified their own objectives, this can reinforce the independent learning process as students realize they have developed their own skills in defining what they believe it is important to learn. In this role, the mode of the facilitator is generally cooperative with outcomes being negotiated and group members being prompted to decide on the programme. However, there is also a hierarchical mode which must be acknowledged in that the boundaries of independence are proscribed by the profession.

Related to linking student and professional objectives is the other important linkage role for the facilitator which is that of providing an overview of the course as a whole and where it fits in relation to the profession. The facilitator can help students see where they have the opportunity to achieve objectives elsewhere on the course, if they are not achieved in a particular unit. The facilitator holds an overview in a way which it is impossible for students to acquire, at least not until they have completed the course, and perhaps not until they are well into qualified practice.

Stakeholders have been less concerned about how students learn than what they learn, tending to leave the process of learning to the 'experts' in education. It is, however, an interesting development that in 'Tomorrow's Doctors', the General Medical Council is essentially recommending a problem-based approach to teaching and learning in undergraduate medical education. As the authors say, 'we have recommended changes in the style of the undergraduate course in the belief that they will bring about the reduction of the curriculum overload which we are all seeking but which has proved so elusive over the years' (1993: 2). Recommending changes in 'style' is an important shift for professional bodies to take.

At the level of the student the facilitator has an important role in encouraging students to explore different ways of learning. Early in the course students need support to move beyond the traditional didactic approach which, as seen in Chapter 5, students tend to initially adopt to share information with each other, to try out other strategies for sharing.

Facilitating personal, process or propositional learning

The facilitating role also emerges as important in enabling students to make the links between personal, process and propositional knowledge. Students have been socialized to expect an emphasis on propositional knowledge. They tend on a professional course to be accepting of the value of process knowledge in the context of the application of propositional knowledge to practice. However, they vary considerably in their readiness to assign equal value to personal knowledge. As seen in Chapter 3, there is a reluctance on the part of some students to explore difficult personal experiences or to share values. At times, facilitators are tempted to collude with this reluctance, as one facilitator said, 'It's too cosy for a facilitator to challenge.'

In managing the competing pulls between the three areas of knowledge, there appear to be three interrelated tasks for the facilitator: establishing a climate of trust; containing difficult feelings; and linking the different areas of knowledge.

The socio-emotional context to learning is important (Boud *et al.*, 1993) and in learning groups, as discussed in Chapter 4, there are many complex elements to establishing effective interdependent learning. Early in the course, the facilitator is in a hierarchical mode and central to the process of establishing trust, actively guiding if not directing the process. Brookfield (1993) suggests that facilitators must earn the right to ask others to share themselves by being ready to share their own experiences and this is essential to establishing authenticity and credibility. Facilitators may view this as undermining student independence. In the first year of EAL, keen to promote independent learning, some facilitators tended to hold themselves back, concerned about disempowering the students. As a result, students were disappointed, as this student said at the end of the first term: 'You want to get to know the facilitators as people, what work they've done, what field they've worked in. I haven't been able to flesh them out as people.' In a transactional relationship, the facilitator cannot be a blank slate, reciprocity is crucial. For authentic dialogue to take place students must get to know the facilitator (Freire, 1981; Mezirow, 1983). With experience and staff training, the Bristol facilitators developed more confidence, understanding the value of sharing themselves without undermining student learning.

Another dimension to establishing trust is agreement about 'rules' for working together. Early in the course the facilitator takes an important lead in initiating discussion of such rules, later the initiative is taken by students. Students also need to feel confident that facilitators will intervene if rules are not kept. It is a challenge for facilitators to know when to do this, intervening too soon might undermine students developing the capacity to take responsibility for this role. The issue of responsibility for learning is discussed later in this chapter.

Containment (Bion, 1970) is a second aspect of the facilitator role important in managing the competing pulls between different areas of professional knowledge. Pietroni defines the term 'containment' in her discussion of reflective learning, as

> The state of calm receptiveness that is required for it to be safe enough for the inchoate and undigested pre-conceptions to be projected, received, reflected upon and given back in an articulate form. As a result of experiencing this containing and reflective process, the subject can introject a capacity for reflection and thoughtfulness in their own right.
>
> (Pietroni, 1995: 40)

Observation of facilitators suggests that a state of calm receptiveness is important, particularly in the face of unpredictable learning events such as students becoming angry with each other or precipitously leaving the room. On such occasions, the facilitator is containing not only the feelings of the individual student but also of others in the group whose feelings are aroused by the experience. An event such as a student leaving the room can be talked through so that students learn from the experience rather than remain guilty, angry and silenced.

Another way that facilitators play an important containing role for some students is in helping them find the public words to describe a private experience (Thompson, 1995). When public words are located, the experience is beginning to be brought within control. This appears to be particularly crucial for some non-traditional students who, as research by Belenky *et al.* (1986) demonstrates, may not yet have developed a public voice (see Chapter 9). Containment involves what Heron describes as working in the feeling dimension and the facilitator is doing this in the cooperative mode: 'eliciting, prompting, encouraging and indicating different ways of managing feelings . . . not managing the dynamic of the group but facilitating cooperative management' (Heron, 1989: 97). On each occasion the facilitator uses containment skills, she or he is modelling these for the group. They are skills the students can use for interdependent learning and they are also skills central to practice in the interpersonal professions.

The third role for the facilitator is to ensure that links are made between the areas of knowledge, particularly between personal and propositional knowledge. As seen in Chapter 3, personal knowledge risks remaining at the individual or anecdotal level if it is not linked with propositional knowledge. This is one of the features which distinguishes sharing personal experience in a learning group from that of sharing experience in a therapy group. It is difficult for students to do this for themselves early in the course when there is a tendency to become overwhelmed by the intensity of shared experience and not know what to do with it. In linking personal knowledge with propositional knowledge, facilitators are helping group members make sense of an experience and give meaning to it.

The facilitator as supportive or critically reflexive?

It is essential for students to feel supported and valued by the facilitator. Once a supportive learning climate is established students are more likely to express their own needs and interests. However, as seen in Chapter 5, in the interests of maintaining a cooperative climate, students hesitate to offer each other critical feedback and the facilitator must actively grapple with pressures towards group conformity (Pietroni, 1994). Yet, it is as important to establish a modus operandi of critical reflexivity as it is to establish a supportive learning climate. Early in the course, the onus is on the facilitator to model and lead in challenging assumptions and critically examining ideas and behaviours (Brookfield, 1986). Heron describes this as the confronting dimension of facilitating learning where the facilitator may act to raise 'consciousness about the group's resistances to and avoidances of things it needs to face and deal with' (1989: 15).

Facilitators who are aware of their own power and concerned about operating from the hierarchical mode and undermining student independence, may be reluctant to be confronting or critically reflexive. As this facilitator said at the end of the first year of EAL,

> Facilitators need to be a little more directive about some of the issues which are around . . . I probably tried to present the alternate views but very ambivalently . . . this is a student activity and I don't want to daunt them. If they feel I've got this information they're not going to discuss freely.

Concerns such as these led new facilitators to be too tentative initially. However, for students, this ambivalence is confusing and frustrating. As this student said in a rather exasperated way at the end of the first term, 'Why can't facilitators facilitate? I just wish facilitators were a bit more proactive and saying "why would you do that"?' There are occasions in professional education, particularly early in the course when the facilitator must be in the hierarchical mode and lead from the front. In doing so it seems important for the facilitator to be proactive rather than reactive, and at the same time be clear about the power and authority associated with the facilitator role.

One simple strategy which is proactive and appears to be effective in both respecting the student position but also challenging it, is to ask questions to stimulate critical reflection (Brookfield, 1986; Jaques, 1992). This establishes the facilitator in the cooperative rather than directive mode. Sophie Freud suggests that good questions may be regarded 'as gifts rather than intrusive assault' (1988: 110). These may be questions which require students to link their assumptions to existing research or frameworks of knowledge. This approach also reinforces the concept that students have access to knowledge, that it does not all reside with the facilitator. If this is established as a norm in the learning group, students adopt a similar questioning stance.

As students question each other and learn to work interdependently, it may be important for the facilitator to mediate between students. Trying to encourage students to express an opinion 'can elicit language and views that upset others (or me). This can't simply be let go' (Pettman, 1991: 158). As mediator, the facilitator builds bridges between students, but more than acts as intermediary. For example as mediator, the facilitator may temporarily join with the more vulnerable students if they are being disempowered by other students in the group. Or, the facilitator may reflect on the impact of language on others. Mediating requires facilitators to actively use themselves to enable students to learn interdependently. As seen in the last chapter, the expression of diversity and difference in a group inevitably leads to tensions and at times to conflict. The role of the facilitator is to normalize this process and model strategies for dealing with conflict.

The expertise of facilitators?

The norm in higher and professional education is for the teacher to be seen to be the expert who delivers subject expertise to the student. Yet in independent learning, the facilitator is expected to be an expert in facilitating and to not provide subject expertise in the context of the facilitator role. Initially on the Bristol course, this was a source of tension and confusion for staff as well as students. For staff there were two areas of concern. First, there was anxiety about not knowing enough about the topics the students would be studying to know if the students were 'on the right track'. Secondly, was the concern about the implications of withholding subject expertise and the risk of students experiencing this as playing games.

It was undoubtedly frustrating for students to be aware that their facilitator either was an expert on the topic under study but would not make the expertise available, or that the facilitator felt she or he knew nothing. As this student said,

> They seem to back off and pretend they're some sort of nuclear scientist who knows nothing whatsoever about social work whereas in practice they have a much better framework than us novices.

It was reassuring for new facilitators to experience for themselves the level of knowledge which as professional educators on a social work course they all shared, a core which can be lost sight of in a higher education context which reveres a high level of narrow subject expertise.

When the topic of the unit touched on the facilitator's own subject expertise, it was frustrating for staff to hold back and to be what was experienced by students as withholding. As this staff member reflected during her first experience of facilitating,

> I have difficulty in knowing how to deal with my own excitement or interest in a question . . . even if it's something I don't know a great deal about. Because it's then about whose agenda are you pursuing.

This concern about undermining student independence held facilitators back from working alongside students, which can be one of the most rewarding aspects of facilitating.

These dilemmas were largely resolved as staff moved away from a too literal interpretation of independent learning as operating only within an autonomous mode, to striving for a more cooperative mode which at times became hierarchical. The skill of facilitation in this arena is providing subject expertise in response to student initiative and acting as a resource for student learning. Facilitators have also come to appreciate the satisfaction of learning alongside students about subject areas previously relatively unknown to both.

Facilitator as assessor

The facilitator role in relation to assessment on a course which is designed to encourage independent and interdependent learning is complex as self and peer assessment must be considered. These issues are fully discussed in Chapter 8.

At Bristol, course planners designed a model which locates summative assessment outside the study group structure in an attempt to separate summative assessment and facilitating, and to support students to take learning risks in the group. The facilitator has a role in giving formative feedback to students in the group. If the facilitator has concerns about individual group members, the policy is to discuss these with the student concerned. Information is only passed on to the student's tutor if there are concerns about unexplained non-attendance, or about unethical or unlawful behaviour such as discrimination against other students in the group. In practice, the latter rarely occurs.

Students, however, do not fully comprehend or trust the separation of assessment roles, or the differentiation between summative and form-ative assessment. They perceive themselves as having to jump a number of hurdles in order to qualify, and staff are perceived as being in an all-powerful position as gatekeepers whether they are providing formative or summative assessment. As this student said,

> Perhaps when a facilitator is in the room we can't be as free as when he's not in the room . . . we can be a bit frightened sometimes to talk to facilitators on an equal level. We feel if we say something wrong, it will go against us.

The anxiety about 'it will go against us' is diffuse and without a rational basis, but it nevertheless shapes student behaviour. Some students do not trust the attempt to separate staff roles in relation to assessment. They see staff working closely together and wonder,

> What do facilitators say to each other? Does any information go back to the tutor? What is being said? We know what goes on at case con-ferences, why not here?

The reference to breakdowns of confidentiality in relation to case confer-ences in professional practice represents a generalized lack of trust in the system. One effective strategy appears to be for facilitators to raise con-sciousness about concerns such as these by tabling them for discussion by group members and clearly delineating lines of power and authority.

The role of the facilitator to provide formative feedback to individual study group members and to the group as a whole is accepted as important by students, and by and large, feedback is valued. Feedback from facilitators is set alongside feedback from other students. Students tend to assign more value to facilitator feedback and early in the course it is important for the facilitator to actively provide guidance in the process of peer feedback.

It is crucial for facilitators' professional development that they invite feed-back about the way they have carried out their role. This step is also important if we accept that students cannot be expected to take risks unless the facilitator does (Brookfield, 1986). On the Bristol course, there was no formal system for written feedback to or about facilitators, although the practice of inviting verbal feedback was common. Facilitators treated such feedback seriously and although, as yet, there is no requirement for such feedback to be made public, evidence of feedback is, for example, included in the evaluation of teaching quality and in applications for promotion.

Facilitating in response to student change

A central feature which shapes the facilitator role is the difference between facilitating independent learning early in the course and in the final term.

By the end of the course, students have developed as independent learners, and they have also developed in their ability to learn and work interdependently in groups.

In the discussion in Chapter 2 about the readiness of students for independent learning, I referred to a number of studies focusing on the development of students as independent learners (Perry, 1970; Belenky *et al.*, 1986; Taylor, 1986). Heron (1989) suggests that early in the course a clear hierarchical framework may be needed within which the development of independence can occur. In the middle of the course more collaboration and cooperation with students may be appropriate in managing the learning process, 'The presumption here is that they have acquired some confidence in the area of learning, with a foundation of knowledge and skill' (Heron, 1989: 18). In this way students are able to orient themselves and participate in decisions about how learning should proceed. Towards the end of the course, group members can be much more autonomous. The facilitator rarely has a central role and often participates as another group member, albeit with special status.

The onus is on the facilitator to monitor and be responsive to such changes. Initially, the Bristol facilitators were surprised and reassured by the sometimes dramatic change in the degree of student independence and interdependence. It is an exciting process to participate in. The only caveat is that there are also times when students are facing a major change and their capacity for independence seems to take two steps back. The challenge for the facilitator is to not make assumptions about the student or the group and to continually check out their position with them.

Who is responsible for learning?

This question was partially addressed earlier in relation to the issue about whether learning in professional education can be independent. A professional education course is about educating for change. 'One of the difficulties of learning for change is not only determining who or what should change, but who is responsible for change/changing' (Pettman, 1991: 161). To suggest that it is the individual student who is responsible for learning is only partially true. As discussed in the previous chapter, on a course which is group based there is the issue of responsibility to the group and by the group. On a professional education course there is the issue of responsibility to the profession and by the profession. The autonomous mode in its pure sense cannot be implemented by the facilitator. The cooperative mode is feasible, but only within externally set limits.

There are occasions when the facilitator must act from a hierarchical mode in the interest of the profession and this may conflict with what the student feels are her or his needs, and with the development of student independence. In operating from a hierarchical mode because this is what the profession requires, the individual facilitator may not feel this is the most productive mode to be in. For example, in social work with the introduction of a narrow task based conception of competence, an increasing number of educators and practitioners are beginning to question the direction the profession is taking.

Whichever mode the facilitator is working from, it is important for facilitators to be clear about the chosen mode and to practice from an ethical base. Pettman, in her discussion of teaching and training in anti-racist and anti-sexist programmes in Australia reflects, 'Do I have any obligation to deal with the effects of my interventions?' She comments on the relatively small amount of literature about the ethics of teaching relative to the ethics of research. Pettman (1991) suggests that as facilitators we have an ethical responsibility to be clear about 'the politics of location' (Rich, 1986). We must be aware as facilitators of how we are located socially in relations of domination and subordination, particularly in relation to gender, race, and class as these relations will 'infuse our dealings with one another' (Pettman, 1991: 164). We must also be clear with students about our perspectives and biases. If we are clear, this enables students to engage with us. One advantage for students working in several different groups over the life of a course is that they have the opportunity to experience the diverse styles and perspectives of different facilitators.

If we accept the premise that personal knowledge is as important in professional education as process and propositional knowledge (Eraut, 1992), this also confronts the facilitator with ethical issues which are less likely to arise in relation to propositional knowledge. Facilitating the development of personal knowledge places a responsibility on the facilitator to be clear about the purpose of doing so and clarifying issues of risk and safety for the student.

A central aspect of ethical practice is the requirement that as facilitators we listen to students, in particular to regularly invite feedback about our practice as facilitators. This process cannot be left solely to the discretion of the individual facilitator. There are limits to the independence of facilitators, as there are to student independence. For example, it is essential to monitor the practice of different facilitators, as increasingly there are moves towards monitoring the practice of lecturers. This is not to suggest there is one way to facilitate, 'there are good and bad methods of facilitating any given group, but there is no one right and proper method' (Heron, 1989: 21).

Rather than agree that facilitators need 'special social and psychological understanding and expertise' (Taylor, 1986: 70), I suggest facilitators need clarity about the activities required in the role, particularly about the modes of facilitation and their implications for independent learning. Opportunities for regular peer consultation and related staff development are essential. Working alongside students engaged in independent and interdependent learning is both challenging and rewarding.

The facilitator role is pivotal and facilitators need to be clear about the centrality of their position, albeit their position shifts over the life of a course. Early in the course the facilitator is highly visible, but surprisingly early, if things go well, she or he moves to the back seat, and only very occasionally will return to the front. As this student commented about the facilitator for her group,

> She took a back seat and we had to work it out amongst ourselves but we did pick her brains when we needed it, her particular expertise. She was really coming in when we asked her and occasionally she might contribute subtly . . . from the back seat.

7
Restraint, Resourcefulness and Problem-based Learning

In the relatively rich countries of the western world we have over the past decade become all too familiar with the impact of reduced resources. In education, the effects have been experienced in the form of diminishing expenditure on materials such as books and audio-visual equipment, a deterioration in the physical environment and worsening staff–student ratios. In the United Kingdom this situation has been exacerbated by the rapid increase in student numbers. Since 1988 there has been a 20 per cent decline in the unit of resource across all institutions as government policy has forced up student numbers and forced down the relative cost of higher education. 'Higher education institutions have been challenged to demonstrate how they can realise the educational potential of many thousands of new learners under conditions of significant resource deprivation' (Robertson, 1994: 26).

There is an inherent dilemma in discussing the challenge of realizing the educational potential of students under conditions of resource deprivation. If creative responses are proposed, does this imply collusion with resource constraints? Would energy be better allocated to fighting cuts? Or, have cutbacks been present for so long, with the prospect of continuing for the foreseeable future, that we are compelled to develop new and creative ways of responding rather than waiting for the proverbial pot of gold? As educators, we have at least a moral imperative to be proactive in our responses for the sake of those students currently participating in courses for whom any future improvement in resources will be irrelevant. As public servants, we also have a moral duty to taxpayers to optimize the service we provide. Finally, proactivity is essential for our own morale as educators in a time of change.

Gibbs and Jenkins (1992) suggest that lecturers in higher education have until recently tried to ignore the problems of increased student numbers and fewer resources, and carry on much as before. Remedial actions have been limited to trimming, reducing, cutting out, and making do. Gibbs and Jenkins further suggest that to respond by continuing with conventional teaching methods and accepting limited outcomes would be to accept defeat. In particular, the continuing pre-dominance of teacher-centred approaches with large classes risks developing in the learner a narrow conception of teaching and a reproductive conception of learning (Gibbs, 1992). We must think strategically and radically and change our approaches to teaching and learning with the aim of retaining quality without staff being central, including exploring possibilities for students using each other as resources (Gibbs and Jenkins, 1992).

We must also examine our beliefs about the nature of resources and access to them. In higher education, students and staff are socialized to expect required resources to be available. Designated resources become over-valued in the pressure to find quick-fix solutions to problems. For example, certain resources, whether they are people or materials, may be earmarked as essential to addressing a particular question. One result is the drive from students, publishers and bookstores for courses to list the titles of a few key texts. This culture encourages a dependency on specified resources challenged by educationists:

> Evidence of inadequate skills in working co-operatively to solve problems, over-dependence on teachers as sources of information, and lack of that self-critical awareness of one's own ignorance in a subject area that is the only true precursor of further enquiry – together these indicate that the standards achieved by our graduates in relation to the resources invested in them are often less than satisfactory.
>
> (Ramsden, 1992: 37)

The relationship between resources and achievement has become a hotly contested political issue throughout education.

In professional education, there are further grounds for developing creative approaches in response to diminishing resources. Students, whether they are entering the fields of health or social care, education, law or business, must be prepared for resources also being increasingly limited in practice. Learning the skills and knowledge of practice in a resource rich environment does not adequately prepare students for the realities of professional practice today. Given the complexity of problems facing practitioners and the pace of rapid change, it is crucial to learn how to address problems, and how to identify and locate appropriate resources, rather than rely on external solutions being immediately available. Problem-based learning is one approach to teaching and learning which enables students to develop these skills.

In the first part of this chapter, I begin by examining the question of what is problem-based learning. I then introduce some research into problem-based learning which is relevant to discussion in this chapter. I go on to discuss the processes of problem-based learning from the perspective of how they enhance students' resourcefulness, and require them to think creatively and act independently and interdependently, rather than depend on traditional external solutions being readily available. Finally, I also examine the nature and structure of resources required to support problem-based learning. If problem-based learning is to effectively develop resourcefulness, it must be underpinned by a resource infrastructure.

What is problem-based learning?

The usual concept of education is that knowledge and understanding are subject-based and the focus is on propositional knowledge delivered by experts. In contrast, problem-based learning is 'a way of constructing and teaching courses using problems as a stimulus and focus for student activity' (Boud and Feletti, 1991: 14). In this approach, expertise is 'the ability to make sound judgements as to what is problematic about a situation, to identify the most important problems, and to know how to go about solving or at least ameliorating them' (Margetson, 1991: 44 in Boud and Feletti, 1991). The focus is on 'knowing how', in addition to 'knowing that', or on process knowledge in addition to propositional knowledge. Knowing how involves being able to take responsibility for learning, including identifying learning needs, setting learning goals, planning learning activities, finding and using the resources for learning and evaluating learning achieved (Boud, 1988). These are all strategies which are central to independent learning and crucial to professional practice.

Problem-based learning involves learning through tackling relevant problems. Engel describes this process in the context of medical education:

> The students will progress from recognition of cues to initial problem formulation, hypothesis generation, enquiry strategy, review and refinement of hypothesis. By iteration they will arrive at a working diagnosis or decision, according to the problem they are asked to tackle.
>
> (1992: 326)

Or, to use rather less logical positivist terminology, students discover what they need to learn about by recognizing what they need to know about a problem, defining their learning objectives, deciding how they are going to find out what they need to know, accessing and sharing relevant information, and assessing what they have learnt. The goal is learning rather than problem solving, the problem provides the context within which learning takes place (Gibbs, 1992: 157). It is therefore interdisciplinary since dealing with problems involves bringing knowledge to bear from a range of disciplines. Typically, problem-based learning involves groups of students working interdependently and cooperatively, sharing ideas, dividing up the learning to be done and briefing each other.

Problem-based learning is establishing an increasingly firm base in professional education. It is best known in the health sciences where the pioneers were North American medical schools: Case Western Reserve in the United States in the 1950s, and McMaster in Canada in the late 1960s (Boud and Feletti, 1991). Problem-based learning has since been adopted by many other medical schools in North America and also in other parts of the world. For example, in Australia at Newcastle University in New South Wales, and in Holland at Maastricht. The United Kingdom has been slower to introduce problem-based learning in medical education, although the General Medical Council (1993) proposes that all medical schools implement a curriculum designed around problem-based learning. This recommendation is slowly being picked up, led by medical schools such as the University of Liverpool. Other health care professions have also introduced problem-based learning. For example, in Canada it is an approach widely used in nursing, occupational and physiotherapy education. Beyond health care, problem-based learning has been introduced in a range of fields including business, engineering, architecture and education (Boud and Feletti, 1991). Social work is a relative newcomer to problem-based learning. It was introduced at Bristol University in 1990 throughout the social work course, and it has also been implemented in parts of other courses, including Newcastle University in Australia and Edinburgh University in Scotland.

Research into problem-based learning

Some of the most extensive research into problem-based learning has been carried out at McMaster University, Faculty of Health Sciences. In contrast to my qualitative study at Bristol, the McMaster researchers adopted a traditional outcome oriented approach, and in particular have consistently compared the outcomes of different approaches to teaching and learning medicine. Their findings clearly indicate that students from a problem-based curriculum are as successful in completing medical education as those in a traditional curriculum (Barrows and Tamblyn, 1980; Ferrier and Woodward, 1987).

A McMaster study particularly relevant to our discussion, compared a problem-based approach to medical education where some guidance about learning issues was provided by staff, with a traditional teacher directed medical education course (Blumberg and Michael, 1991). Learning issues were defined as factual or conceptual material which students decide must be understood in order to respond to the case under discussion. It was found that students in a programme where learning issues were identified by a mix of staff and students, develop self-directed learning behaviours to a greater extent than students in a teacher-centred programme. Self-directed learning behaviours include recognizing the need for new learning, setting one's own learning objectives, defining relevant questions for study, accessing relevant information and testing one's depth of understanding about what one has learned. The researchers suggested there are several aspects of problem-based learning which foster self-directed learning. First, students themselves set their learning objectives based on what they think is relevant and are therefore more internally motivated. Secondly, students access material on their own. Thirdly, the need to contribute to group learning motivates them to acquire the content and this process also gives students feedback on their level of understanding.

This study is of particular interest here because generally in professional education there is a core of identified knowledge students are required to learn in order to qualify. Yet, the availability of course objectives does not seem to undermine the development of independent learning, assuming student generated issues and course generated objectives are consistent. These findings will be returned to later.

The processes of problem-based learning

Problem-based learning relies on the development of process knowledge, in particular the three processes of acquiring information, handling information and giving information (Eraut, 1994). These processes are similar to the self-directed learning behaviours outlined in the Blumberg and Michael (1991) study. It is through observation of Bristol students using these processes that I have come to view problem-based learning as playing an important role in both developing independent and interdependent learning and contributing to student resourcefulness.

Acquiring information

Students must acquire information in order to understand fully the problem. The emphasis is on students actively seeking out relevant information rather than being provided with that which the subject expert deems to be important. The problem provides both the context and the guide for acquiring information. The body of knowledge relevant to the particular profession in question will also be highly influential in shaping the information sought. Eraut (1992) identifies four types of process knowledge essential to effectively acquiring information: an existing knowledge base in the area concerned; a conceptual framework to guide enquiry; and skills in collecting and interpreting information. For our discussion here, I am locating the centrally important skill of interpreting information with the process of handling information.

Early in the course, students' existing knowledge base is, as would be expected, varied, ranging from minimal to extensive depending on the relatedness of pre-course experience and education and the topic under study. Inevitably, many students lack a conceptual framework to guide enquiry. Furthermore, few students have pre-course experience of problem-based learning where independent enquiry was expected. However, even if students have an existing relevant knowledge base or conceptual framework, the level of anxiety about beginning a course and the lack of understanding about where knowledge might fit tends to contribute to a generalized feeling of anxiety about not knowing.

As seen in Chapter 3, a significant number of students feel disoriented in the first term, describing this in terms of not knowing enough to know what information to seek, where to go for it, or how to set boundaries on the information they are looking for. McMaster research (Neufeld and Chong, 1984) indicates this is a confidence issue and that students are very efficient in generating hypotheses early in the course and using them to collect further information. They found that even early in the course the patterns of clinical reasoning of medical students were remarkably similar to that of experienced physicians. The key difference between the beginning student and the experienced practitioner was in the quality and accuracy of the hypothesis, dependent on increasing knowledge and experience (1984: 251–2).

Initially, Bristol staff were also concerned about whether students knew enough to know what information to acquire. One example of staff concerns arose in a study unit on mental health. If students alone identified the learning issues, there was a risk that some students would ignore, or view as uniformly negative, mainstream approaches to treating psychiatric illness and focus on alternative therapies. On the other hand, there was also concern about whether staff guidance would undermine student generated learning objectives. This dilemma about how much information students should be expected to gather for themselves and how much they should be given is common in problem-based learning courses (Coles, 1991: 300). It was exhaustively debated by the Bristol staff with agreement that more guidance should be provided early in the course and later on, students could be expected to gather it themselves.

An outcome of the decision to provide more guidance was to offer a 'frameworks lecture' which would introduce each problem-based theme, and meet Eraut's (1992) requirement for a conceptual framework. The lecture was envisaged as a map which would signpost students about the various possible directions and routes to take. This was seen as important for those students who lack a conceptual framework to guide enquiry. It also addressed the need to frame learning within the context of a set of learning outcomes defined by the professional accrediting body. By and large frameworks lectures have been a well received addition to the course, particularly in the first year when students are seeking a way into the knowledge underpinning a problem. This confirms the McMaster study (Blumberg and Michael, 1991) where identification by staff of some learning issues appears to complement student led learning rather than undermine it.

A further challenge for students in acquiring information is setting boundaries on the almost infinite store of knowledge potentially available in relation to a problem. This can be daunting and an initial objective is to learn to be realistic about what can be achieved. This student's comment at the end of the first term was typical of that of her peers:

A lot of us are feeling we don't quite know what level of learning is expected. We're just testing all the time. Sometimes we set standards too high for ourselves, and then we ease off a bit and then we sometimes feel we are lowering standards too much and are getting a wishy washy overview.

The facilitator has a role to help students set boundaries. For example, as seen in the previous chapter, the facilitator has an overview of the course and can reassure students that they are not expected to learn all there is to know about a problem at a particular point, there are other opportunities elsewhere on the course.

One of the crucial determining boundaries on a professional course is time. The processes of problem-based learning are time consuming compared to the time spent in a lecture. Students can work together very efficiently and effectively once they are familiar with problem-based learning and know how to work together as a group. However, for a new group, particularly early in the course, the process of problem-based learning can be slow and confusing. As seen in the previous chapter, the facilitator is central to shaping these processes early in the first term.

Students become very resourceful in collecting information. Students acquire information from traditional resources including written materials and videos, and from a developing bank of information technology resources. Blumberg and Michael (1991) found that the use of study resources varied quite significantly between students in a traditional course and those in a problem-based course. The former most frequently use material developed by staff and two-thirds of their most used resources are staff directed. In their use of textbooks, they read for specific assignments. In contrast, problem-based learning students frequently use the library and use various types of library resources significantly more often than the traditional group. They also read primary research literature much more frequently than traditional students which may be indicative of their resourcefulness in locating such sources.

Problem-based students learn to view each other as resources. Their scope of enquiry is as broad as the capacity of the students in the group, and they support each other to expand beyond the suggestions for sources provided by course planners. They also develop systems for sharing materials, an important feature of interdependent learning in contrast to traditional models where learning is a private and competitive activity. The Bristol students used each other as consultants, extending the concept of peer tutoring which has been used successfully with same age students in higher education (Falchikov, 1986). Falchikov found that, in addition to tutees, tutors benefited from peer tutoring, 'experienced' tutors felt themselves to be more confident and critical as a result of the experience. This process was evident among the Bristol students.

Students also acquire information from expert consultants in the field of enquiry. They develop skills in consulting, and learn how to determine what questions to ask and how to obtain information relevant to the problem. As this black woman student commented as she looked back on her first year of the DipSW,

Being able to do it [obtain information from a resource person] systematically without much thought or panic, 'Oh, God, I've got to speak to a consultant, what am I going to ask him?' That's not been a problem for me. Most of my training in the first year has contributed to my confidence . . . and also what you do with information once you've got it. Sifting out what's relevant and what isn't has been very crucial. In our Study Units when we decide what's relevant, what do we have here, we use the board and we brainstorm and we think about what we are going to have to know about.

In a society where we have been socialized to view particular kinds of experts as intimidating and hard to reach, the process of learning how to access consultants is important to learning and to practice. This process also contributes to interprofessional practice, to working with professionals where there are status differences of the kind described by this student which often create barriers.

Handling information

Handling information includes being able to interpret the information acquired and critically evaluate it:

We do not only want people who can find resources for themselves, arrange their time appropriately or set learning goals, but rather we want learners who know and understand enough to be able to distinguish plausible from implausible knowledge claims or convincing from unconvincing evidence.

(Boud, 1988: 60)

This is particularly crucial today when we are subject to information overload and to very sophisticated marketing strategies.

There are two complementary approaches to learning to critically evaluate information in problem-based learning. The traditional approach is to use propositional knowledge as a resource and examine information in the light of existing knowledge, identifying where there is agreement or disagreement and where there are gaps in knowledge. For students who are strong conceptually and familiar with handling abstract theory, particularly those with recent academic training, this approach is familiar and usable. For other students, this process can be mystifying and intimidating. As a strategy to develop analytic skills, it was agreed by Bristol staff that each study unit would include one learning activity which requires students to critique a piece of research. This provides an opportunity for students to practice skills of analysis and to observe others modelling this process.

Secondly, learning in groups offers significant opportunities to develop skills in interpreting information as group members will inevitably interpret information differently. Perry's research (1970) suggests that students are at different stages of readiness for accepting a diversity of opinions and perspectives. It was evident in my research that the expression of difference was at times avoided by students, or brought to premature closure, a theme discussed in Chapter 5. However, as the course progressed, various strategies and learning activities in relation to the 'problem' were successfully used to encourage students to express difference, including structuring debates or activities which required students to take a position and then discuss it.

Students use the information acquired to work towards understanding the problem. Their task is to link aspects of the information together, relating what they are learning to what they know. Among the students there were different levels of activity and participation, as reported in other problem-based courses (Coles, 1991). As seen in Chapter 5, factors influencing group participation are complex and varied, and the different levels of participation can be a source of tension in a group. The Bristol students were very concerned about students participating equally and became creative in tackling less than good enough participation without necessarily challenging it. For example, they clearly identified in writing early on who was responsible for what, and thus attempted to introduce elements of a contract and associated accountability.

Giving information

The process of giving information has taken on a new importance in professional practice in recent years with the increased emphasis on good quality communication between professionals, and between professionals and service user. Eraut (1994) identifies that the skills needed for giving information are to be intelligible, to select the information most needed, and to be able to give information orally and in written form. Observation of the Bristol students suggests that these skills, although important, are not sufficient to enable students to develop the full range of information giving skills. Students need to develop a range of strategies for giving information, in part for interest and variety, and in part to be sensitive to the nature of the information and the varying needs of the recipients. Furthermore, the process of giving information must be managed so that the information given can be received.

Early in the course students tended to provide information to the group in a fairly stereotypic way, often presenting it orally in the form of mini lectures, sometimes with accompanying handouts. Typically, towards the end of the first term they became bored with the routinization of this format and, encouraged by facilitators, discussed alternative strategies. The timing of rethinking their processes was concurrent with them gaining confidence in the requirements of problem-based learning. Their increased confidence was noticeable and appeared to enable them to take more risks and become more creative in their strategies for sharing information. For example, students made a video, or developed a role play. Some students continued to feel it was important to acquire briefing notes, much as one files away lecture notes in a traditional approach.

Related to the strategies for sharing information is the issue of accessibility of language used. Presenting information to a range of students, including students from ethnic minorities and from different social classes, requires the presenter to pay attention to intelligibility beyond that typically required in presenting an essay to a subject expert. The experience lacked by students in organizing and presenting material is more than adequately compensated for by their ability to talk in a straightforward, jargon-free way. It seems likely that developing these skills will contribute to skills of giving information to a range of service users.

Giving information in a way which enables it to be received also requires the learning group to be managed. I was impressed on a number of occasions by the skills of chairpersons managing a group. When the chairperson was responsible for activities such as time-keeping and managing the demands of the total agenda, it enabled the student presenters to focus on delivering their information.

The students were universally positive about the skills they developed in giving information. As will be seen in Chapter 10, when interviewed at the end of their first year of qualified practice, they viewed this skill as essential to practice with colleagues and service users, and were clear that they had developed it on the course.

Problem-based learning, independence and interdependence

Discussion in the previous section identified the various processes involved in the development of process knowledge. The risk of discussing these separately is that the value of the integrated experience of problem-based learning is lost. There are some key features of problem-based learning which contribute to the ability to learn independently and interdependently. These features closely link with those identified by Bligh (1992) in his survey of self-directed learning among trainee doctors in general practice.

First, problem-based learning generates enthusiasm and excitement among students and is positively received by most if not all students. Its relevance to practice appears to reinforce motivation to learn. As this student said, 'I'm very interested in sociology and psychology, but I have to be able to see the person in the street in relation to theoretical ideas to understand them.' Problem-based learning relates directly to the person in the street. Early in the course, before assessment begins to play a dominant role, the interest in learning is evident and students work very hard to address the learning issues generated by the problem. This would appear to be 'deep level learning' as described by Entwistle and Ramsden (1983), and noted by Bligh (1992) as an intrinsic interest in study.

Secondly, by the end of the first term, the students have significantly developed their confidence in working both independently and interdependently. Bligh (1992) discusses the importance of a positive self-concept as a learner. One of the most noticeable features of the Bristol students, remarked on by staff, agency supervisors, and the students themselves, was the confidence of the students to acknowledge they did not know the answer to a problem, but were confident they could find out. Blumberg and Michael (1991) also noted student willingness to admit and consequently pursue lack of understanding. Experience with problem-based learning appears to make it easier for students to tolerate the anxiety of not knowing because students become familiar with the process of moving from not knowing to knowing.

Thirdly, working interdependently encourages discussion and the opportunity to learn from each other which many students enjoy. This also develops an openness to feedback and criticism. Whereas for some students this may never reach the point of comfort, it is integrated into their expectations of the way they work together. They understand the enabling and disabling factors and some students become very skilled in managing these in the role of chairperson, or simply as an enabling group member.

Finally, problem-based learning enables students to bring together personal, process and propositional knowledge, and to value each for its contribution to understanding the problem. Problem-based learning enables more than the integration of different areas of propositional knowledge, it enables the integration of different kinds of knowledge.

The resource infrastructure

Much of the discussion so far has been about student responsibility for learning. There is a risk that this implies students can manage without resources. Whereas I am arguing that problem-based learning enhances student resourcefulness, a coherent resource infrastructure to support and underpin problem-based learning continues to be necessary. It is also essential for the infrastructure to be apparent and accessible to students. In the first year of implementation of EAL, some students were disparaging about the course being a DIY (do-it-yourself) course. In more recent years this diminutive has all but disappeared. Initially, the resource infrastructure was not clearly and firmly enough in place to be visible and since then several years of experience have enabled staff to refine it. Like McMaster, the infrastructure includes four broad categories of resources: problems presented in various formats; reference and information resources; support resources; and evaluation resources. To this list I add the fifth resource of the physical climate. These are separately discussed with the exception of evaluation resources which provide tools for formative assessment and are fully discussed in the next chapter.

Problem format

Problems can be presented in various formats, including written case studies, simulated patients and audio-visual presentations. On the Bristol course, each problem is presented in the context of a 'study unit' which includes learning objectives for the unit, suggested activities to extend learning about the unit, assessment tasks and suggested learning resources (Burgess, 1992). The most important features of the study unit are that it is relevant, varied and forms an intelligible and achievable unit which is part of a larger whole.

For students in professional education, the relevance of problems to practice is crucial. This not only requires attention to the different dimensions and levels of practice but also regular updating as new knowledge emerges. Designing problems is a complex art because not only must a range of problems be represented, but also a diverse range of people and contexts. For example, there is a risk that people featured in the problem scenarios are always represented as members of a white heterosexual majority culture. Student feedback about problem scenarios has underlined the importance of representativeness, a difficult issue if tokenism is to be avoided.

It is also important that the study units link together to form a coherent whole. As mentioned earlier, it is not easy for students at any one point in the course to have an overview of the whole, and it is helpful if staff can clarify how a problem at one point in the course might link to another. For example, in the first term a study unit focuses on understanding children and families, whereas later in the year another unit focuses on child abuse. Engel describes this as cumulative learning, where a subject is not studied in finite depth at any one time but is reintroduced repeatedly and 'with increasing sophistication whenever it contributes legitimately to reasoned decision making in a problematic situation' (1991: 29).

Finally, variety of format is important. If problem outlines look the same at the end of the course as they do at the beginning, they do not continue to generate the same kind of enthusiasm in the student.

Reference and information resources

On a problem-based learning course the ready availability of up-to-date reference and information resources is important. On the Bristol course, extensive reading lists are made available so that students have a wide range of texts to draw on, and little or no use is made of core texts. Students are also actively encouraged to go further than reading lists and pursue their own resources. As discussed earlier, Blumberg and Michael (1991) found that problem-based learning students used a wider range of resources than students on a traditional course who were considerably more wedded to staff-directed resources.

Gibbs (1992) recommends the strategy of widening the range of resources so that not all students are chasing the same materials at the same time. At

Bristol, a decision was made for the course to be organized so that groups focus on a different theme at any one time, therefore spreading the demand for resources over a longer period. Complaints about the lack of availability of books diminished following the introduction of this system.

'Ephemeral' material is held in Resource Boxes and in addition each group collects material during the period of their work together. These are materials which libraries usually do not hold, such as newspaper articles, newsletters, materials developed by practitioners and agencies, photocopied articles and student notes. Such materials generally have a short-term shelf life but they have the value of being current and may be the precursor to more formal material being produced.

The other essential element in the resource bank is people. One central resource is the 'expert' consultant who may come from the university staff or practice. On a professional course this offers a rich opportunity to increase diversity of expertise beyond that represented by course staff who are typically criticized by students for not being close enough to practice. This is also an ideal opportunity for practitioners to contribute their expertise. In planning consultations attempts are made to include a range of perspectives. For example, within a mental health unit, consultants include a university researcher, a hospital based psychiatrist, an approved social worker from a statutory agency, a psychiatric survivor representing a self-help group, and a social worker from a voluntary agency specializing in tackling homelessness. This diversity of expertise could not be replicated among university staff running a conventional lecture based course.

Support resources

Support resources for students are essential in all professional courses where students face a range of pressures, including personal pressures such as student poverty and caring responsibilities, and course pressures such as expectation of success and fear of failure. Support resources are varied on the Bristol course, based on the philosophy that sole reliance on the traditional resource of the tutor encourages student dependency. Furthermore, it may set up an expectation of a dependent relationship of the kind increasingly unavailable in practice where practitioners are having to locate their own support systems.

Emphasis is placed on the support students can offer each other, particularly in the context of the learning group which very often becomes a core support for the student and lasts beyond the formal life of the group. Although group membership changes throughout the course, ongoing contact with members of the first study group is clearly a significant resource for many students. In addition to providing emotional support, group members provide each other with tangible help such as writing skills. The potential significance of peer contact is indicated by Smith and Hatton's (1993) research into teacher education which suggests that more course reflection may occur with 'critical friends' than through interaction with staff or written assignments.

Support is also available through a structure of student support groups. For example, when the Bristol students were researched there were groups for black students, and since then groups for gay and lesbian students and disabled students have been introduced. The support groups vary to include student led groups, groups with a paid facilitator who is an 'expert' on the focus of the group, and groups which may have a staff member playing a facilitator role to help it get started. The groups vary each year in their viability and meaning to individual members. They can become very active, as for example, the gay and lesbian student group did in relation to advocating for curriculum change. In this way they can begin to experience the power of the collective (Mullender and Ward, 1991).

Study skills

A form of student support which merits specific attention is support with study skills. Study skills input is designed to help students overcome skills and knowledge deficits. With the diversity of routes into higher education, discussed in detail in Chapter 9, the range of educational backgrounds of students is increasing at a time when opportunity for individual staff contact is decreasing. There is a debate in the literature about whether special provisions should be made to counter individual difficulties for non-traditional learners.

On one side of the debate are those who believe non-traditional learners lack 'ideational scaffolding' (Entwistle, 1983: 23), and particular attention needs to be paid to remedying this situation to enable students to organize their developing knowledge effectively (Percy, 1985). Yet, Ramsden (1987) reported on research into first year students who participated in a learning skills programme at the University of Melbourne in 1984. The programme addressed managing study time effectively, reading strategies, note taking, examination preparation, and writing effectively. The academic progress and approaches of this group of students was compared with that of a comparable group of students who did not take study skills and found that those who attended performed no differently.

On the other side of the debate are researchers such as Mills and Molloy who suggest that,

> Non-standard entrants have no greater need to acquire study skills than do standard entrants. Conventionally aged and qualified students have just as much difficulty in adjusting from the teacher-centred modes of A-level teaching to the student centred modes of higher education learning, as the non-standard entrants do . . . There need be no elaborately different response from institutions with assumed initial difficulties of non-standard entrants.
>
> (Mills and Molloy, 1989: 52)

Mills and Molloy determined that the greatest difference between non-traditional learners and others is that the former have no clear expectations about how much needs to be learned and understood, and no reserves of self-confidence to fall back on so that when the going gets tough, they have 'an extremely high tendency to attribute all learning difficulties to their own personal inadequacies' (1989: 52). They propose including study skills as a central feature of a programme and something from which all students can benefit.

The Bristol course opted for the latter point of view. Study skills were offered in the first term, both in a small group and individual format, to any Bristol student who wanted it. However, take-up by students was surprisingly low. This may be explained by the preference expressed by the students for individual help relevant to specific pieces of assessed work, rather than more generalized skills courses. The other major barrier to participating in study skills sessions appears to be that it makes a public statement about students who self-identify as needing help and who have often already had a history of being labelled as failures in the education system. Being a student on a professional course may bring an additional barrier to identifying the need for help. Similar to the findings of Mills and Molloy (1989), the lack of confidence of this group of students is significant. Non-traditional students often prefer the option of individualized private help from within or outside the university system.

Physical climate

The other important resource for adult learning, not mentioned by the McMaster researchers, is the physical climate. Hammond and Collins (1991: 34) suggest important elements of the physical climate include: comfortable lighting, temperature, seating and ventilation; and, access to parking, canteen, library and storage. A survey of concerns raised by Bristol students at course meetings demonstrates the importance to them of the physical climate. Early in Year 1, student concerns were dominated by concerns about their environment, including requests for example, for more cafeteria facilities, lockers, bicycle racks, parking space, and private study accommodation.

It is speculated that these issues may be more important to mature students, who predominate on professional courses, because they have become socialized to expect a certain level of provision in their pre-course experience. It is also possible that the focus on practical concerns provides an acceptable way of expressing anxiety about the system they are entering.

Staff become frustrated with a predictable litany of complaints and requests over which they have little control and many of which also negatively affect the quality of the staff environment as they double up on office space, relinquish common room space to teaching, and wait for years for a parking space. However, it is clearly essential not to invalidate student concerns with 'we've heard all that already', or to suggest that the 'real' problem is their anxiety, but rather to take time to hear and acknowledge students' concerns, and to respond with suggestions about how students might advocate on their own behalf, as well as provide information about what has previously been tried to tackle the problems.

Conclusion

Like the problem-based learning students in medical education (Blumberg and Michael, 1991), the Bristol students developed independent learning skills which include the ability to tolerate not knowing initially how to respond to a problem, to identify their learning objectives, and to identify, locate and use resources in a given situation. Crucially, acquisition of these skills generates student confidence in their ability to learn independently and interdependently. As this woman student said as she reflected at the end of her first term,

> I've got used to the EAL method now and I've got more faith in it. One thing it's done for me is give me more confidence in my own resources and that's been good. I don't feel I've been a passive creature who has just been fed a whole load of information. I've actually had quite an active role in my own learning.

This confidence in her own resources increased as the course progressed.

The skills of learning independently and interdependently are also essential for professional practice. It is important to note that problem-based learning students require a resource infrastructure, partly because when time to study is finite there is a limit on the amount of time which can be spent on identifying and locating resources. However, problem-based learning students are not dependent on staff directed or controlled resources. They range as far and wide in their search for relevant resources as the restraints of time will allow. As this student commented at the end of her first year on the course, 'EAL is about finding out for ourselves. This process may take longer but we do think for ourselves.' These are crucial qualities in professional practice when neither answers nor external resources are immediately available.

8

Assessment: The Crux of the Matter

The social and political context for assessment

Assessment has acquired an 'overwhelmingly powerful role in education' (Broadfoot, 1984: 2). It has become a political tool to control both the process and outcome of education. Politicians have realized that,

> If the stakes are high enough with individual life chances depending on the outcome of such assessments, any changes in the form or content of what is to be measured will bring about equivalent changes in curriculum emphasis.
>
> (Broadfoot, 1994: 3)

Furthermore, assessment has become a potent tool in dictating institutional and professional goals, with educational institutions from primary schools to universities being assessed and publicly compared on the basis of student results, and professions being required to introduce specific learning outcomes.

In professional education, the way courses have been designed and students assessed has more to do with power sharing between higher education and professional bodies than any analysis of what professional education should consist of, or how any model of expertise should develop (Eraut, 1992). Assessment in professional education reflects the tensions in the relationship between higher and professional education. Increasingly the professions, influenced by stakeholders, require the student to achieve particular learning outcomes. Yet, these learning outcomes may be at variance with those of higher education. A primary concern of the latter is ensuring that academic standards are maintained and outcomes can be measured in ways which are seen to be objective, reliable and supportive of merit and equal opportunities. This is most easily achieved in relation to propositional knowledge. However, professional knowledge is also about personal and process knowledge.

Although assessment is seen as more important than ever before, there are many criticisms of the assessment system, and there is probably more bad practice and ignorance of assessment issues than any other issue in higher education (Boud, 1994). This is surprising given that we place high value on critical analysis in our own work, but we are in general uncritically accepting of our assessment practices (Boud, 1996). Increasingly, staff development is being offered for new staff in universities. It might be illuminating to survey what proportion of this time is spent on developing staff expertise in assessment practices, as opposed to the usual focus of learning how to deliver lectures or use audio-visual resources.

Boud (1996) suggests that assessment involves two key elements. The first is the development of knowledge and the identification of standards and criteria which may be applied to any given work. The second is the capacity to make judgements about whether the work meets the required standards. In professional education, strongly influenced by the host setting, the focus by staff and students tends to be on the latter element, with standards and the criteria which underpin them not being clearly defined. The emphasis on standards is reinforced by the interests of stakeholders concerned with protecting service users and ensuring good practice. Assessment will always result in learning, but as we shall see later, the kind of learning generated by assessment may not be that desired by professional educators or students (Boud, 1994). There is too often a disturbing gap between what we require of students in assessment tasks, and the kind of learning necessary to professional practice.

Assessment and professional education, three basic premises

There are three basic premises which underpin assessment in professional education. First, assessment must bear a direct relationship to the way professional practice is assessed in the workplace. If we accept Eraut's (1992) premise that professional knowledge is derived from the three elements of propositional, personal and process knowledge, it is clearly crucial to develop appropriate criteria for meeting standards which can be applied to all three elements. It is also essential to develop the capacity to make a judgement about whether the work meets required standards. It is not defensible to summatively assess students only for entry to a profession, they must also be prepared for practice in the profession. For example, it is not defensible in either the content or structure of assessment tasks to give priority to the acquisition of facts which are likely to quickly become outdated, or which place a premium on memorization skills.

Secondly, in a course which is concerned to encourage independent and interdependent learning, staff, self and peer assessment all have a part to play in an assessment repertoire (Boud, 1996).

Once a varying mixture of self, peer and collaborative assessment replace unilateral assessment by staff, a completely new educational

climate can be created. Self-determination with respect to setting learning objectives and to programme design is not likely to make much
headway, in my view without some measure of self-assessment.

(Heron, 1988: 85)

Assessment by staff is the norm in higher education. The ability to self-
assess is a key foundation to lifelong learning (Boud, 1996), it equips the
learner to continue education after initial professional education has ended.
The rhetoric of self-assessment is increasingly voiced by all the interpersonal professions. For example, it was recently endorsed by the General
Medical Council who said that initial undergraduate medical education
'must provide the graduate about to embark on a professional career with
the capacity and the incentive to acquire and apply new knowledge and
with the ability to adapt to changing circumstances, many as yet unfore-
seen' (1993). Furthermore, in education for the interpersonal professions
which is preparing students for independent and interdependent practice,
peer assessment is a central element of self-assessment.

Thirdly, it is essential to hold in balance both the formative and summative
dimensions of assessment. The concept of formative and summative assessment was developed by Scriven (1967) over 25 years ago and remains useful
to a discussion of assessment in professional education. In particular, the
concept of formative assessment as the feedback and response designed to
help improve performance is essential to professional development, and
plays a particular role in relation to personal and process knowledge. It can
be provided by peers in a group learning context, or by staff. Summative
assessment relates to the judgement of performance and is essential to
ensure that qualifying practitioners meet required standards for entry to a
profession. In both cases, judgement is involved, but in the first it directly
serves the needs of the student, and in the second it primarily serves the
need of the university and/or profession.

Three stages of assessment

There are three key stages in the assessment process which, although relevant to higher education, take on additional significance in professional
education. The three stages include selection, continuous assessment once
the student has been accepted for the course, and 'certification' prior to
being licensed to practice. The balance between formative and summative
assessment shifts during the career of a student in professional education,
with one or the other being accorded priority at different stages. I will
explore the tensions and possibilities of complementarity between formative and summative assessment at each stage, focusing on assessment of
classroom based learning as opposed to practice based learning. Boud (1994)
suggests that summative and formative assessment cannot be separated and
both aspects must be considered together. In practice this is true, but for
clarity of discussion about a complex issue it is useful to separate formative

and summative assessment before examining how they come together and complement or undermine each other.

Selection

Selection is the first assessment point where the power of assessors is paramount. Selection of students involves a summative judgement which results in a student being accepted or rejected for a course. Selecting students takes on a heightened importance in professional education because it is making a public statement about the kinds of applicants who are or are not appropriate for education for a particular profession. One memory of my own application to an initial professional education course, well over 20 years ago, is the anxiety generated by the fear of being rejected at the selection stage by a profession to which I was committed, and within which I had already spent some time working in an unqualified capacity. The prevailing myth at that time was that if one could gain acceptance to the course in question, one could count on qualifying. Selection was viewed as a greater hurdle than finally qualifying.

Surprisingly, in view of the significance of this crucial stage, little research has been carried out into selection or admissions procedures, except perhaps in relation to access to higher education. The marginalization of selection procedures was confirmed by a study which found that admissions policies and practice take low priority in higher education and consequently few universities have formal admissions policies, there is great variation between departments in admissions procedures within one institution, and outcomes are not monitored (Fulton and Ellwood, 1989).

Professional education courses may have complex selection procedures which absorb considerable resources on the part of course staff who attempt to manage the perhaps insurmountable challenge of making the 'right' choice for the 'right' applicant. Gatekeeping to the course is only a few steps away from gatekeeping to the profession. As at other assessment points, good practice requires selection to be on the basis of agreed and explicit criteria, and in recent years this has increasingly required attention to equal opportunities issues. In contrast to higher education generally where criteria may be defined only in terms of propositional knowledge, professional courses are likely to be seeking applicants who also have personal attributes which signal potential suitability for a particular profession, and relevant experience which provides the applicant with a basis of understanding of what the profession entails. The concern to select an applicant with appropriate potential and to avoid admitting someone who is manifestly unsuited for a particular course results in a range of admission procedures. In addition to standard admission forms, references, and evidence of academic prowess or potential, there may be procedures such as personal statements and interviews.

One of the most complex and well-documented admissions procedures for professional education is that for entry to McMaster Medical School.

The procedures involve several stages with reduced numbers at each stage: an initial screening on the basis of academic standing and an 'auto-biographical letter'; then a group interview which comprises a 'simulated tutorial' observed by assessors, and a personal interview; and the final stage where all the existing data is thoroughly reviewed. At each stage members from two of the three constituencies, a faculty member, a medical student, and a lay or academic member of the community, are represented among the assessors. The selection process also includes information provided to the applicant to assist self-selection. Whereas it is common practice for courses to provide applicants with information, McMaster is unusual in that applicants receive a letter from Year 2 students spelling out the differences between the McMaster approach and conventional approaches to medical education. The final paragraph compellingly exhorts applicants to,

> Be honest with yourself. If you think you cannot adjust to the McMaster programme, you may wish to reconsider your suitability for the pro-gramme, and/or the programme's suitability for you. This is not a case of 'better' or 'worse' education, rather, each mode is appropriate to the needs of a different kind of student.
>
> (McMaster, 1989/90)

This is important information for potential applicants to consider, although in a market context where different institutions are competing for the same student it may be difficult to definitively advise applicants to seek an 'appro-priate' course elsewhere.

Selection has a potential formative dimension, both for those applicants who are refused a place and those who are accepted. Regardless of its genesis, it can be assumed that motivation to be selected as a candidate for a profession is high, and whether the applicant is accepted or rejected, the impact of the process and outcome is likely to be significant. One woman social work student in her 30s vividly described the intense emotions she experienced in the selection process. She did not have a prior degree and had negative early experiences with school which made acceptance for higher education seem an impossibly daunting hurdle. She initially kept the application forms for a social work course under her mattress for two weeks before bringing herself to fill them in. Once she had received the acceptance letter, she carried it round with her for days, expecting the words would change.

Assuming applicants' motivation will be high, the energy generated by the intensive scrutiny they receive at the point of selection could be put to positive use if those who are accepted or rejected are given formative feedback about their application. In my experience there is a keen wish on the part of rejected applicants to understand where they failed. Feedback for those refused a place might include clear indications of what the applic-ant needs to do to enhance her/his eligibility. Feedback for the successful applicant could be the initial step in orienting a candidate to the course, encouraging her/him to do some focused preparatory reading or writing.

In both instances, if a proforma is used at the selection stage which includes clearly defined criteria and a rating scale, a copy could be returned to the applicant, successful or otherwise.

Tension between summative and formative assessment is likely to arise from workload concerns if staff are expected to give formative feedback. This tension may be avoided if the issue is viewed over the longer term and resources expended at this point are seen as possibly preventing the need for later staff support. Formative feedback may also prevent an applicant re-applying inappropriately. The pressure on course staff may further be relieved by the appointment of a designated admissions officer so that academic staff are not expected to carry the total load of admissions responsibilities.

It seems likely that as stakeholder pressures on the professions increase, pressure on summative judgements at the selection stage will mount. This may influence who is selected or how the selection procedure operates and may, for example, dictate numbers of applicants admitted to a profession to reflect projected levels of need or a change in priorities, aspects such as age, race and gender of applicants selected, or the relative weighting assigned to various criteria. Already, the provision of funding by government for students in professional education indirectly controls who does or does not enter.

Continuous assessment

Once on a professional course, students are likely to expect continuous assessment. Continuous assessment may be a series of summative hurdles on a course towards a final destination. However, in a professional education course which is designed to encourage students to learn independently, it is essential for the student to not only be summatively assessed but also to receive formative feedback. What is necessary for both formative and summative assessment to occur at the continuous assessment stage and what undermines this occurring? How can summative assessment coexist with formative without the formative side being severely compromised (Brown and Knight, 1994: 21)? I will begin by discussing the structure and content of assessment tasks, and then in the following section examine formative feedback.

What is being assessed and how are tasks designed to achieve this? Whereas we have considerable experience of assessing propositional knowledge, we have little experience of assessing personal or process knowledge, particularly in the classroom based parts of the course. Each profession will have its own desired learning outcomes but there are some common criteria which might be applied to assessment in the interpersonal professions, and also meet Boud's (1996) proposal that assessment tasks should be designed with a 'high consequential validity' for learning. High consequential validity refers to assessment procedures which have consequences for learning beyond those which are immediately evident. This may relate to the content of the task as well as the processes built into the task which the student will need to complete in order to be successful. This concept is important to assessment in professional education because it indicates how a task might be constructed so that all three areas of professional knowledge are assessed.

The following criteria for assessment in professional education are adapted from Eisner's (1993) recommendations for criteria for assessment practices in schools. I have adapted them for our purposes here as they suggest ways in which the notion of high consequential validity might be applied:

1. Tasks should reflect both in content and structure what the students will encounter in practice and relate to the central outcomes for the profession. For example, rarely will a professional be required to write a 5000-word essay, much more likely to be required is a briefing paper or a report.
2. Tasks should allow for the student to make observations about the essential process of reflection in approaching a task. For a professional who will be continually encountering new problems, the development of the skills of approaching a problem are as important as the outcome. Schön's (1983, 1987) work on the importance of reflection is referred to by a number of professions, including teacher education (Calderhead and Gates, 1993), nursing education (Palmer *et al.*, 1994); and social work (Gould and Taylor, 1996).
3. Tasks should reflect the values of the profession from which they are derived, encouraging students to contextualise their ideas within the larger field. Given the shifting boundaries of the professions and shifting values, this area assumes particular importance. For example, the recent legislative and policy developments discussed in Chapter 2, must be integrated into assessment tasks.
4. Tasks necessarily focus on the part rather than the whole but should be related to the overall 'tapestry' (Eisner, 1993: 227), and in totality portray the desired outcome of the course. This underlines the importance of specific units forming a whole, particularly in relation to modularization, if we are to avoid a fragmenting experience for the student.
5. Tasks should make possible more than one acceptable perspective on a question and encourage the student to develop an argument for her/his judgement and interpretation rather than arrange a set of facts and ideas (Hounsell, 1987). This criteria is important to developing independence in relation to propositional knowledge.
6. Tasks should enable the student to vary the medium through which what has been learnt can be demonstrated. Brown and Knight (1994) give many useful examples of creative activities for assessed work such as developing a course reader or a poster display. The breadth of the medium adds to the possibilities for high consequential validity.

On the Bristol course some of these criteria were successfully met. The second criteria of requiring the student to reflect on the process of approaching a task was built in to criteria for the summative judgement, and also included expecting students to reflect on the role their personal knowledge played in their work on the task. This criteria was linked with the criteria that tasks should reflect professional values, a theme which has a long history in social work education. For some students, particularly those with undergraduate academic training which had not included such criteria, this was a difficult transition to make. The fifth criteria of encouraging students to develop an argument or a critique, rather than 'arrange a set of facts and ideas', was also specified in the summative criteria. In contrast to the second criteria of allowing for reflection, the fifth criteria tended to be where students with prior undergraduate training were confident.

There was an attempt to meet Eisner's first criteria and to introduce what, in the context of higher education, were innovative tasks of the kind students would expect to encounter in practice. It was recognized that students in practice are rarely expected to write essays, but they are expected to carry out activities such as writing reports or preparing briefing papers. Introducing assessment tasks of this kind also met Eisner's fifth criteria, that students should be enabled to vary the medium through which what has been learnt can be demonstrated. However, these steps forward were undermined by the range of choice at each assessment point, as students were not required to undertake a particular kind of task and could always avoid an undesirable one.

The notion of choice was deceptively seductive in its promise and its ease of implementation. A wide range of choices was introduced, including some interesting and innovative assessment tasks, based on the notion that the process of choosing and the opportunity to select from a range of options to meet the needs of the individual student would encourage the development of independent learning. However, staff failed to predict some of the problems which would result from this strategy. Some students opted for safety and always chose the same type of task. For example, some students always chose essay type tasks, particularly if they had prior experience of higher education, whereas other students always avoided the conventional essay. Some students avoided particular topics because they were too difficult or painful to deal with, or chose topics because they had prior relevant experience to draw on. Students were often very aware of the implications of their choices, but opting for safe choices had an obvious appeal even if it meant the task had low consequential validity for the individual student. One student described the liberation of being able to make a choice for the more unknown and risky at the time when a task was not being summatively assessed. The range of choice negated the fourth criteria that tasks should form part of an overall tapestry, and in totality portray the desired outcome of the course.

In addition to establishing assessment tasks with high consequential validity and agreeing criteria, of central importance is that the objectives on which students are assessed do not differ from those of the overt curriculum. If there is a difference between what students are actually assessed on and what the curriculum states they are assessed on, there is a risk of a gulf developing between desired learning outcomes and what students actually learn. 'To please teachers, students have to study the overt curriculum; to pass examinations, they have to study the hidden curriculum' (Elton, 1988: 217). The overt curriculum is usually concerned with deep learning and with creativity and originality (Marton and Saljo, 1976), whereas in the hidden curriculum (Snyder, 1971) grades are the 'currency of the campus' and pressure to obtain good grades and to focus on the extrinsic rewards of learning rather than their intrinsic worth is likely to result in short-term, surface memorization.

A split between the hidden and overt curriculum was evident to the Bristol students and it undermined the impact of interdependent learning in relation to the problem scenarios. Students were only too conscious that, 'when you're doing assessed work, it does take priority'.

They resented the intrusion of summatively assessed work on the 'real' work of the learning group which they viewed as tackling problem scenarios:

> I felt I couldn't really put as much as I wanted into the second unit because I had that deadline and I really had to get that work finished.
> I would have wanted to put much more work into that second unit.

Of most significance was the conviction that their learning in groups focusing on the problem at hand was centrally important to preparation for professional practice, yet they were prevented from fully exploiting the potential of this learning because the structure of summatively assessed work remained individual and private. One student framed this tension very clearly: 'I'll be more productive with assignments if I stay at home. If I come to study group meetings, I'll be a better social worker.' This statement reflects the dilemma for students and professional educators of an approach to summative assessment which does not value interdependent learning. In study group meetings, students valued giving and receiving formative feedback but ultimately this was undermined by summative assessment which assigned value to different criteria.

Linked with students negotiating the gap between the overt and the hidden curriculum was 'cue consciousness' (Miller and Parlett, 1974). Research showed that Edinburgh University students fell into three categories: cue seekers who actively decide which pieces of work can be selectively neglected, or which method of working will get highest marks; cue conscious who were aware of the cues; and cue 'deaf' who did not play the game at all. The structure of the learning group may reinforce the existence of some of these categories. For example, it provides the forum for impression management by the cue seekers: 'I'm showing off a bit when the tutor is there. I say the right things.' This student was in fact talking about his facilitator rather than tutor, but his confusion about role and title may signal that any member of the academic staff, regardless of the role they are carrying at any one particular time, is seen as being in an assessment role which compels the student to say the 'right' things when the staff member is present.

Saying the 'right things' was an issue which stirred up very strong feelings among students, particularly in relation to discrimination and political correctness: 'If people say the right things they'll pass, but in their hearts they may be thinking other things but they're too frightened to say it.' Students were perturbed if not angry by this dynamic. They wanted staff to be able to cut through the rhetoric of political correctness rather than confront it themselves. This issue demonstrates the difficulty of feeling safe enough in an assessment situation to publicly reveal personal knowledge, yet it is one which must be dealt with adequately if personal knowledge is to be equally valued with propositional and process knowledge.

Why does the hidden curriculum remain? At Bristol, in spite of the significant degree of innovation in the overt curriculum and limited change in assessment practices, some traditional assessment practices persisted which undermined the impact of the innovation. In particular, the focus for summative purposes remained predominantly on propositional knowledge and on work completed privately and individually, although work on the course was undertaken predominantly in groups where there was considerable emphasis on personal and process knowledge. In part, continuing with a traditional model of assessment reflected a lack of specialist staff expertise about assessment. The lack of knowledge was compounded by the lack of resources within the development team to enable them to find out enough about new assessment methods. In addition, there was no central provision within the university to provide this expertise.

The most significant reason for the enduring gap between the hidden and overt curriculum was that assessed work did not consistently directly link to problem-based work carried out in groups. There was some staff resistance to moving forward to consider innovations such as self and peer assessment. The staff were imbued with traditional academic notions of fairness, justice and equal opportunities and this became a barrier to introducing innovative assessment practices which appeared to jeopardize reliability. This barrier is confirmed by Broadfoot who suggests that the overwhelming emphasis in assessment is on efficiency and reliability and the need to 'be seen to be operating fairly and consistently in the crucial business of determining life chances' (1994: 4), although the link between reliability and equal opportunities may be more apparent than real. This may result in the concern of teachers to encourage deep learning and divergent thinking being overridden by concerns to structure assessment tasks which are straightforward to assess and easy to compare with that of other students. Efficiency is also becoming increasingly important to academic staff whose resources are severely stretched.

Two kinds of assessment task, the multiple choice exam and the essay, are appealing because they appear to be efficient and to meet criteria for reliability. However, they have other negative indications. Multiple choice exams were not used on the Bristol course. As Rowntree (1987) comments, he would prefer a doctor capable of divergent thinking about diagnosis and treatment than one who is confined to choosing the best of a number of alternatives suggested by someone else. Alternatively, the essay appeared to offer the student the opportunity for deep learning and much more room to pursue particular interests than the exam. However, Hounsell (1987) researched essay writing among students of history and psychology at Lancaster University and found that student interests may conflict with the stipulations of the tasks assigned. This finding was also borne out in the Bristol study where students complained that having to meet a range of stipulations about content and structure of a task encouraged a checking-off approach rather than a full exploration of what interested them.

It is essential in assessment of professional education that the pressure towards reliability and what is easily measurable be counterbalanced by assessment tasks which are valid and measure what they are intended to. It is also essential to assess those abilities and skills which are not as easy to measure as knowledge and understanding, but which are essential to professional practice.

> There are more ways of coming to know a person than through poring over his recorded products – words on paper, drawings, models, etc. Many people best reveal their powers – for example of creativity, fluency, imagination, reasoning, drive, persistence, empathy – only in interpersonal situations.
>
> (Rowntree, 1987: 64)

To return to the example of the doctor, we would surely all prefer to consult a doctor who in addition to being capable of divergent thinking, has well-developed problem-solving skills and an ability to relate to the patient. Increasingly these skills are included in the curriculum in medical schools, but are they assessed in a way which counts or does the hidden curriculum devalue them? It seems that for summative and formative assessment to be complementary at the continuous assessment stage, the gap between the hidden and the overt curriculum must be closed. In addition, the belief in the reliability and efficiency of certain methods must both be examined closely and weighed against the importance of assessment methods which are valid and meet the Eisner (1993) criteria.

Formative feedback

I have referred to feedback as intrinsic to formative assessment but how are assessment tasks responded to in a formative way? Accepting that 'one of the most valuable contributions anyone can make to another person's learning is constructive comment' (Boud, 1986: 32), is formative feedback provided in a way which makes it usable by the student? Is it linked with the criteria for the assessment task? Is it enabling, reviewing achievement and identifying new goals, or does it always tend to be final and summative?

Students' wish for feedback from staff can at times appear almost insatiable. One Bristol staff member likened it to a parent bird continuously facing a nest full of open beaks. Staff approval is 'reified' (Rowntree, 1987). Students complained that there was not enough feedback from staff: 'from the people we see as significant . . . we can all give ourselves constructive feedback but it's not enough'. Cowan (1988) suggests that if staff feedback is on offer at the same time as student feedback, the latter will be under-valued. This appeared to be the case with the Bristol students, compounded by some of the barriers to peer assessment discussed later in the chapter.

Students are not only seeking feedback on completed assessed work they are also, particularly early in the course, seeking feedback on their initial planning for an assessment activity. They may already have a successful academic history behind them before joining the course, but the unfamiliar professional context often creates significant anxiety. Students who had achieved considerable academic success in their undergraduate courses talked about their difficulty writing essays where one of the criteria they were marked on was their ability to reflect on and integrate personal experience.

There is a tension between summative and formative assessment at the continuous assessment stage. It is unquestionably quicker for a busy aca-demic, under increasing pressure from a range of demands, to summatively assess a piece of work. Furthermore, giving formative feedback requires criteria to be clear and explicit to provide the pegs on which to hang the feedback. Finally, as most academics have had significantly more practice with summative than formative feedback, both in their own education and now as providers, it is often easier and more familiar to provide summative feedback. Yet, it is at the continuous assessment stage that students are most eager to receive formative feedback and most vulnerable to receiving inad-equate feedback on a piece of work where they have not done well and where they want to improve for next time. It can be quite devastating for students to fail assessed work, even when it is not critical to their overall success. One student who failed an oral exam at the end of her first year had done well in every other assignment that year but was crushed by this single failure. These feelings remained throughout the second year, her confidence was severely shaken.

Formative feedback is a skill which should be central to professional development for academic staff. Not only is it crucial to professional edu-cation but in practice professionals are regularly required to give formative feedback, written and verbal, whether to colleagues or service users. On professional courses we have the opportunity to model for students the skills of providing feedback.

Self and peer assessment

A central thesis of this book is that students of the professions must develop independent and interdependent learning skills as both are essential to professional practice. Core to this is self-assessment. Boud proposes the following defining characteristic of self-assessment as,

The involvement of students in identifying standards and/or criteria to apply to their work and making judgements about the extent to which they have met these criteria and standards.

(Boud, 1996: 12)

Boud differentiates between self-assessment as a practice in which students engage, and a goal to which they aspire. In professional education it is essential for courses which are designed to facilitate independent learning, to both hold self-assessment as a goal and include activities which develop self-assessment skills.

Self-assessment is taking responsibility for establishing criteria and monitoring and making judgements about one's own learning. Through actively setting goals and assessing themselves, students will be more committed to their learning (Boud, 1992). The need for professionals to be able to accurately assess their own practice is directly related to lifelong learning, 'Self and peer assessment is in my judgement the central way of maintaining and developing standards of professional practice' (Heron, 1988: 87). This begs the question about why self-assessment has not yet become a well-established part of the process of assessment on professional education courses?

What constitutes self-assessment? For this discussion I draw extensively on the work of David Boud, in particular his recent book *Enhancing Learning Through Self-Assessment* (1996), which brings together much of his earlier work. For self-assessment to take place, students must be involved both in setting the criteria on which they will be assessed and making the judgements about performance. Criteria should include the area to be assessed, aims to be pursued and standards to be reached. These must be spelled out at such a level of detail that it will be possible for the person making the judgement to know whether they have been reached. The objective ultimately is for students to be able to reach their own decisions about criteria, a skill essential for self-assessment in practice. It may be desirable to agree on criteria as a class group and Boud suggests structured group activities for achieving this, such as students each adding their suggested criteria to a flip chart and arriving at an agreed and composite list. The advantage of this approach is that it enables the facilitator to comment on omissions. On a professional education course where learning outcomes are often specified by professional accrediting bodies, it will be necessary for the facilitator to be active in ensuring that key criteria are given appropriate weighting, or are not omitted.

On the Bristol course, self-assessment was on one level integral to student learning. For example, in learning groups working on problems, students had to make decisions about what to learn and how to go about it, which included assessing what they already knew and what they needed to find out about. They then had to evaluate as a group whether they had achieved their objectives, as well as individually consider their contribution to group learning and to their own overall goals. At specific stages in the course, students were expected to self assess in relation to their progress on the course and discuss their views with their tutor. However, the activity of students participating in establishing criteria against which to make judgements, was relatively undeveloped. As this was not clearly identified as a course activity, it was dependent on the knowledge and understanding of individual facilitators about the value of agreeing criteria.

There was enough experience with self-assessment on the Bristol course to begin to see what some of the issues were for both students and staff. The students were, with few exceptions, positive about learning the skills of self-assessment, and believed them to be essential to professional practice. Boud points out that self-assessment will only be acceptable if students appreciate its value and see it as based on student priorities rather than institutional priorities. Students are rightly suspicious of measures which appear to be based solely on cost-cutting motivation. However, early in the course they needed help with learning the skills of self-assessment. The wish of one student for a 'self-assessment kit' is unrealistic but nevertheless represents a culture seeking do-it-yourself packages which promise to deal with uncertainties.

When first introduced to expectations of self-assessment it can be confusing and overwhelming, particularly in a context where students feel challenged on many counts. This comment made by a student in the first term typified the feelings of the majority of her contemporaries: 'I don't know when I've made mistakes and I don't know when I've got it wrong.' Such uncertainties are frightening and anxiety provoking, particularly for those students used to staff being in a directive role. This student may have been at an early stage of development as an independent learner (Perry, 1970) and looking for right and wrong answers, but it would be naive to attribute this concern to students only at an early stage of development. It is possible for students at all stages of development as independent learners (and for staff) to make mistakes, and a particular worry for students of the interpersonal professions is about making mistakes and unintentionally harming others.

Another set of worries which is linked with not knowing enough to differentiate between 'right' or 'wrong', is a concern about setting boundaries on learning and knowing when and how to limit the search for new knowledge. As this student commented at the end of her first term,

> It's knowing where to go into things in depth and where to skim over the surface and all those decisions you have to make yourself as a student. Whereas in another model of learning the staff would make it for you. It's taking responsibility which is a good thing but it's a bit frightening at times.

Students share a strong conviction that taking responsibility for learning and making decisions about what they will learn and how they will learn is important, based on their expectations that in practice they will often be taking decisions on their own. However, making decisions of this kind without direction from the 'expert' can be challenging and frightening, and may involve risks which are not perceived to be there if staff take responsibility for the choices.

One concern often raised by staff about self-assessment is that students will be unrealistic or inaccurate in their views. Research into this issue comes up with interesting, if not conclusive, findings. In a review of literature on self-assessment Boud and Falchikov (1989) found a general trend of high achieving students underestimating their performance and low achieving overestimating. Stefani (1994), suggests that Boud and Falchikov's survey was limited and highlights the fact that studies were inconsistently reported and their parameters unclear. Stefani set out to evaluate a peer, self and tutor marking scheme where students defined the marking schedule for reporting laboratory experiments in the biological sciences. She found that self-assessed marks were more stringent than tutor marks, and that both high and low achievers tend to mark themselves down. She also noted that students were more highly motivated and more interested in the task than those students not self-assessing, they also rated the scheme highly and although they found it time consuming and hard, they found it made them learn more. As a result, Stefani supports Cowan's (1988) argument that 'the benefits of self-assessment are so great that we should trust students to act appropriately even when there is a risk that there could be differences between the student mark and the tutor mark' (Stefani, 1994: 74). It is easier to adopt this position if self-assessment is only one of a repertoire of tools.

Boud (1996) describes the use of a 'self-assessment schedule' as a qualitative and discursive personal report which aims to provide a comprehensive and analytical record of what the student has learnt. It can be for the student's own record or be used as part of assessment. The schedule consists of a framework which identifies students' process and outcome goals, including those which were identified at the beginning of a course and those which emerge during the course, criteria by which achievement of the goals will be evaluated; evidence for attainment of the goals; judgements or reports about what others have said and analysis of extent to which goals have been met; and statements about further action. Boud notes that a possible problem with the schedule is that some kinds of information such as what students are reading tend to be omitted; there is also a tension between providing students with considerable detail about how to use the schedule and leaving it open hoping students will use it creatively. Nevertheless, these difficulties appear to be far outweighed by the opportunity the schedule provides for students to look back over their learning. 'It is common for students to report that they only start to become aware of what they have learned when they look back on the course in a systematic fashion as a prelude to completing the schedule' (Boud, 1992: 191). The emphasis on process as well as product not only encourages students to be reflective about their learning, it also values those aspects of student work which have not necessarily contributed to a summative grade but have contributed to learning. The intention on the Bristol course is to adapt this schedule and link it with the use of a portfolio.

The purpose of peer assessment is to inform self-assessment. Boud (1996) suggests that reactions to peer assessment are most positive when students give each other specific feedback and no grading has taken place, and recommends avoiding peer assessment which leads to peer determined grades. Students often have the opportunity to observe their peers in the learning process and may acquire considerable knowledge of their work, particularly in situations of group learning. However, to be able to give and receive feedback requires interpersonal as well as intellectual competence (Heron, 1988).

With few exceptions, Bristol students valued peer feedback, although as discussed earlier, when combined with staff feedback, the latter was typically assigned more value. The students shared a conviction that feedback is essential to learning the skills of working collaboratively, and in turn this is essential preparation for practice. This male student talked about the value of learning collaboratively,

> which I never did as a schoolboy or as a student. That was completely alien. I still have the odd flicker of thinking that somehow working in a group is cheating, because that's what I was taught as a child, if you weren't working alone, you were cheating, someone was helping you and that was wrong, and one of the real richnesses for me is actually working, not just in a group but in the pairings that come out of groups, of going through an essay plan with another student and picking holes in it and filling up the holes again. That's obviously the way people work in life, we're all going to be working in teams.

One of the interesting questions raised here for future research is the influence of gender differences on working collaboratively.

However, in spite of a prevailing belief that peer feedback is a useful and important process, as seen in Chapter 5, its implementation raised a number of issues. In the early weeks of the course, learning group time was allocated specifically to focusing on feedback skills. This did not mean that all students were able all the time to say what they meant to other students. One student looking back on the course reflected on peer assessment:

> Part of it's been a good process because it's been about trusting each other and being prepared to listen and not fly off the handle . . . but some of the conflict goes underground which is a bad thing.

Negative feedback goes underground in part because of students loyalty to each other and the compelling requirement not to 'rat' on their friends:

> I found there was a real dilemma there because I was quite keen to give positive feedback but I would have felt a lot more comfortable to give whatever feedback I wanted without the facilitator being there because there is this power structure, the facilitator is there to assess and I didn't want to have to rat on my friends and write the assessment for the facilitator.

Attention needs to be paid to how to get beyond what appears to be loyalty, although it may also be fear on the part of the individual student about possible repercussions of giving 'negative' feedback. Students share equal status as students but there may be significant differences in the informal power they each hold. This is a crucial issue to recognize in relation to peer assessment.

Informally, when it was not related to any real or perceived summative assessment of individual students, peer assessment worked well. An example was provided by this student who was academically able and had a prior degree:

> I suppose I've spent a lot of time working with other students which in a way involves giving quite a lot and they give back to me. You give someone your time like I read this person's essay three times and then I wrote a page of notes on it and then I spent one and a half hours discussing it with her. That's a lot of time. Whereas in the old model I would have put that into a book or making some notes.

This student positively compared the competitiveness of the 'old model', by which she meant her first degree, with working more collaboratively. She had put a great deal of effort into providing peer feedback and certainly the student who was the recipient would be very unlikely to have received the same quantity of attention from staff. Boud cites research by Smith and Hatton (1993) which suggests that 'students engage in a greater level and depth of reflection when they discuss their work with a peer as distinct from discussion with a specially trained staff member or in a specially designed written assignment' (Boud, 1996: 200). This would support the importance of peer assessment.

One of the criteria often selected for peer assessment is feedback about class participation. Bristol students believed that participation in groups is important, and because they spend a high proportion of their time in learning groups, it should contribute to summative assessment. However, Bristol staff had two concerns about this. First, the recognition that for assessment of participation in groups to be equitable, personal factors have a bearing on participation and must be taken into consideration. Secondly, was the inhibiting effect assessment of participation might have on teaching and learning if facilitators were required to assess participation. Nevertheless, recognizing the importance of interdependent learning to the learning of the individual student, the need to address this issue was established.

Staff new to self-assessment also need support and guidance in knowing how to facilitate the process. Common themes among the Bristol staff beginning to work with self-assessment echo those described by Cowan (1988) in his description of his attempts to introduce self-assessment into an engineering course. Notable was staff concern about how to be facilitative and not prescriptive, an issue fully discussed in Chapter 6. A particular issue in professional education is likely to be that some criteria for self-assessment are prescribed by the profession. This requires staff to be clear about external requirements which are not negotiable. As Cowan reflected on his own experience, 'I should have differentiated more clearly and carefully between the features of our agreement which were renegotiable (or open to unilateral rejection) and those which were immutable' (1988: 195).

Assessment for certification

In professional education, the issue of certification assumes a level of significance which may not be the case in higher education generally. Assessment at the stage of certification or accreditation is primarily for the profession and society as a whole, to designate the student as ready to practice. It is also important to the student as confirming they have reached this point, validating their learning. Professional education students are working to achieve certification in their chosen career and failure to achieve this is likely to have significant implications for their future. The student risks not only failing a course but also failing to become a nurse, doctor, teacher, social worker and so on, careers which may have a significant vocational component. Another dimension of failure for the professional education student, in contrast to other students in higher education, is that failure may not necessarily be on academic grounds but may be related to skills or values and attitudes. Failure on these grounds may be experienced as a personal assault.

Grading for certification is inevitably public, however much the reasons for failure and the process of informing students about their marks is private. Final grades have become not only a public statement about the individual but also about the success of the institution. This also applies to the individual student where the effect of summative certification is that the beginning point of the student is ignored, even though a simple pass for students who have entered a course through access routes will reflect significant success on their part (see Chapter 9).

Is there a place for formative assessment at the certification stage? If qualifying is conceptualized as a beginning of practice and continuing professional development, rather than an end of professional education, then certification is an opportunity for the student to review strengths and areas to continue to focus on in future employment. This can be reassuring for the qualifying practitioner who is likely to be feeling very apprehensive about meeting the demands of practice. Such a discussion is also particularly useful to the preparation of references, a task which will be much less onerous for the provider of the reference if there has been a process of continuous assessment. It will also be a much more straightforward and satisfying experience if the student is skilled in self-assessment and has developed a portfolio which can be used as the basis for references.

Conclusion

If Broadfoot (1994) is right and assessment is on the agenda because change is on the agenda, the rapid developments in higher and professional education may provide the opportunity to address assessment practices and bring about required change. However, the risk is that at such a time of far-reaching change, instead of moving forward and experimenting with innovative approaches, we entrench ourselves for safety's sake, and our practices become more rigid and narrow.

Furthermore, the pressures on educators are significantly increasing and there are compelling reasons to seek efficiency which may not always be consistent with good assessment practice. It is much easier for example, to set and mark an exam which may test propositional knowledge, than an oral assessment activity which may also assess personal and process knowledge. The inclination to opt for the former is particularly strong when it can be defended on grounds of fairness and equal opportunities. In this context, our assessment practices and our professional education practices generally risk becoming ever more irrelevant to and distant from professional practice. 'Assessment is fundamental to teaching. Get the assessment right and the teaching, by and large, follows' (Brown and Knight, 1994: 149).

Part 4

Promising Outcomes

9

Non-traditional Learners:
Valuing Diversity

My attention now turns from the learning infrastructure which supports independent and interdependent learning to examining three quite different outcomes of this approach to learning. In this chapter, I look particularly at the outcomes for non-traditional learners. This group of students caught my attention early in the research because their responses to learning independently and interdependently were at times dramatic. Also, the outcomes for this group of students appears to have implications for the learning of all students. At present, however, higher education and professional education is designed for the majority group, and as will be seen in this chapter, this effectively denies access and accessibility to students from minority groups.

There appears at first sight to be almost universal consensus that ways must be found of attracting a larger and more diverse population into higher education (Wright, 1991). However, if consensus really existed, we would be seeing considerably more diversity in the student population than is currently the case. 'Class, gender and ethnicity are now the three giants in the path of aspirations towards equity, replacing what was the major focus of traditional concern with social class' (Halsey, 1993: 129). A fourth giant, that of disability, is now emerging, and has been given some prominence as a result of the disability rights movement. There is increasing recognition that sexual orientation and age are also factors which influence the path to equity in higher education. The evidence is that for some groups, structural barriers to access to higher education continue to be formidable.

Even if access is successfully navigated, university courses have a long-established tradition of being designed to meet the needs of the dominant group with potentially negative consequences for non-traditional students. 'When one is forced to learn and be a learner within a framework which is dominated by the dominant value system, one's identity as a learner and one's capacity as a learner within that system, may be put at risk' (Weil, 1986: 232). Greater than the risk of lack of fit, or 'disjuncture' (Weil, 1986), is that of reinforcing the structural disadvantages women, black, working-class or disabled people already experience in society as a whole.

Inequities in access to higher education and inaccessible courses have particularly serious implications for professional education. In education for the interpersonal professions it must surely be a matter of some urgency to ensure that practitioners more closely reflect the groups they are serving. The same must be true of the importance of the staff profile on professional courses reflecting the profile of the student population. The philosophy of equality of opportunity upheld in the UK by recent legislation will remain notional as long as professional education at the levels of students and staff remain in the hands of an elite. This is not to suggest that selection requirements are waived, but that we must seriously address issues of both access and accessibility. Bird suggests that we are at risk of selling a 'false prospectus' (1996: 30) if we focus only on opening the doors to higher education, and are guilty of discrimination if we do not address those barriers internal to the institution which impede the progress of black students.

Wright (1991) distinguishes between access which focuses on helping individuals or groups to enter higher education, and accessibility or the 'transformation of higher education in such ways as to make it more attractive, relevant and open to all sections of the population' (1991: 7). In this chapter, I begin by reviewing the issue of access to higher education for non-traditional students. My primary focus, however, is on accessibility which I discuss in relation to findings from a small exploratory study of non-traditional students, examining them particularly in the light of an earlier study by Weil (1986). I suggest that non-traditional students benefit from a balance between personal, process and propositional learning (Eraut, 1992), and from being encouraged to learn independently and interdependently.

Questions raised about the goodness of fit between non-traditional students and traditional courses inevitably raise questions about the appropriateness of the traditional higher education model for all students. Perhaps what is needed are courses which accept students for what they are, and are responsive to their learning needs, rather than an approach which assumes that all students have the same beginning point.

Who are the 'non-traditional' students?

There is a noticeable lack of a developed discourse in this area of higher education, symptomatic of the marginalization in higher education of the groups who are the focus of attention in this chapter. The terms 'non-traditional', 'non-standard', and 'drop-out' convey omission. This marginalizes certain groups by viewing them against a norm established by the dominant minority who successfully complete their schooling using conventional routes and continue into higher education. The term 'mature students' has more positive connotations, although older students may experience ageism and be marginalized (Richardson, 1994). However, 'mature students' is not adopted in this chapter because it includes students who successfully completed their schooling.

'Non-traditional' learners are those who did not achieve the standard school leaving qualifications; particularly represented in this group are older women, manual workers, certain ethnic minorities and disabled people (Wright, 1991). Between leaving school and re-entering formal education they will have had many different experiences and Weil (1986) suggests they are of necessity experienced learners. While acknowledging that the term 'non-traditional' can also be used to marginalize certain groups and can mistakenly convey a notion of homogeneity, 'non-traditional' is used in this chapter because it highlights the diversity issues of pre-course experience (Weil, 1988).

The other variable associated with non-traditional students is their age. By virtue of not having followed the traditional route, students enter higher education at a 'mature' age. Richardson (1994) defines this as over 21 for admission to undergraduate courses and over 25 for postgraduate courses. Over the last decade, from 1981–89, the numbers of mature students admitted to higher education in Great Britain increased by 55 per cent (Richardson, 1994). These figures do not differentiate between those students who achieved school leaving qualifications in the conventional way and those whose entry to higher education is through a non-traditional route. It is the latter group I now go on to discuss.

Access of non-traditional students into higher education

During the 1980s the sponsor and provider groups (Watson, 1992) of government, industry and educational institutions all made clear their support for increased access of non-traditional students to higher education (Wakeford, 1993). A profusion of schemes has sprung up designed to widen access including Access, CATs, APL and Open College (Wright, 1991). However, research suggests these schemes are as yet having surprisingly little impact on the representation in higher education of non-traditional groups (see for example, Butler's (1993) study of the marginalization of APL discussed in Chapter 4).

The picture of access in relation to gender is the most encouraging. Gender inequalities have decreased rapidly over the last two decades (Halsey, 1993). However, set against this advance it must be noted that there continues to be a skewed distribution of women towards less prestigious courses and institutions (Blackburn and Jarman, 1993). There is confidence that increasing participation of women in higher education will continue and the experience of other countries supports this view. However, it is startling that in Britain we lag so far behind. As early as 1979 women caught up with men in the numbers entering Australian universities, while the number of undergraduate degrees awarded to Canadian women passed the number awarded to men in 1981 (Blackburn and Jarman, 1993).

With respect to ethnicity, considerable advances have been made in access to degree courses 'it may even turn out on further evidence that ethnicity per se is not a barrier: only the asymmetric fit of race to class produces apparent inequality of access' (Halsey, 1993: 131). However, Modoods' (1993) analysis of the ethnic origins of those students admitted through UCCA and PCAS (central admissions systems for universities and polytechnics respectively) in 1990 and 1991 suggests that the admission pattern of ethnic minority students is complex. There are significant differences in admissions between ethnic groups, between institutions, and between subjects. In the ex-polytechnics, or 'new universities', all ethnic minority groups, with the exception of Bangladeshis, are over-represented, with the concentration being regional rather than institutional, and over-representation in some subjects (business, engineering, law and medicine), and under-representation in others (languages, humanities, arts). In the 'old university' sector, while most minorities are not underrepresented, they are there in half the proportion they are in the other sector, and African Caribbeans and Bangladeshis are significantly underrepresented.

The selection rate for old and new universities shows that the data on ethnicity must be treated with some caution. The selection rate for admission to old universities shows a hierarchy with white applicants at the top, and for example only half as many African-Caribbean as white applicants are likely to succeed. UCCA explains this by the fact that fewer individuals from minorities apply to courses with relatively low entrance requirements such as teaching, whereas application rates to medicine and law, the two hardest subjects in which to gain acceptance, are three times higher for minorities than for white applicants (Modood, 1993). Modood also notes that ethnic minority applicants are at least twice as likely to have re-sat exams and they also have a lower average A level score, all factors which do not appeal to admissions officers. Some of the factors in lower rates of selection, such as type of school and non-A Level qualifications, are also factors in low rates of acceptance of working-class applicants, 'yet it is striking that most ethnic minority groups have worse class profiles than whites, but produce much larger proportions of applications and admissions in the national higher education system' (Modood, 1993: 181).

The giant proving particularly impervious to change is that of social class. There is evidence that trends in access by social class to universities are relatively unchanging (Blackburn and Jarman, 1993) as they are in entry to higher education generally (Egerton and Halsey, 1993). Whereas, the chances of the working-class student going into some form of higher education has increased in absolute terms, 'class inequalities, measured in relative terms, have apparently remained stable for the past three generations' (Halsey, 1993). Further research is needed to determine why working-class students continue to stay away from higher education in large numbers, and to examine the influence of factors such as parental expectation and quality of schooling.

The issue of disabled students has only very recently begun to be identified, largely as a result of the work of the disability rights movement. As a result there is very little research available about disabled students in higher education. The Department of Education does not keep statistics about disabled students, although according to unofficial figures produced by UCCA, disabled people constituted 4 per cent of students in higher education in 1992/1993 (cited in Phillips *et al.*, 1995). In 1993, statistical information on disabled students applying to social work courses was collected for the first time identifying a range of impairments. Out of a total of 10,410 applicants, 651 declared they had a disability, of these 198 were accepted. This represents 30.4 per cent of disabled applicants compared to a 35 per cent success rate among those who were not disabled. The largest proportion of disabled students experience dyslexia.

For disabled students, issues of 'access' in the literal sense of the word, are clearly central and here there is evidence of significant barriers. Barnes (1991) in a review of higher education for disabled people found that most British colleges and universities are inaccessible and many are unable or unwilling to introduce the necessary changes. Courses may be concerned about the costs of adaptation. However, Skill, the National Bureau for Students with Disabilities, emphasizes that accessible provision is more to do with the existence of disability policies, the level of awareness about disability issues by staff and their readiness to undertake disability awareness training (1992). Phillips *et al.* (1995) in their study of disabled social work students in Scotland, identify five barriers to disabled people training as social workers: a disabling environment in the context of a disabling wider society; problems of typification or stereotyping associated with individual impairments; a failure of application of equal opportunities policies; assumptions about non-disablement which underpin selection and training; and self-limitation, for example reluctance to disclose an impairment or to ask for specific consideration.

Access of students with particular impairments is beginning to be examined. Corlett (1991) examined the access of deaf students and found a poor level of support services, an ignorance of the support needs and a low representation of deaf people in higher education. Etheridge and Mason (1994) identify the need for a curriculum for visually impaired students which recognizes the specific needs of the student as well as the rights of the student to be 'equal'. However, Low (1996) in her study of disabled students at McMaster University, identifies the inherently contradictory process of negotiating both a disabled and non-disabled identity. This issue must have relevance for all students who enter higher education from a disadvantaged position.

Access courses

Access courses allow a potential student to prepare for entry to higher education but bypass the traditional qualifications (Wakeford, 1993). They were introduced in the late 1970s to provide the option of a one-year preparatory course leading to entry to higher education. They were introduced in the social sciences but there are now over 600 Access courses and the range of courses has expanded to include maths, science and technology (Wakeford, 1993). There is a surprising lack of national data about who attends Access courses. The relative importance of Access routes is not well documented nationally, neither is information about students on Access courses consistently collected at the institutional level. The lack of data is perhaps again a reflection of the marginalization of access issues in higher education.

One study completed by Nina Wakeford in 1991 (Wakeford, 1993) does, however, provide some useful data. Wakeford surveyed a sample of Access courses and compared her findings with the only other national survey (Millins, 1984) of the first Access courses developed between 1979 and 1983. The most significant finding emerging from Wakeford's study is that further expansion of Access courses does not necessarily mean proportionately increasing participation in higher education by those 'groups who are currently under-represented in the higher education system as a whole' (1991: 228). With respect to the 'three giants' (Halsey, 1993), Wakeford found that since 1983 there has been a shift in participation away from women in favour of male students, although Access courses still favour a larger proportion of women than men. She suggests this is probably a by-product of expansion of courses such as maths and science which are more likely to attract men. Secondly, there is also a shift away from participation by ethnic minorities. The average proportion of ethnic minorities across all courses sampled in 1991 was 17 per cent, less than half the proportion found by Millins (1984), 'the majority of Access courses may not have retained what for some has remained their mission to contribute to ethnic minority participation in higher education' (Wakeford, 1993: 224–5). Wakeford suggests this is probably due to the expansion of Access courses outside the original areas of high ethnic minority residential concentration in the areas surveyed by Millins. Thirdly, the social class profile of Access students has also changed and now reproduces the class distribution of non-graduates found in the general population. Wakeford found that Access courses are less likely to under represent men and women from manual class positions than higher education admissions as a whole, but they do not overrepresent students from manual class backgrounds to the degree suggested by Millins' earlier study.

To help contextualize the following discussion about non-traditional students, the main concerns emerging from a developing critique of Access courses (Wright, 1991; Tight, 1993) are highlighted here. First, Access may in reality lessen accessibility as some groups of students are counselled to enrol in Access courses who could choose another, perhaps more direct, entry route to higher education. Secondly, Access may marginalize students. In colleges or new universities, 'they are effectively in an educational ghetto, with a restricted set of educational opportunities open to them, both during and after their studies' (Tight, 1993: 66). Thirdly, the focus of

Access courses is on preparing students for higher education and encouraging their accommodation to the system rather than focusing on changing the culture of higher education itself. To be truly accessible, courses need a different pedagogy, curricula, counselling systems and staff development which are at variance with traditional institutions (Harrison, 1990). This argument about the importance of accessibility is the focus for the balance of this chapter.

Accessibility – what we know

Transforming higher education to make it more attractive to non-traditional students (Wright, 1991) shifts the focus in the access debate from the institutional barriers to entry, to the social and cultural barriers of the traditional curriculum. Wright (1991) suggests that the success of access courses has hindered the fundamental transformation of higher education by its focus on the demand for educational resources, rather than the supply, and the requirement for change in course structure, curriculum and learning methods.

Woodley and colleagues carried out a comprehensive study of adults in education and suggest that if the actual experience that students have on courses are not addressed then 'the open door will become a revolving one' (Woodley *et al.*, 1987: 168).

In spite of this debate, there is a notable absence of British research which studies the experience of non-traditional students. We know little about 'attrition' or the relative 'success' of non-traditional students in graduating from higher education, with the exception of one study (Mills and Molloy, 1989) which compared the successful completion of a DipHE course by 'non-standard' entrants with those with standard entrance qualifications, looking at 1000 students over a 10-year period from 1975 to 1984. No statistical difference was found between the two groups in either their completion of the course, or the overall level of marks attained by each student. Mills and Molloy compare their results with other studies of mature entrants (Lucas and Ward, 1985; Woodley *et al.*, 1987) and conclude their findings are 'fairly typical of the national picture' (1989: 50). Mills and Molloy stress the importance of analysing the impact of higher education programmes on non-standard entrants, or 'the experience of the experienced' (1989: 50). They conclude that of overriding importance is an access-oriented culture which is evident in the readiness of staff to welcome non-standard entrants, and a willingness and competence to respond to their needs. One important aspect of such a response is recognition that the students' lack self confidence and 're-assurance and competent guidance need to be offered in generous quantities' (1989: 52), including some attention to study skills.

The Mills and Molloy finding that staff responsiveness and guidance is important to the success of non-traditional students is replicated in smaller studies. James Pye in his study of 'returners' (1991) identifies the relationship with the teacher as central and suggests returners begin to succeed when they experience optimism and interest from their teachers, in contrast to their expectations based on previous experiences of impatience, boredom, sarcasm, terrorism and distance. Weis (1985) found that the black students who succeeded in the United States were close to staff and given a disproportionate amount of time and energy by them. Rosen (1993) in her study of black Access students comments on the importance for students of personal contact with staff to facilitate learning. Phillips *et al.* (1995) in their study of disabled students make a number of recommendations for change which require increased staff support.

A US study by Berger (1992) examines five variables which might be significant in the 'retention' of students in a university in the Bronx, New York, where since 1970 admissions policies were intended to increase opportunities for minorities. The study included 352 students admitted to an undergraduate social work course in New York between 1980 and 1986, predominantly female (87 per cent), over the age of 25 (64 per cent), and from minority racial or ethnic groups (49 per cent African American, 35 per cent Hispanic). The variables which Berger hypothesized might classify students as being at risk of not graduating included: demographic or predisposing factors; school background; post-school and pre-admission education; social work course factors; and, academic achievement during the course. Two variables were found to be associated with success. First, the students' past history of marks was a significant predictor of graduation, although for some students the 'second chance' phenomenon appears to have been present and they were able to overcome earlier academic problems (1992: 93). Secondly, the other predictive factor was age, the relatively older and relatively younger students were most likely to graduate. Berger speculates that for the age group 35–44, life stage factors such as the demands of older children, particularly adolescents, influence graduation. Berger also suggests that retention appears to have been promoted by programmatic and institutional supports, and notes that faculty–student relationships were an important part of the experience of many students, helping support students to deal with critical issues relating to economic and family problems affecting academic performance. Berger did not explore curriculum issues.

Weil (1988) carried out a multi-site qualitative study in England where she investigated the perspectives of 48 learners who returned to do some kind of higher or continuing education after an interval of at least five years, 23 of whom had left school with no or few qualifications. Of the sample, 37 were women, 30 were working class, six were Asian or African-Caribbean. Weil was concerned to know if and how the students' prior learning within and outside formal education had a bearing on their expectations and experiences of returning to a formal learning context. Weil's thesis was that in the period away from formal education, the experiences of the students became shaped by alternative values and alternative experiences, 'and by a sense of self that is rooted in the differential access to opportunity' (1988: 28). Her purpose was to contribute to a database which would guide the direction of teaching and learning of adults from different social backgrounds and to inform planning for institutional change and staff development.

For analysis purposes, Weil (1989) developed a framework of disjuncture and integration which is described in detail here as it is drawn on in the next section of this chapter to illuminate the experience of the students in my study. Disjuncture arises from mutually interacting influences, it is the feeling of being at odds with oneself and involves issues of identity and how one's present experience relates to one's previous experiences. If disjuncture interacts with miseducation then the overall sense of identity as a learner is undermined. Adults in Weil's study experienced disjuncture in relation to the following: their expectations of and initial encounter with the formal learning context; their expectations and experiences of teaching and learning approaches; the ways in which social differences and power relations were experienced and managed; the extent to which core aspects of identity felt threatened; the management of multiple and conflicting roles; the kinds of knowledge allowed and disallowed; and the impact of contradictions between tutors' private and public stances. Alternatively, Weil suggests that disjuncture can be anticipated and managed and result in learning and integration. Of particular importance to integration is the active use and appreciation of different kinds of knowledge, making connections across disciplinary boundaries, and the positive valuing and use of personal and social difference within the group.

An exploratory study of the experience of non-traditional learners

In 1991, I began an exploratory qualitative investigation of the experience of 12 non-traditional learners in the Bristol course. Of the 12 students, all had the equivalent to four GCSEs or less on leaving school and had not since completed A-level or part-time university courses, seven had taken Access courses. The sample included nine women and three men, nine white and three black students, 11 were working class and one middle class, the average age was 35, with the range of 26–46. Whereas the students did not disclose impairments, it is acknowledged this may be because the relevant questions were not asked. The purpose of the study was to begin to assess whether the nature of the course itself was significant to a successful outcome, in addition to looking at the impact of the variables which the students brought with them to the course, including previous academic history, demographic, environmental and psychological variables. The objective of the study was to contribute to our understanding of the teaching and learning of non-traditional students.

Data was obtained largely through in-depth interviews which for half the students in the sample occurred at intervals throughout the two-year course, and for the balance occurred at the end of the course when the students were asked to take a retrospective look at their experience on the course. The group were also interviewed once in the post-qualifying year. In addition to individual interviews there were focus-group interviews and extensive observation of students in formal and informal learning situations.

Experiences of disjuncture

The experiences of disjuncture discussed in this section include those factors identified by Weil (1989), in addition to factors such as role conflict and lack of adequate economic resources which Weil does not mention. Individual courses have relatively little control over these latter areas of a student's life, although undoubtedly could do more collectively to influence provision of resources such as creche facilities and holiday play schemes. The other areas of disjuncture fall more within the control of individual courses who have a responsibility to recognize the needs of non-traditional students in relation to course management, curriculum and support.

Multiple and conflicting roles

Non-traditional students carry multiple and often conflicting roles with significant potential for disjuncture. Of the 12 students in the Bristol sample, seven were married at the beginning of the course, three marriages ended during the course (all female students), and three experienced considerable turmoil. Woodley *et al.* (1987) found that one in 10 mature students in their survey reported that study had moved them further apart from their families. In family systems terms it is predictable that roles and relationships are disturbed when one member of the family enters into the process of professional education with the potential this has for individual growth and change.

With the exception of three students, two of whom were young and single and one of whom was divorced with adult children, the other students were all carrying significant caring responsibility for family members, including children, partners and ageing parents. Yvonne, a black single parent mother graphically described her frustration with role conflict and its intrusiveness into her life as a student:

> You can't shut off your life outside. You're worrying about the kids, you're worrying about this, you're worrying about that, you're too tired to study because you've been up the night before.

Caring responsibilities were not only a problem for the women students, men were also in a caring role. Of the three men in the sample, two had partners and children and during the course both were temporarily in the position of being primary carer due to illness of their partners, causing periods of absence from the course.

Phillips *et al.* (1995) do not discuss the issue of multiple roles for disabled students, but they comment that a constant theme running through the experience of disabled students is needing more time than other students, to travel and to complete tasks, 'the possibility of disabled students producing work of the same quality as students without impairments was thus reduced' (p. 22). Lack of time to manage the various commitments clearly emerged from the Bristol students:

> It's very hard to find your own space. When you leave here and you go home you haven't got time to study. By the time you've got home from school, you've cooked, you've tidied up, it's time to go to bed. When do you have time to study? Weekends are even worse, you're on your feet twenty four hours a day then.
>
> (Yvonne)

Course design provided students with considerable unstructured time to support reflection and self-directed learning. However, for students dealing with multiple roles, the temptation to use the time for purposes other than study was sometimes difficult to resist.

Role conflict may be exacerbated by the student's family or friends who resist the entry of the student to university, an experience not discussed by Weil. Three women in the Bristol study were experiencing active resistance from their husbands. This dilemma was most powerfully expressed by Yvonne, who described being told by both her husband and mother that she was 'getting beyond' herself and was going to become 'one of them'. Yvonne's achievement of being accepted for the course was attributed by her relatives solely to her being black rather than any recognizable ability on her part. This message was eroding Yvonne's belief in herself: 'If you hear messages like that for long enough you believe it. It's hard to shake off.' Similar experiences were identified by Rosen (1993), who describes the strain on family relationships of black students being perceived as going over to the other side, to the establishment towards which they and their families felt distrust (1993: 187). A study of black students in an American community college (Weis, 1985) found that readiness to 'leave' their own community was positively associated with success in college.

Time is another factor in managing multiple roles. The theme of lack of time to manage learning and other commitments recurs in studies of mature students, 'Perhaps the most intractable situational problem facing mature students is that of time and family commitments both as a barrier to entry into education and as a difficulty on the course once the barrier is overcome' (Woodley *et al.*, 1987: 177). It is difficult to assess whether role conflict is greater for non-traditional students. However, it seems likely that because of the number of different areas of disjuncture experienced by non-traditional students, the burden of any one area is experienced as qualitatively greater.

Lack of resources

Percy (1985) identifies finance as one of the main barriers to access to higher education where there has been no real progress, as grants decrease in value and paid educational leave becomes a rarity. Weil (1988) does not address the disjuncture created by economic resources inadequate to maintain a reasonable standard of living for the student and her/his family. Neither does Berger (1992) link the at risk variable of age range of 35–44 with it being a time of financial pressure on growing families. However, a survey by the National Union of Students and the National Westminster Bank conducted in February 1994 found that debt increases considerably with age, the average level of student debt for those aged 22–26 was £4856 and for those aged over 26 it was £6105 (AUT *Bulletin,* January 1995).

My study suggested that economic issues were of central importance. It is much easier to be a student if adequate child care is affordable, or if sufficient creche or after school child care facilities are available in the higher education facility. As full-time students, the majority were receiving very limited grants from either local or central government which were totally inadequate to cover the costs of supporting a family. The situation for the non-traditional student is made worse by having limited resources prior to beginning the course. The small minority were two students with partners with earning power sufficient to sustain them through the course. The more common scenario is reflected in this statement: 'I don't know what it's like not to worry about not paying this bill or that bill, not to have to struggle to put food on the table every day of my life.'

One of the outcomes for students with severely limited financial resources, was that although they were full-time students they felt there was no choice but to obtain part-time employment, and this often meant shift work with its disturbance of sleep patterns. This experience is shared by the wider student body. The phenomena of the impact of employment on study is under-researched. It inevitably erodes study time, and may therefore add to the stress levels for students. Non-traditional students are caught in a vicious circle in their attempts to move out of a cycle of disadvantage.

Initial encounters with professional education

The degree of disjuncture at the beginning of the course was very noticeable with significant potential for fragmentation and an assault on the identity of the learner (Salzberger-Wittenberg, 1983). They all had negative experiences with schooling and left school feeling inferior, demoralized and devalued. A white woman working-class student described how she felt ignored at school because she was working class, even 'nicking off' (truanting) did not generate much enthusiasm by the school authorities in bringing her back into school. The students had in common a negative self-image as non-achieving, and for black students particularly this was compounded by being labelled as inferior.

The combination of an unsuccessful early experience with education and coming from a socially disadvantaged group who traditionally remain outside higher education means that beginning a university course represents an enormous step into foreign territory. Rosen describes how black students entering higher education 'were entering unknown territory and feeling their way blindfolded through what they understood to be a minefield, intended to explode their aspirations at the first chance' (1993: 182). Phillips *et al.* (1995) identify the poor quality of information about the learning environment and the lack of focused assistance at the interview stage as important barriers for disabled students at the initial stages.

For some students the feeling of disjuncture was so strong it was more a dislocation than a disjuncture, they felt they were in the wrong place and did not belong:

'People like me don't go to university'.
(Susan, white working-class woman)

'I was surprised all the time . . . I was surprised I was still here and able to carry on'.
(Jean, black working-class woman)

The feeling of being in the wrong place was compounded by terror of it being confirmed that they were indeed in the wrong place;

'I was terrified, would I be bright enough or intelligent enough?'
(Hannah, white working-class woman)

Disjuncture early in the course is experienced by many students and Chapter 3 discusses some attempts made by course planners to begin to address this.

Expectations of teaching and learning approaches

Although some effort had been made to prepare students for the kind of approach to teaching and learning they would be participating in, it was evident that few students had grasped the nature of the course they were embarking on. As Hannah commented, 'I knew everything was going to be strange and different so I didn't have any preconceived ideas, I just came.' Sue reported that the only fact about the course which stuck in her head as important was that there were no exams at the end, a crucial consideration as she had suffered immobilizing exam anxiety at school. The lack of preparation was striking, and although on the one hand the lack of academic training of the non-traditional learners was positive in that they did not have to unlearn an approach to teaching and learning, on the other hand their expectations of assessed work were of huge hurdles to be jumped, often with little anticipation of success. Failure is devastating and for non-traditional students who lack academic confidence the fear of failure is ever present (Percy, 1985; Woodley *et al.*, 1987). This is discussed further in the section below on the threat to a core aspect of identity.

Ways in which social differences and power relations are threatened

Analysing and critiquing social differences and power relations was a core feature of the curriculum, with an emphasis given to building on personal knowledge. However, even given the best of attempts to manage this learning, the material emerging was raw and threatening for students who had experienced first-hand the impact of often multiple oppressions. The black students became more aware and angry about racial discrimination. As Yvonne said,

> Too much learning is not too good. What I've learned, it's divided my feelings and it's making me very distrustful of people, especially white people. I see them in a different light than I did three years ago.

Rosen, herself a black woman, describes how black students began to speak freely for the first time, exploring ideas they had not been able to in mixed-race settings. As they began to argue and discover their own powers and found staff prepared to listen and take them seriously, 'they found themselves changing profoundly and in the process they began to express fear, grief and a new sense of self, but most of all they began to vent anger' (1993: 179). The degree of anger can be very challenging, and even frightening, for staff who are trying to address students' learning needs.

Interestingly, the experience of a non-traditional white male student was also one of disjuncture. Steve, a white working-class man who had spent many years working in a macho environment on building sites, was confronted with the implications of gender socialization and its relation to the abuse of women and children. He felt responsible for this and experienced considerable disjuncture and distress as he questioned his masculine identity and the values attributed to maleness by society.

An optimistic view is expressed by Weil who describes how re-entry into the formal education system 'can result in disappointment, dislocation, and ultimately re-discovery – the process of which seems to result in renewed value bases upon which to make choices as a learner' (1986: 224). Whereas both Yvonne and Steve appeared to go back and forth through these stages, they did not find ultimate resolution of the kind suggested by Weil, hence Yvonne's comment at the end of the course,

> One part of me wishes I never came here and the other part of me is glad I did . . . I can't go back because of what I know, I can't go back to where I was three years ago.

It seems likely that for some students, if they have been exposed to years of multiple and interacting oppressions, resolution will not occur by the end of the course, in particular because discrimination from wider societal structures continues. Their experience suggests that the possible optimum outcome is to develop the ability to manage the fluctuating contradictions in their lives.

Areas of knowledge allowed and disallowed

This area of disjuncture is closely related to the ways in which social and power differences are threatened. Non-traditional students did not just bring their experience with them, in a very real way they were their experience (Knowles, 1973). Although the course philosophy and structure encouraged the students to build on personal knowledge, the non-traditional students did not feel that all experience was allowed, particularly in relation to social and power differences. Given the risk of generating the kind of anger and intense feelings described above, it is not surprising that staff may hesitate to encourage expression of personal knowledge. The students raised concerns about contradictions between the actual and espoused behaviour of both staff and other students. They did not always experience being heard, and it is likely the non-traditional students are particularly susceptible to feeling ignored and invalidated, and to reactivation of old feelings of being inferior.

Another dynamic may reinforce student perception that their experience was not allowed. Phillips *et al.* (1995) suggest that the politics of equality risk reproducing inequality, and for disabled students this results in an assumption that all students are non-disabled. For example, in 'group' interviews used to assess candidates, the needs of those with sensory impairments were not identified, and as a result they may be at a significant disadvantage. Students may be reluctant to identify their needs, for fear of being labelled a nuisance or inadequate. Low's research (1996) into the experience of disabled students highlights the dilemmas they face in negotiating their identities.

Furthermore, non-traditional students face a significant dilemma in seeking support from staff. 'Who could they trust with their uncertainties without being labelled as failing?' (Rosen, 1993: 179). As this student said, 'I've got this thing about appearing stupid if I have to ask questions, so I don't ask too much.'

It is perceived to be risky to reveal needs. Sue described not seeking help from staff until she was at crisis point. Based on earlier experiences in education, she was afraid of being rebuffed if she sought help earlier. Another possible barrier to students seeking help from staff is the degree of difference between them. Bird suggests that lack of black staff is still a central issue in the support of black students, 'while the presence of black staff may well not be a sufficient condition for dealing with the isolation of black students, it is probably a necessary one' (Bird, 1996: 24). Finally, staff may not proactively invite students to seek support, or create the opportunity for them to do so, although they may be responsive to direct requests for help from students assertive enough to express their needs. As staff contact time diminishes due to the pressure of other demands, this situation is likely to worsen.

Threat to core aspects of identity

For non-traditional students, entering education appears to promise fulfilment and improvement in life chances, yet it also threatens personal identity:

> We cannot underestimate the power of the formal system – to define and undermine identity and status (or lack of it), to frame the criteria by which success should be judged, to influence the extent to which learning is allowed to be a process rather than just a means to an end.
>
> (Weil, 1986: 232)

Success or failure was perceived by the students in absolute terms, or in comparison to other students, not in relation to individual learning objectives or starting points. The high value placed by higher education and the professions on assessment of propositional knowledge relative to personal and process knowledge contributes to this. As Rita, a black woman from an Access course commented,

> Students can identify themselves as the all right students, the not so bad students, and the students that rarely do well and unfortunately the students that rarely do well are the Access students.

The risk of failure is terrifying, as Joanne, a white working-class student said, 'Each piece of work is frightening because we've come such a long way. If I fail what would I go back to?' The theme of 'what would I go back to?' was a recurring one in discussions about failure. Successfully completing the course with a professional qualification promises a way out of a life which may be typified by lack of power, status and economic resources.

A core aspect of identity is language, yet the spoken and written language of non-traditional students may not fit conventional academic norms. As Yvonne said, 'I didn't have confidence in my own language, I felt I wasn't good enough'.

The capacity to write in a conventional academic style, presented significant difficulties to students not trained in using standard English. In her study of black students in an urban community college Weis (1985) found that willingness to change aspects of their culture, for example written English, is associated with success. In her view 'dominated groups must become familiar with the discourse of dominant groups if they are to challenge the class structure effectively' (1985: 166). In professional education this is not only an academic issue but one in which the professions and accrediting bodies are concerned. Whereas the humanistic ethos of independent learning might argue for the student being able to express her or himself in their own language, which may of course be a language shared by the service user, patient, client or student group, the sponsor and provider groups of universities, professions and employers are likely to insist on particular standards and conventions which meet the norms and requirements of professional practice.

Integrating factors

Higher education has tended to respond to the needs of non-traditional learners by building in supports such as student advisers or study skills programmes to help the student adapt, problematizing students whose 'ways of knowing and relating to the world, and whose conceptions and expectations of learning' are different (Weil, 1988: 37). This approach reflects the view that there is little evidence that adult learners learn differently and need different learning and teaching methods (Percy, 1985). Yet, my observations would suggest that adult learners vary considerably and are shortchanged when treated as a homogeneous group by educators.

The alternative approach is to change the higher education system not only so that it provides a learning context sensitive to the needs of non-traditional students (Weil, 1989; Wright, 1991), but equally is responsive to the needs of all students. In this section I discuss some aspects of the Bristol course which appear to be responsive to non-traditional students and enable them to successfully complete the course. Weil (1988) proposes that integration occurs when the new situation compensates for prior feelings of disjuncture and identifies four integrating approaches: positive valuing, the appreciation of different kinds of knowledge, the active use of different kinds of knowledge, and making connections across disciplinary boundaries. I will look at each of these areas in relation to my research.

Positive valuing of students

There is considerable evidence to suggest that positive valuing of students by staff is of prime importance (Weis, 1985; Mills and Molloy, 1989; Pye, 1991; Rosen, 1993),

> Enabling teachers and groups can go a long way to counteract the impact of disjunction arising from forces that seem outside the bounds of one person's agency, and to create an oasis of integration in which the experience of other kinds of disjunction can be made sense of and more effectively managed.
>
> (Weil, 1989: 143)

Support from enabling teachers was certainly crucial for the students, particularly early in the course. This was available from facilitators in addition to tutors. Recognizing that some students are likely to require more staff support than others, the course planners began to differentiate this in work-load weightings. For example, tutors for disabled students are allocated more workload time to enable them to give proper attention to the role.

A central feature in the student's experience was of positive valuing by other students. The interdependent and relational aspect of learning was crucial. 'The psychological need for reassurance in the early stages of return, the stage before 'self-directedness', could be supplied by students for students, one often taking the role of a teacher for another' (Pye, 1991: 153). The model of learning in small groups of about 10 students with membership of the group remaining constant for a term provided the student with a base, particularly significant in the first term when disjunc-ture was at its peak. The non-traditional students were, with very few excep-tions, positive about learning in groups and often the connections made in the first term remained significant sources of support throughout the course. They all reported seeking support from other students, finding students more readily accessible and available than staff.

However, groups did not always provide a positive experience, and at their worst they replicated the experience the students had with lack of opportunity and power in society. Sarah thought middle-class students in her first group were inclined to make the non-traditional students feel even less able. Joanne described feeling at times that other group members were talking over her head. On occasion it was possible for students to raise these issues, or for facilitators to identify group dynamics and intervene. As dis-cussed in Chapter 5, initial experiences with group membership led course planners to ensure that members of minorities were not knowingly placed in isolated positions in groups. For example, black students were always placed in groups with at least two other black students. However, issues of power and oppression are very difficult to resolve and at times inevitably go underground.

The course also encouraged the development of student support groups, allocating meeting times on the timetable, as well as funds for start-up or ongoing consultants. One of the most active groups was for black students which advocated on its own behalf in course matters.

One form of staff support offered to non-traditional learners and to any student who felt he or she would benefit, was a study skills programme (see Chapter 7 for further discussion about study skills). The non-traditional students were very mixed in their responses to the study skills programme. Some students sought as much assistance as possible, but others avoided it and sought their own external supports outside the course. The latter alternative was taken particularly by students concerned about appearing stupid, and/or because they had established study skills support outside the university prior to joining the course.

Integration of propositional knowledge into the curriculum about minor-ity group issues also emerged as important to non-traditional students feel-ing valued. In scenarios developed for use in problem-based learning it is essential to ensure they do not predominantly represent white majority culture. They must reflect the diversity of society, including particularly those groups with which non-traditional students identify.

Finally, although not identified by Weil (1988), positive valuing by the student's family or friends was also crucial for some students. Yvonne was determined to do well for the sake of her children: 'If I fail, I fail the kids, they're dependent on me.' Mirza (1992) in her analysis of the achievement of young black women at work and school presents a picture of second generation African Caribbean girls in Britain, regardless of class, being positively influenced by their parents' strong orientation to work and education.

Appreciation and active valuing of different kinds of knowledge

Directly related to the experience of positive valuing in the group was the priority given to integrating personal knowledge (Eraut, 1992) into learning. Considerable emphasis was placed in the first term on students identifying their pre-course experiences and being supported to view their experiences as relevant and worthwhile, 'whilst experience may be a learning resource the confidence to use it is not always present' (Usher, 1989: 66). In the first term, before assessment factors became intrusive, this had a distinctive levelling effect. As Sarah commented, 'I never felt in any way inferior because I haven't had formal education. Compared to other people, I've got lots of work experience.' Rita, who had completed an Access course, had arrived at the university anticipating she might experience an 'us and them' and instead found that her skills and experience were valued – 'Qualifications don't really come into it'.

The levelling experience of the students was also experienced by facilitators who did not read student files before a group began and reported often being unable to tell from student participation in the group which students were graduates and which were not.

Students were expected to use their pre-course experiences as resources for learning and, given the diversity of non-traditional students in each group, there was a great deal of experience which could be drawn on. Learning from each other appeared to be particularly important to these students. The experience that was being shared had both cognitive and affective meaning which gave it an impact rarely achieved in a lecture. It was also shared in accessible language as opposed to academic jargon which can be alienating and intimidating:

It's [sharing] sort of easier to take in than reading books and trying to remember for myself. It's easier to listen to other people and how they put it in context.

(Jean)

The emphasis on sharing prior experience and positively valuing what each group member brings within the context of a small group had another very important effect of 'unlearning not to speak' (Weil, 1989: 121). A noticeable feature of non-traditional students early in the course was their reluctance to speak up for fear of saying the wrong thing, appearing stupid, as Yvonne said, 'You daren't open your mouth for fear of saying something stupid.' Inhibitions of this kind tend to reinforce the negative self-image they brought into the course.

One of the most significant changes for the women students, was learning to speak out and to use their voice in the process of learning and creating knowledge. The importance of the voice in learning is highlighted by Belenky *et al.* (1986). As a result of their study of the experience of black and white women learners, Belenky and her associates developed a framework of five stages in the epistemological development of women. The first stage is that of silence 'a position in which women experience themselves as mindless and voiceless and subject to the whims of external authority'. The next stage is that of received knowledge, 'a perspective from which women conceive of themselves as capable of receiving, even reproducing, knowledge from the all-knowing external authorities but not capable of creating knowledge on their own' (1986: 15). At the third stage of subjective knowledge, women begin to question external knowledge and acknowledge private authority, and in the final two stages they arrive at 'real talk' and move towards creating knowledge.

The learning group provided a safe place to experiment with speaking out. The change in those women students who in the first term moved from being silent to beginning to speak out and even to chair group sessions was dramatic. As women students looked back on their course experience this was frequently a change they noted in themselves: 'When I've got something to say I try to say it. Before I used to hold back.' One of the most eloquent exponents of the power of learning to speak out was Yvonne:

> I've got a voice and I'm going to make sure I'm heard ... I've learned about people, I've learned about organizations, I've learned about theories and even though I may not believe some of them I can understand them. I know how to present myself and not present myself. I know how to read people a bit more. I know how to survive.

This statement conveys an impressive synthesis of the personal and the political, of personal, process and propositional knowledge.

Problem-based learning requires the bringing together of different kinds of knowledge, it also supports different students' strengths and allows them an opportunity to practice what they are less familiar with. For the non-traditional students, whose preferred style tended to be doing rather than conceptualizing, this offered an effective means of learning. As Yvonne commented, 'If I don't get up and do it, I'm not going to get it. Because EAL makes me go out and research and do things, I'm learning more things.'

Yvonne was learning about the process of learning, as well as acquiring propositional knowledge. Lectures were in general not enthusiastically received by these students. It was often a major challenge to keep up and understand the lecturer who was experienced as not talking in an accessible language, going too fast, and not addressing the needs of the individual. Lectures were described as either an intimidating, boring or irrelevant experience.

Learning across disciplinary boundaries

Problem-based learning also enables the crossing of disciplinary boundaries and helps the student do some of the integrative work which learning within disciplines so often does not do. This is significant in many professional education courses which draw on different disciplines and which in a traditional course structure typically leave it to the individual student to make the links and do the work of integration. Problem-based learning enables integration as part of the process of learning and was experienced as highly relevant to practice, offering non-traditional students their chance to learn in order to achieve an ambition to become a social worker. Woodley *et al.* (1987) found in their survey of mature students that two out of three students in qualifying courses were studying for instrumental reasons mainly connected with career improvement. For the Bristol students, learning built on case studies drawn from practice felt real and built on the motivation they brought to the course.

Conclusion

> How do we know if we offer to new kinds of students an education that enables, rather than compounds, previous disabling forces? What more do we need to do, and which of our many strengths do we need to build upon?
>
> (Weil, 1989: 143)

We can only know if education is enabling by listening to its users. It is not enough to measure the success of non-traditional students by indicators such as access, outcomes or retention, the accessibility of courses is equally important. The exploratory study of the Bristol students would suggest that an enabling education is one which has in balance personal, process and propositional knowledge, where pre-course experience is integrated into new learning, where there are opportunities for independent, interdependent and dependent learning, and where learning begins with the problem related to practice and builds on motivation to learn at the same time as providing a framework for integrating learning from different disciplines. As has been discussed, there were also disabling forces in the Bristol course, notably associated with assessment processes, a point developed in

Chapter 8. It is very important to conceptualize success and failure differently for non-traditional learners.

> If the individual can demonstrate an increased set of competencies from that on the point of entry into higher education then he or she should not be considered a 'failure' or a wastage statistic irrespective or not of whether the end point qualification has been reached.
>
> (Harrison, 1990: 10)

The growing number of non-traditional students may provide a catalyst for important reforms in higher education generally (Weil, 1988). The Bristol students identify experiences which must to a greater or lesser degree be significant to all students in professional education. Perhaps most crucially for professional education, given the appropriate initial professional education, students want to continue to learn. As this non-traditional student said, 'I'm hungry. I missed out early on.'

As will be discussed in the next chapter, it is crucial in professional education for the individual and the system to sustain the motivation for lifelong learning.

10

Perspectives on Education as Preparation for Practice

If a primary objective of professional education is to prepare students for qualified practice, then a central question for evaluation is its effectiveness in doing this. The ultimate evaluation of effectiveness must lie in the effect of professional education on practice with service users, as perceived by the users themselves. However, it is also important to examine the students views of the impact of their education on practice, as they are a significant group of stakeholders in professional education.

It has been suggested that students are not well placed themselves to evaluate the impact of professional education on their practice. Over a decade ago, Davies suggested that, 'Students in training are not ideally placed to judge the efficacy of their course against the demands of future practice, the true nature of which they can only guess at' (1984: 12). He surveyed former social work students about how they felt their training helped them with their practice three years on. Whereas Davies' point is an important one to consider, a wait of three years before surveying practitioners' risks ignoring the possibly substantial influence of the employing organization on the views of the practitioner. Also, many students have a good understanding of the nature of their chosen profession prior to entering professional education and can do more than guess at the nature of practice ahead of them. Indeed, understanding of their chosen profession and relevant experience may be included in selection criteria. Furthermore, the requirement for students in professional education to undertake supervised practice prior to being accredited as qualified means they become familiar with the nature of practice, albeit they are placed in agencies as students with protected workloads, and are not carrying an employee role.

I believe that the students' views of the impact of their education on practice, both during the course and in the year immediately post-qualifying are significant, and as educators we can learn from them. In evaluating EAL, there were two opportunities for me to survey student views. Field placements are an integral part of social work education and they provided the first opportunity. Initially, I did not assign high priority to evaluating the impact of EAL on students in field placements. My intent as a researcher with a utilization focused agenda (Patton, 1986) was guided by the priorities of course planners who were primarily concerned with the university based curriculum. Although some initial orientation to EAL had been provided for practice teachers, there were few major changes in the form or substance of practice learning introduced as a result of the curriculum changes at the university (Baldwin and Burgess, 1992). However, if I was to understand fully the impact of EAL on the cohort of students in my interview sample, it was important to gain some understanding of the impact of EAL on student performance in placement, from the perspective of both student and Practice Teacher. This objective was incorporated into the initial research strategy.

The second opportunity was provided by the experience of newly qualified practitioners. Following the students from graduation into qualified practice was not part of my initial remit as a researcher. However, fortunately the Sir Halley Stewart Trust agreed to invest further in the initial research and fund an exploratory study to examine what newly qualified social workers thought of EAL as preparation for practice. The general hypothesis to be explored was that this approach produces social workers who feel themselves to be, and are considered by their managers to be competent to practice. Within this general proposition the intention was to explore four more specific areas, including the contribution to practice of problem-based learning, independent learning and learning in groups. The fourth area related to the hypothesis that the practice environment influences the ability of newly qualified workers to practice in the way they have been trained.

Relevant findings from McMaster research into medical education

I was aware of the various outcome studies carried out by McMaster researchers during more than 20 years of the McMaster approach to medical education. Given the existence in Canada of a national qualifying exam for medicine, it was possible to compare outcomes from different medical education programmes in a way which is not possible with social work education in the UK. Furthermore, there now exists in Canada a considerable data base about graduates from medical schools to enable comparisons to be made for example about the different career paths of McMaster graduates and those of other programmes (Woodward and Ferrier, 1982; Ferrier and Woodward, 1987; Woodward, 1989). This again is regrettably not available in social work education in the UK.

I have selected findings from three McMaster studies as particularly relevant to my research and briefly summarize them here. Although I used a different methodology than the McMaster researchers, there are some interesting similarities in outcomes which I refer to later in this chapter.

The first study relevant to this chapter is the survey of six classes of graduates for their views on the medical curriculum as preparation for postgraduate work (Woodward and Ferrier, 1982). Three classes were surveyed five years after graduation, and three classes two years after graduation. The graduates reported feeling very well prepared compared to fellow postgraduates in independent learning, self-evaluation and problem-solving skills. They also judged their preparation in data gathering skills, behavioural science knowledge, ability to deal with social and emotional problems of patients, medical record keeping skills, preventive, follow-up and in-patient care as very good compared to peers. They identified two content areas, pharmacology and basic medical sciences, as requiring more attention.

Teaching staff were also surveyed by McMaster researchers. A sample of faculty members were surveyed in 1981 for their perceptions of the McMaster programme (McAuley and Woodward, 1984). Problem-based learning was the most frequently identified strength of the programme, followed closely by tutorial learning. The most frequently identified area of weakness was evaluation of student performance, followed by the fast pace of the programme and its short length.

The third study relevant for our purposes is a comparison of the career paths of McMaster graduates from 1972–79 with those of graduates from other Canadian English-language schools (Ferrier and Woodward, 1987). It was found that McMaster graduates were more likely to have chosen internal medicine, less likely to have chosen surgery and equally likely to have chosen primary care as their medical field. While the nature of practice and time spent on patient care did not vary between the two groups, several variables including time spent on professional activities other than patient care, proportion of time spent on research or classroom teaching and proportion of salaried physicians employed by universities indicated a higher than average interest in academic medicine among McMaster graduates. 'This could be partially explained by differences in the student profile if students who are interested in education are more likely to choose an educationally innovative medical school' (Ferrier and Woodward, 1987: 39).

In spite of the large number of research studies carried out by McMaster researchers, they have not followed a group of graduates into practice and looked in-depth with them at their views of the usefulness of their training for practice. It is hoped that the findings from interviews with the Bristol students, summarized in the next section of this chapter, complement the McMaster findings.

EAL as preparation for practice – research approaches

To examine the impact of EAL on field placements, as perceived by students and practice teachers, the second placement was selected as the initial focus for attention. The first field placement lasted only three months and was seen as too short and occurring too early in the course (after one term in the university) to be confident that student experience would substantially reflect university based work. In contrast, the second placement lasted five months, occurred in the second year of the course and was usually in an area of work in which the students intended to practice following completion of the course.

My plan was to interview at the beginning and end of placement, the cohort of students I followed through the course and in addition, their practice teachers following satisfactory completion of the students' placements. I anticipated that interviews with the practice teachers would provide information about the students from a group of experienced practitioners who it could be assumed would be very familiar by the end of the placement with their students practice.

At the point of completion of the course, my plan was to interview the cohort of nine students I had followed through the course, adding a further six students randomly selected on a stratified basis to balance the gender and race mix of the initial interview group, and the balance of students specializing in general social work or probation. It was not possible to control any further for the kinds of agencies students would be working in, as at the point of graduation most students did not know where they would be working.

Unfortunately, for reasons of illness and personal problems, it was only possible to follow five of the initial cohort into employment which meant that ultimately I followed 11 students through their first period of qualified practice. The destinations of the newly qualified workers included, four in the probation service (two women and two men), six in social service departments (four women and two men), and one in the voluntary sector (woman).

I planned to interview the former students again at the end of nine to 12 months of practice. This period of time was selected because it was felt that newly qualified workers would be close enough to their education to comment in detail, yet not too far away from the impact of their training for it to have become inseparable from the impact of the employing organization. It was also anticipated (mistakenly as it turned out) that they would still be in their first job.

A surprise and a significant setback to the research plan was the difficulty in obtaining data because of the shifting nature of the newly qualified workers' pattern of employment. As mentioned above, it had been anticipated that interviewing graduates nine to 12 months into qualified practice would ensure that they would still be in their first post. However, the picture in reality was significantly different. Only two students (probation) went into posts which they still held nine to 12 months later, and one of these was planning an imminent move to another authority. Of the remaining two probation students, one had changed teams within the same authority and one had begun in a non-probation post and then managed after several months to obtain a probation post. The other seven newly qualified workers had changed jobs at least once, and four of these had changed jobs twice. Of this group, with the exception of the newly qualified worker in the voluntary sector, all had moved posts within the same local authority. In the total group, all of the job changes, with the exception of one, were due to the initial posts being temporary. The one exception had made a planned change to a post with more predictable day-time working hours which suited her needs as a single parent. The one newly qualified worker who began work in the voluntary sector remained in the voluntary sector, albeit in a different organization. She was by the end of the study anticipating a move into the statutory sector where she felt she would have the opportunity to practise 'real social work'.

Regrettably for my initial research plans, this pattern of change was mirrored by changes in line manager. Only one newly qualified worker (probation) had the same senior or supervisor throughout the research period of twelve months. Not only had the other newly qualified workers changed jobs, they all told a very similar story of changes in line managers. Interviews with the newly qualified workers indicated little was to be gained from interviewing managers who it was felt did not know the workers in question, and who were either acting managers or on the move themselves. This pattern brought into question the original plan to seek the views of managers or supervisors about the competence of EAL trained staff to practice. It was decided that in the circumstances little was to be gained from pursuing this objective. The effect of this all encompassing picture of change will be explored further in my discussion of the impact of the organization on newly qualified workers.

In addition to interviews, all students who completed the course in 1992 were asked to complete a questionnaire about how well they thought EAL had prepared them for practice. This questionnaire was administered at the point of qualifying and again 16 months later. Of the initial cohort of 40 students group, 34 qualified after two years on the course, and of these, 21 students (62 per cent) returned both questionnaires.

Views of EAL as preparation for practice

In the following section I discuss findings in relation to perceptions of the impact on practice of problem-based learning, independent learning and learning in small groups, at both the placement stage and the newly qualified stage. I then go on to discuss the perception of the influence of the organizational context on practice.

Problem-based learning

It was seen in the earlier review of the McMaster findings that problem-based learning was perceived by its graduates as a strength (Woodward and Ferrier, 1982), and it was also rated as a strength by McMaster faculty

(McAuley and Woodward, 1984). This picture is remarkably similar in the Bristol study. In interviews with students in placement and their practice teachers, and then at the point of qualifying and again after nine to 12 months in practice, the views of problem-based learning were consistently very positive.

In examining the data from students and practice teachers, I first review the areas of process knowledge required for problem-based learning, including acquiring information, handling information and giving information (Eraut, 1994). I then go on to explore the use of propositional knowledge in practice on the basis that a central rationale for problem-based learning is that it facilitates the integration of theory and practice (Burgess, 1992). In his study of learning to use propositional knowledge in nursing and midwifery, Eraut *et al.* (1995) clarify the confusion about the 'theory-practice gap' and identify a number of distinct issues wrapped up in this phrase. I use the term 'integrating knowledge in practice' to refer to knowledge used in guiding or reflecting on practice.

The Bristol students believed that the process knowledge integral to problem-based learning would be useful to them in practice and it can be speculated that such conviction enhanced their motivation to learn. As a student at the end of the course commented,

> It's [EAL] prepared me for going into future work in the probation service. It's equipped me with skills normal first year officers will take a while to have . . . not being afraid to ask for help, using resources, using people, asking questions.

As a result of pre-course experience as a volunteer in the probation service and subsequent placement experience, this student felt knowledgeable enough about the probation service to predict that her process knowledge would give her an advantage over first year officers from other courses.

Students were very positive about their ability to acquire information. They viewed the skills of seeking and obtaining information in practice, whether on placement or as newly qualified workers, as directly transferable from the classroom,

> When you're on placement you're doing EAL . . . The way you work on placement is an EAL way of working because you are actually doing things and you have to find out things for yourself.

This student was making the link between 'doing things' such as acquiring information, and being able to work independently.

At the point of qualifying, the newly qualified workers described how their confidence in their process knowledge played an important part in job interviews. This confidence in acquiring information fits with the report by McMaster graduates that they are skilled in 'data gathering' (Woodward and Ferrier, 1983).

A significant finding from the Bristol study is the students' confidence in acknowledging not knowing, and not being afraid to ask for help. If they did not have the necessary answers they knew they would be able to acquire the relevant information. As a student on placement said, 'I don't always have to know, I don't have to be an expert.'

It was very reassuring for students to be in this position. Whereas it might be expected that students on placement could acknowledge being in the learner role, they often experience a significant pressure to know and it may feel risky to reveal not knowing when there is so much invested in success. This theme of not being afraid to acknowledge not knowing, or asking for help, continued into the initial interviews with the workers in employment when they were often acutely aware of all they did not know, 'I don't feel frightened when I don't know certain things.'

In the final interview 12 months into practice, a male social worker who was employed by a social services area team, and had begun the course very lacking in confidence commented, 'I feel very confident in finding information because I know I will get the information I want eventually. I will always be able to find out.' Given the pace of change and the inevitability of not having knowledge at one's fingertips or readily available from others, this confidence about being able to find out is essential to practice. It also seems possible that readiness to acknowledge not knowing is a precondition to continuing learning, an issue I will return to later in the chapter.

Another area of process knowledge where students experienced the skills of problem-based learning transferred into practice, was in the ability to handle information. In Chapter 6, I discussed the specific difficulties which students reported early in the course with being able to handle information, particularly being able to identify what was important and what was peripheral, and in being able to set boundaries on information they were seeking. At the three interview points respondents were positive about their developing ability to handle information. During the second placement students were positive about learning to distinguish what is of central significance in practice. One student talked at the point of graduating from the course about developing process knowledge,

> The way of looking at problems, of taking apart problems. It has given me insight into taking away the fluffy bits . . . the things which are distracting and aren't relevant and given me ways of getting at what is relevant.

In employment this confidence in handling information continued: 'I can take almost any subject now and think it through.'

One newly qualified worker employed by a local authority social services department felt that the ability to identify the most important aspects of the problem, be able to contextualize it and then make sound judgements was the most useful outcome of his learning on the course,

> Everything we deal with is a problem . . . you have to analyse the problem, prioritize the problem, look at the surrounding issues. That's all we're doing in social work.

Similarly, a newly qualified probation officer also commented in the final interview on the value of being able to transfer process knowledge from problem-based learning to practice,

> Everything we do has to have a plan of action and information about how you're going to implement it. It includes looking at what resources are available, what you can do. You have to include strategies and objectives and who you can resource.

Practice in professions such as social work, nursing, teaching, and the health care professions is becoming increasingly oriented to developing plans which include aims, objectives, strategies and means of evaluating whether the objectives have been met. A problem-based learning framework provides university based opportunities for practising this approach.

Another increasingly important aspect of handling information in professional practice today is record-keeping. McMaster graduates perceived themselves as skilled in 'record-keeping' (Woodward and Ferrier, 1982). Evidence of these skills was also reported by the Bristol students, most clearly by the probation students who were required on their placements to write detailed 'social inquiry reports'. They described how tackling these reports was similar to tackling a problem based scenario in university work, and again the skills were experienced as directly transferable to practice.

Respondents at all three interview points were positive about the usefulness in practice of developing the third area of process knowledge of being able to give information. Some newly qualified workers had been asked as part of the job interview process to make a presentation to the interview panel and reported positively on the value of rehearsal on the course. At the end of their first year in practice, all reported having been required to present information to a variety of audiences including such diverse groups as team members, local councillors and groups of service users. Interview data was supported by questionnaire data with a large majority of practitioners reporting they felt well or were adequately prepared to present information. Interestingly, after 15 months in practice, the proportion of practitioners feeling well or adequately prepared to present written information had dropped, whereas they felt their skill in presenting verbal information had increased. These practitioners seemed well equipped to meet the increasingly emphasized requirement in professional practice today of being able to provide accessible information in a variety of ways to a diverse range of groups.

Practice teachers of the cohort of students I followed through the course were also consistently positive about their students' process knowledge, although understandably hesitant about attributing this to EAL based on their limited experience of supervising only one student. The comment of this practice teacher about her student was typical:

> It very quickly became evident at how able she was in finding information. It was very noticeable. It was her biggest strength. She got on with the work very quickly.

Practice teachers commented on how students were systematic in their approach to their work, active, enquiring, able to consult and able to work on their own.

The ability of students to use their initiative and work independently is particularly important to practice teachers who often take on the role from interest or commitment to professional education, but are typically not provided by their employing agency with compensation in the form of workload relief or financial reward. This practice teacher, experienced in supervising students, favourably compared the EAL student with others she had supervised: 'Some students, especially early in the placement, come and ask you about everything. She didn't do that.' Interestingly, another practice teacher suggested that this kind of resourcefulness and initiative reduced 'the omnipotence' of the practice teacher. If true, then EAL training might have unexpected implications for employers.

The main criticism from newly qualified workers about problem-based learning was that the pace of learning was too fast and there was not enough time to address the problem scenarios in depth. These concerns echoed those of McMaster faculty members (McAuley and Woodward, 1984). Similar to the McMaster students, the Bristol students identified specific gaps in their knowledge, including for example knowledge of legislation relevant to social work. Newly qualified workers could not see a solution to the problem of lack of time, other than extending the duration of the course, and several of them identified the desirability of a third year of social work training. Alternative possibilities, which will be discussed later, include a more coherent approach to induction and continuing professional development.

The criticism about lack of time also relates to students and newly qualified workers feeling there simply was not enough time to deal adequately with the amount of propositional knowledge. In particular, they voiced the frustration of not being able to pursue topics in depth. Given the rapid pace of development and change in knowledge, it is conceivable this picture is inevitable. However, more encouraging is that at the point of qualifying, 85 per cent of the graduating class perceived themselves as being able to use theory in practice well or adequately. This proportion had dropped slightly after 15 months when 72 per cent reported being able to use theory in practice well or adequately.

There is a need for further research here which focuses specifically on the use of propositional knowledge to guide or evaluate practice. Eraut *et al.* (1995) in his study of the use of 'scientific knowledge' in nursing and midwifery, provides some useful suggestions for how this might be done. For example, asking a practitioner to discuss a recent case for which knowledge from university based work might have been important and asking him or her to talk about it in some detail, seeking in particular to identify what knowledge was drawn on and how it was interpreted and used. An extension of this approach is 'concept mapping' where one person conducts the interview and another maps the concepts used 'to record an evolving description of the knowledge elicited' (Eraut *et al.*, 1995: 19).

However, these approaches are very labour intensive and require significant research resources to pursue them, of a kind which were not available to this study.

Independent learning

I suggested earlier that the process knowledge developed in problem-based learning contributes to being able to practise independently. In this section I examine four other abilities which are significant to independent practice: the ability to take the initiative; the ability to reflect critically on information; the ability to evaluate one's own practice; and the use of supervision.

Similar to their belief in the value of problem-based learning for practice, students believe that learning to work and learn independently will be valuable in practice,

> I suppose what's been most helpful is the fact that we haven't been like students in a way. We've had more opportunity to find out for ourselves which I feel has been more useful because it's like that in the real world. You have to find out for yourselves . . . It's more geared towards getting me to think how do I tackle this right from the word go rather than be spoon fed and not actually thinking.

This belief that spoon feeding will not be available 'in the real world' appears to help motivate students to overcome difficulties in learning to work independently.

A theme which recurred in interviews with students, practice teachers and newly qualified workers was of the importance of initiative and being able to 'get on with it'. Some students entered the course with initiative, others did not but felt that the course helped them learn some of the skills of developing it. As this student commented during her placement: 'I don't feel I'm naturally a person with a lot of initiative . . . EAL has taught me that I don't come here [placement] expecting everything to be set up for me.' The expectation of students that they function independently influences their performance in placement, they expect themselves to get on with it: 'I felt the onus was on me to be quite autonomous and find out what resources were needed . . . to just get on and do it.' This theme is mirrored by practice teachers who, perhaps not surprisingly, use a similar discourse. One experienced practice teacher commented on her usual experience of being 'constantly bothered and pestered' by students, but her surprise in discovering that the EAL student did not do this. Another practice teacher, unfamiliar with EAL and with Bristol students, assessed her student as having good initiative and good decision-making skills. At the newly qualified stage, one worker in social services described how her team manager had been against hiring a newly qualified worker because of concerns about the anticipated level of dependency and consequent degree of support which would need to be provided by the team. However, the team manager had been surprised by the confidence and ability of this practitioner to work on her own. The team had also commented favourably on her ability to use her initiative. The ability to use initiative would seem to be essential in practice, characterized by frequently having to respond to the unfamiliar and unexpected and where a consistent other person is unlikely to be immediately available to provide direction.

It seems possible that those practice teachers knowledgeable about EAL tended to expect students to be more independent than students from other courses, although the degree of understanding of EAL varied considerably depending on whether they had attended orientation sessions at the university. As this very experienced probation service practice teacher said,

> I have an expectation of students working with the EAL curriculum ... that it's so close to the reality of placement, the practice of the job that they will assimilate what's going on more quickly, that they will need less direction ... they will seek advice and consultation elsewhere than the practice teacher, that they are allowed greater freedom too.

This practice teacher, who had interviewed the student prior to placement, in fact found that early in the placement the student did not live up to these expectations, resulting in some tensions in the relationship. Moving into a placement is an anxiety-provoking experience and dependency needs of even the most independent students are likely to increase initially as a result.

An important aspect of learning to work independently is developing the skills of critical reflection and self-evaluation. At the level of university based work, this is one area where there appeared to be a difference between the graduate and non-graduate students, with the former having learnt skills of critical analysis during their undergraduate education and the latter initially accepting the voice of the expert as a given and later struggling to challenge this. At the end of the course a male non-graduate student described an important outcome of the course for him as having developed the skills of being able to reflect critically on material,

> If somebody says something that sounds very good and is worded well and everything, I try and work out exactly what they are saying, whether it does make sense and it is the right thing. People are very clever with words ... it's easy to want to believe someone.

Both graduates and non-graduates identified an increase in their confidence in practice in raising questions or concerns with high status professionals, whereas before the course they might have remained silent. This is important particularly in fields of practice which rely on interprofessional collaboration and where power differentials, such as those between doctors and nurses, have traditionally influenced decision-making (Hugman, 1991).

Linked with the capacity to critically reflect is the ability to challenge policy or practice rather than accept the status quo. At the point of graduating from the course, 85 per cent of newly qualified practitioners reported that they felt well or adequately prepared to challenge policy and practice. A year later this had dropped slightly to 76 per cent. It would be interesting to monitor whether the proportion continues to decline as either practitioners become institutionalized, or those who challenge practice without the desired results leave the field for another career.

The area of independent learning where there was a discrepancy between interview and questionnaire data was in relation to the ability of students and newly qualified workers to evaluate their own practice. The questionnaire data indicates that at the point of qualifying, 93 per cent felt well or adequately prepared to evaluate their practice and a year later this had dropped very slightly to 88 per cent. This picture is consistent with the McMaster graduates who identified self-evaluation as a strength of their course (Woodward and Ferrier, 1983). However, among the interview group there was evidence of ambivalence about their ability to accurately self-evaluate. This may not be surprising given the discussion of assessment issues in Chapter 7 where there was concern that insufficient attention had been paid on the course to the processes of self-evaluation, such as setting criteria against which to self-assess. The shifting pattern of employment may also have contributed to an ambivalence about self-evaluation, as external expectations and performance criteria were continually changing.

Finally, the use of supervision is an indicator of independence, although views about this were only available from practice teachers and not from line managers as had originally been planned. Supervision on field placements is the responsibility of the practice teacher and in social work the practice and theory of practice teaching is well developed (Bogo and Vayda, 1986; Shardlow and Doel, 1996). In social work, the practice teacher is responsible for enabling the learning of the student and included in this is the responsibility to assess the student's practice and make a pass or fail recommendation. The practice teachers all felt their students used supervision appropriately. This included behaviours such as students coming to supervision sessions prepared with an agenda, and consulting outside of regular supervision sessions as appropriate. There was a perception that students were ready to ask questions, perhaps more so than students from other courses. Two practice teachers noted how self-contained their students were, and one noted how the student never gave the impression she could not cope, unusual among students. These are in themselves very small pieces of data which cannot be definitively causally linked with EAL. However, the readiness of students to work independently and to seek direction when appropriate suggests their education may have been significant in this.

Learning in groups

McMaster graduates perceived tutorial or small group learning as a major programme strength (Woodward and Ferrier, 1982) and similarly there was a consensus that working in EAL groups was good preparation for working collaboratively in practice. All the respondents to the questionnaire at the point of graduation felt well or adequately prepared to work with social work colleagues and with colleagues from other professions. A year later the response about colleagues from other professions remained the same overall, although there was a big increase (45 per cent) in practitioners who felt they could do this well, compared to adequately the previous year. However, 6 per cent reported they felt inadequately prepared to work with social work colleagues.

Students in the interview sample talked positively about the transfer of skills and knowledge in learning groups to work groups, both at the placement stage and at the beginning and end of their first year in qualified practice. Familiarity with groups was an important element of this. One student in placement on an interprofessional team described, 'that familiar feeling of being in a group of people'.

Another student who had worked as a member of a team in placement said, 'It seemed very natural. I almost felt I was quite used to working in that way.'

One newly qualified worker on a recently constituted social services team which was having significant difficulties forming as a group, commented that she felt other team members, although more experienced practitioners, were also more anxious about the confusion engendered by the new group than she was. She felt confident that they would form into a functioning group, as she had experienced on the course on several occasions.

One unexpected gain from learning in groups was that at the stage of being interviewed for jobs, newly qualified workers were typically being interviewed by a panel and felt their experience with groups on the course helped them manage this. Other features of learning groups which they felt transferred to practice in work groups included the ability to understand and deal with group dynamics, to negotiate tasks and share their work, and to report back to group. They also felt they knew how to use team members consultatively, and to give feedback.

The skill of chairing groups was particularly appreciated by newly qualified workers. At the point of qualifying, 87 per cent of graduates felt well or adequately prepared for this task. A year later this had fallen slightly to 81 per cent, although within this, the proportion who felt they were able to do this well had increased by 10 per cent. A newly qualified probation officer commented favourably on the opportunities he had to rehearse the role of chairperson while on the course:

> trying to be clear, trying to keep to the point and trying to be considerate, trying to allow people to have their say . . . I like being able to direct it and keep it on track . . . I've got permission to do that by being chair.

Again students worked hard to develop these skills, often going through a steep learning curve, convinced they would be useful in practice.

A perspective on learning in groups as preparation for practice which might be construed as negative came from a newly qualified worker who reflected on the 'collective cocoon' of study group sessions, and how far this was from the reality of practice in work groups or teams. Certainly interviews with other newly qualified workers revealed that as places to explore personal knowledge, work groups were not experienced as providing sufficient time, opportunity or safety. However, as seen in Chapter 5, neither did learning groups always provide a 'collective cocoon'; they were often difficult and uncomfortable. This student at the end of the course expressed her anger about lack of confidentiality among group members by commenting,

> I've learnt a lot from groups. I've learnt people to avoid and people not to avoid; things to say and things not to say; things like basic ground rules – people don't stick to them; groups are supposed to be confidential but there's none of that so I've learnt what not to disclose and what to disclose.

She is talking here about the important skills of clarifying personal and professional boundaries, essential for practice. When she looked back on the course a year later from the vantage point of qualified practice she felt that learning in groups had been very positive in helping her learn to understand and work with the perspectives of others.

The final feature of learning groups which emerged as significant to practice in the short term is the ongoing availability of network support long after the life of the group as a formal entity has finished. In particular, the first study group remained an important informal source of support for many students throughout the course. It was apparent that supportive contact also continued following qualifying. At a time when agency supports are severely constrained by lack of resources it seems possible that an informal support network will be crucial particularly to newly qualified workers, and also in the longer term.

The influence of the agency on newly qualified practice

The referent point of the professional course remains strong in the first year of practice. Increasingly today, stakeholders criticize initial professional education as inadequately preparing students for practice, and in the UK, recent targets for this criticism have been teaching and social work. But what of the employing agencies and their impact on the newly qualified worker? What do they provide to support the newly qualified worker make a transition which will inevitably, by the nature of transitions, be anxiety provoking? How do they socialize newly qualified workers into the organization? What opportunities do they provide for continuing professional development? What supervision is provided?

The four organizational issues which emerged from interviews with newly qualified workers as having a significant impact on practice include the pace of organizational change, the lack of supervision, high caseloads, and the requirements of recording and paperwork. The theme of induction and continuing professional development cuts across these issues and is discussed separately at the end of this chapter.

Early in the chapter I described the pattern of instability and change which characterized the experience of the newly qualified workers in their first year of practice. The pattern was one of temporary or locum posts, agency restructuring, changing teams, shifting supervisors and acting managers. In part this can be attributed to recent major policy and legislative changes which have had far reaching implications for practice. Even in the probation departments where in 1992/93 there was relative stability, there were changes in line manager. Of 11 newly qualified workers it is remarkable that one year after qualifying, only one worker (in the probation service) was still in his first post and had a constant line manager over that period. What was not fully apparent in 1993, when I was conducting the final interviews, was that the pattern of upheaval would increase with the impact of Local Government Review and the subsequent demise of some major local authorities. One hospital social worker I interviewed was prescient in her view that her position was in a 'time warp' and was inevitably going to change, but for most of the interviewees such changes were not yet anticipated. Furthermore, the probation service was on the brink of several years of destabilizing intrusion by central government. A culture of increasing instability and change was rapidly developing.

The most significant impact on newly qualified workers was that they could not rely on the system for support but had instead to find their own: 'EAL has made me more self-sufficient and in social work you have to be.'

Although the lack of supervision was not a surprise, there was a common experience of disappointment about the availability and quality of supervision from line managers. One probation officer talked about his ability to work autonomously and be self-monitoring and also his worry that his supervisor did not know what he was doing and whether he was acting appropriately. Acting on one's own is particularly stressful in the context of the very complex situations newly qualified workers are coping with. Although their agencies had policies about not allocating particularly complex kinds of cases, such as child abuse, to newly qualified workers, in reality these kinds of boundaries are not always easy to implement. A newly qualified child care worker had been supervising child abuse cases; a newly qualified probation officer was supervising a convicted murderer. In both cases these were contrary to agency policy about newly qualified practitioners and the work which should not be allocated to them.

When supervision was available it tended to be task focused on case management, and did not provide an opportunity for reflection. Yet, the need for newly qualified workers in any profession to have the opportunity to reflect on their practice is crucial, particularly in professions where they are dealing with difficult interpersonal material. Tickle (1994) suggests that learning how to handle emotional responses is as important for newly qualified teachers as learning how to handle the tasks and recommends a 'curriculum for the emotions' which is 'intertwined with a curriculum for clinical and technical competencies' (1994: 156). A newly qualified male worker on a child protection area team recognized this need: 'I've realized my own limitations. I do need quite a bit of support. I'm quite vulnerable in certain areas and I recognize these.'

He was referring particularly to his emotional vulnerability in working with children in need of protection, partly due to his own childhood experiences. His primary support came from another newly qualified worker who he had met on the course and who was working in a neighbouring area. In fields of practice as sensitive as child protection it is crucial to recognize the need for consistent supervision of a kind which provides an opportunity for newly qualified workers to develop personal knowledge. The only social worker in the voluntary sector was at another kind of disadvantage as she did not have supervision available from anyone with a social work qualification, nor was there another social worker in the system she could draw on.

The days of sufficient resources to support regular and ongoing one-to-one supervision may be over, and may not even be desirable in that they can encourage a counterproductive dependency for the practitioner. It may be unrealistic given the many pressures on line managers to expect them to provide individual supervision of a kind which supports reflection. One alternative may be the model which the teaching profession espouses of designating experienced workers as mentors. Within large agencies such as social services where there will be a number of newly qualified workers at any one time this could be provided on a group basis.

Another disappointment for the newly qualified social worker was the size of caseload compared to the protected caseload of field placement. This was similar to the shock for new teachers of abruptly assuming full responsibility (Tickle, 1994). Workloads may be protected throughout an induction period, but this was often cut short due to the needs of the agency to allocate cases in situations of overstretched resources. Furthermore, as seen earlier, the degree of complexity and severity of the cases the newly qualified workers were dealing with was significant. As this probation officer commented, 'There is so little time to do quality work it is unbelievable.' This was very frustrating and disillusioning for newly qualified workers who were keen to try out their newly acquired knowledge and skills and found they did not have the time to do so. For example, the child care worker mentioned earlier was very concerned about the amount of surveillance and monitoring work he was expected to carry out. This did not fit his concept of social work and was not the helping role he had foreseen for himself or spent so many years working towards. His solution was to plan to transfer as soon as possible into community practice in the voluntary sector.

Finally, the volume and nature of recording and paperwork caused significant concern to the newly qualified workers. Its purpose was often unclear, other than for reasons of accountability. This worker suggested that the paperwork was increasing 'to prove we are doing the job properly'. Certainly demands for paperwork are increasing throughout the professions to meet increasing expectations about the need for accountability and audit mechanisms. Newly qualified workers reported that form filling was dominating practice and impeding work with service users. A social services social worker expressed concern about becoming deskilled in practice and skilled in filling out forms. It is paradoxical that, on the one hand, the picture given by the newly qualified workers is that they are having to work independently as supervision for educational or supportive purposes is not available. On the other hand, the bureaucratization of the agencies and in particular the requirements for record-keeping are proliferating with an increasing emphasis on accountability. This is an important issue and one which it would be valuable to research over a longitudinal period.

In spite of the concerns about the pace of change, lack of supervision, high caseloads and the volume of paperwork, by and large the newly qualified workers at the end of the year were still attempting to adopt a proactive and optimistic position. At the point of qualifying, 73 per cent felt that EAL had prepared them to be proactively involved with service or policy development. Just over a year later this proportion had risen slightly to 76 per cent, with an increase particularly in those practitioners who felt well prepared. One probation officer said at the final interview, 'The course has given me the confidence to say, this is what I want to do, this is the right idea . . . and to try and persuade people.'

A social services worker talked at the end of her first year in practice of her conviction about the importance of new ideas and brainstorming, although she was also aware that established workers tended defensively to view these as criticisms. It is encouraging that at the end of a year or so in practice, newly qualified workers continued to believe that they could influence external events in their agencies.

If the newly qualified workers were not able to develop a practice role of the kind they had anticipated, or to influence the organizational context, then the response tended to be to consider an alternative post. The child protection worker was considering moving into the voluntary sector feeling that the monitoring and surveillance role was immovable in the statutory sector. The worker in the voluntary sector was planning to move into the statutory sector feeling that the voluntary organization would not change to recognize the value of a social work role. Seeking the elusive post where newly qualified workers can practise what they were trained for can only increase the climate of change.

At the end of the first 15 months, these social workers were by and large not questioning the adequacy of their preparation for practice, other than criticisms mentioned earlier about the omission of specific propositional knowledge and the fast pace of learning. Yet it is easy to see how this process begins to develop as a way of encompassing the gap between education and practice. Eraut suggests that the gap between idealized practice and practice considered acceptable in most service settings 'can be accounted for by practitioners' unwillingness or unpreparedness to attempt 'ideal' practice or by the impracticability of the 'ideal' in service settings' (1995: 9). It is perhaps appropriate that professional education courses uphold an ideal for practice to aspire to. One student said at the end of the course that she valued the idealism of the course and felt it counterbalanced the cynicism of practice,

> They [the staff] tend to be very idealistic on the course, maybe we need their idealism. People in practice are jaded and disillusioned. If staff were jaded, we wouldn't stick at it.

Very often this pendulum swings and university staff are accused of being too idealistic and out of touch with practice and practitioners are revered for presenting reality. The size of the gap and the kinds of bridging mechanisms available seem important. It is essential that professional education critiques existing practice, presents good practice, and makes possible new practice possibilities. However, if professional education is too far removed from day-to-day practice realities, students will inevitably be critical.

Continuing professional development

So far, I have suggested that various fields of professional practice have recently come under sustained attack by stakeholders, especially by government. In particular, questions have been raised about the adequacy of initial preparation for practice. Criticism of professionals such as teachers and social workers has focused on the knowledge and skills of the newly qualified or newly trained, with criticism more or less explicit that their training and education is misguided, ill conceived, or even unnecessary. This scenario begs the question about what should and can reasonably be learnt as part of the basic curriculum and what should and can be addressed under the banner of continuing professional development (CPD)?

Houle (1984) describes how the history of each profession shows that formal means of providing continuing education were created early in the life of the profession and often became the chief responsibility of the bureaucracy which maintained the organized profession. With this development, the nature and the degree of complementarity between initial education and CPD clearly becomes essential. The effectiveness of the complementarity between initial and continuing education depends on three key questions (Houle, 1984). How can a professional school choose entrants who are likely to be continuous learners throughout their professional lives? How can this trait be encouraged by basic training? What learning is appropriate at each stage? These questions are particularly relevant to students graduating from an EAL approach as the course philosophy is designed to encourage development of the skills of independent learning seen as essential to life-long learning (Burgess, 1992).

Newly qualified workers in my study were asked at the point of qualifying if they felt EAL had prepared them to continue professional development and training. Of the total, 73 per cent felt well or adequately prepared and 27 per cent inadequately prepared. Some15 months later, 88 per cent felt well or adequately prepared and the proportion who felt inadequately prepared had fallen to 12 per cent. This data is encouraging and suggests the newly qualified worker is likely to participate in CPD.

In the interview sample, all the newly qualified workers in the statutory sector had been provided with induction programmes. The probation officers were the most satisfied with the process of induction. The newly qualified workers in social services had a more chequered experience with a pattern of induction being curtailed because of the pressure to take on a full caseload and begin work. Tickle in his study of the induction of new teachers found that teachers were left to work things out as best they could and suggested that 'such lonely decisions and solutions will be affected by personal qualities and predispositions such as confidence, perceptiveness, energy, commitment, and perseverance' (1994: 106).

Closely linked with induction is the provision of ongoing training. Perhaps to be expected in the first year of practice, all the newly qualified workers shared a conviction about the importance of ongoing training and viewed this as part of being a professional. By and large, they were pleased with the training they had received in the first year of practice and they also described a picture of professional development they had initiated, reading relevant materials, viewing videos and attending courses. Again newly qualified probation officers were most satisfied and participated in a surprising degree of training. Whereas, in social services the picture was more arbitrary and even within the same social services department there were considerable variations in practice. For example, one newly qualified worker had been given time off to complete a Masters in Social Work, whereas another working in a different part of the same organization had not. Unlike probation staff, social service staff could not assume that training would be prescribed and provided. Newly qualified workers described having at times to 'make a case for' training, identify their own needs, locate the opportunities available and access the training budget. One newly qualified worker was particularly dissatisfied about the lack of training opportunities in a large social services authority. In her first year of practice in child protection she had participated in a total of one and half days training. She had taken the initiative to write a letter to her team manager to complain, but after three months at the time of our interview still had not received a reply.

A year into practice is too early to know the answer to the crucial question about whether graduates from a course which emphasizes independent and interdependent learning have acquired the skills of lifelong learning and are more open to continuing professional development than graduates of other kinds of courses. The early signs are optimistic, particularly the willingness to acknowledge not knowing, the ability to evaluate their own practice, the ability to work independently but seek guidance when appropriate, and the ability to advocate for learning opportunities and take advantage of them when available. Interestingly, the propensity for lifelong learning is one outcome which McMaster has not yet researched.

Certainly the degree of change experienced by the newly qualified workers would confirm openness to and ability to initiate lifelong learning is essential. As Parton, in his analysis of the implications of post-modernism for social work practice, suggests,

> Where nothing can be taken for granted and where there are no self-evident truths available or waiting to be found the reflexive, self-monitoring, individual becomes crucial to making sense of the world and trying to impose a degree of consistency and control upon it.
>
> (1994: 106)

However, clearly the onus cannot rest entirely with the practitioner. Stakeholders, particularly employing agencies, must also recognize the crucial importance of continuing professional development and make the resources available to support their staff. Failure to do so is unprofessional and unethical.

11

Partnerships with Users of Professional Services

In this final chapter my attention turns to the theme of partnership between professional educators and service users. I view this as one of the most challenging issues to confront professional educators as we approach the millennium. My attention in this book has until now been directed towards student–student, student–facilitator, and group–facilitator partnerships. In Chapter 2, I introduced the concept of partnership collaboration as resulting in either value capture where one organization takes resources from another, or value creation where collaboration results in increased value (Haspelagh and Jemison, 1991). In this chapter, I move to exploring partnership with service users in professional education as another strategy which results in increased value for students, staff, users and the professions. As discussed in Chapter 2, partnership does not mean each party has equal power which is clearly not the case in either professional practice or education, but rather a negotiated agreement about roles and responsibilities, and a clear understanding about where power is located.

Service users are relative newcomers to partnerships, both in practice and education. Yet, there are strong parallels between partnership in both arenas:

> Collaboration with service users and carers and collaboration between different groups of practitioners, should not be treated as two separate issues, but as part of a *single* [authors' italics] transformation of the whole way in which we think about what has come to be known as community care.
>
> (Beresford and Trevillion, 1995: 7)

Whereas these authors are commenting on partnership in relation to community care, part of my thesis in this chapter is that partnership with users is central to all fields of practice in the interpersonal professions.

In Chapter 2, I referred to the recent legislative changes in the UK which are permeated with a philosophy of partnership, empowerment and consumerism. The Children Act (1989) emphasizes the requirements for partnership and involvement of parents in decision making. The Education Act

(1993) spells out the duty on providers of services to involve parents and support them. The National Health Service and Community Care Act (1990) endorses participation by users in decision making, viewing users as experts in identifying their own needs and having a voice in the services they receive. This has implications for the relationship between users and professionals, as the following statement from government guidance for practitioners involved in implementing community care reflects,

> The rationale for this reorganisation is the empowerment of users and carers. Instead of users and carers being subordinate to the wishes of service providers, the roles will be progressively readjusted. In this way users and carers will be enabled to exercise the same power as consumers of other services. This redressing of the balance of power is the best guarantee of continuing improvement in the quality of service.
>
> (Department of Health, 1991: 9)

There is of course a debate about whether users who are not directly purchasing a community care service will ever have the same power as consumers of other services.

Increased user participation in professional practice inevitably has direct implications for professional education and training, as discussed in a recent report on users views on training for community care:

> User involvement is about changing the whole culture and attitude of workers to recognise user expertise and needs to start where users are. This has clear implications for who gets trained, who does the training and how the training is organised.
>
> (SSI, 1994: 5)

However, partnership with service users in professional education has only very recently begun to be considered by professional associations. The Central Council for Education and Training in Social Work identify 'Assess and Plan' as one of the six Core Competences which students must provide evidence of in order to qualify. This competence is defined as 'work in partnership to assess and review people's circumstances and plan responses to need and risk' (CCETSW, 1995: 16). The General Medical Council in its recommendations for undergraduate medical education, identifies one of the attributes of the independent practitioner as the maintenance of attitudes and conduct which include, 'recognition that good medical practice depends on partnership between doctor and patient, based upon mutual understanding and trust' (1993: 26).

In spite of the rhetoric of user participation in education and training, its extent in professional education is unknown and its effect remains largely untested empirically. Critical analysis of the involvement of service users in professional education from either the perspective of the user, student or educator is, with few exceptions (Beresford and Harding, 1993; Beresford, 1994; Hopton, 1994/1995), relatively scarce.

There are interesting parallels between partnership of student and facilitator in an adult-learning approach, and user and practitioner in a user-led approach to practice. Clearly, if users are to be viewed as the experts in defining their own needs, the role of professionals must change to reflect greater appreciation of users expertise and a refocused emphasis on assisting the expression of need and on coordinating services on behalf of the user (Fisher, 1994). This change in the role of the professional mirrors the change in role of the educator in adult learning:

> Educators have to assume the role of commentators and interpreters rather than knowledge legislators. Educators rather than being producers of knowledge, the gate keepers, boundary maintainers and arbiters of acceptable learning, instead become 'facilitators' . . . They become part of the culture industry where the consumer (learner) rather than the producer (educator) is articulated as having greater significance and power.
>
> (Johnston and Usher, 1996: 13)

In addition to being commentators and interpreters, the educator as facilitator ensures the provision of an appropriate infrastructure for learning and supports the students to identify their learning objectives, sort out how they will be met, and evaluate whether they have been achieved. Furthermore, in contrast to the above statement by Johnston and Usher in relation to adult education, in professional education as in professional practice, practitioners and educators are gatekeepers to desired resources and arbiters of acceptable learning.

In this discussion of shifting power from the expert to the user it is important to clarify that there are two related but different ideologies influencing these changes. Beresford and Trevillion (1995) identify an important distinction between the market vision and the collaborative vision of user involvement. Hopton (1994/1995) similarly comments on two different but related ideologies in the field of mental health and suggests that the rise of the user movement is less the outcome of a successful struggle by users towards self-determination and more the result of the wider social, political and economic impetus towards a free market. The market vision is based on the view of the consumer as customers, or 'supermarket style consumerism' (Walker, 1993: 22 in Beresford and Trevillion, 1995). Although there are few examples of customers actually purchasing services in community care, the contract culture has had a significant impact on the ways services are 'designed, purchased and packaged' (Beresford and Trevillion, 1995: 6).

The collaborative or user led vision is one where power is shifted from professionals to communities, users and carers and is often linked with the concept of empowerment. Empowerment is a slippery concept, there is a risk of it being 'a linguistic technique used as a political ploy' (Jarvis, 1993: 30) and as a result the term has come to be viewed with some suspicion.

Empowerment and partnership are both attractive rallying points, particularly by professions beleaguered by criticism from all sides (Fisher, 1994: 279). Both terms have roots in Freire's (1981) educational model of social change in which awareness of choice has a critical role in recognition of powerlessness. Fisher (1994) in his research into partnership practice suggests, however, that partnership and empowerment diverge in the means of achieving their goals. Empowerment calls for people to free themselves from oppression and emphasizes the need for structural change to reduce social inequality and change society. Partnership relies on a humanist emphasis on the value of common experience and implies a recognition of inequality in interactions. Partnership practice seeks a change in power systems and is committed to participative methods. Partnership may result in participants experiencing empowerment and may contribute to recognition of inequality and the introduction of more egalitarian approaches.

In this chapter, I focus on partnership in professional education, examining partnership practice by users of professional services and professional educators. I begin by defining who the users are and the different levels of user participation in professional practice. I use research into community care as a case study of user participation because in the absence of such research in education it provides some clues as to important considerations. The community care field includes some of the most well-developed analyses of user participation, although there is also an increasingly developing literature about participation of parents in education and child welfare. In particular, I highlight findings from a recent study (Smith *et al.*, 1993) which examines how professionals, users and carers worked together in six innovative community care projects in England and Wales. I have selected this study because its findings mirror some of my own observations about involving users and carers in the delivery of professional education. Based on my experience over four years of involving users and carers in a professional education course for social work students specializing in the field of community care, I discuss the gains to be made from the participation of users in professional education, the strategies adopted to facilitate such participation, and the institutional, organizational and psychological barriers encountered.

Who are the users?

This question is important to a discussion of users in professional education because the answer is indicative of the complexities of user participation. Throughout this book I have selected the term 'service user' in preference to others, including 'patient', 'client' or 'customer'. Whereas I recognize that different professions employ a particular discourse which reflects the culture and ideology of their profession, it is not my purpose here to explore the differences but rather to suggest that whichever term is selected, service users are not a homogeneous group and they include a number of different kinds of users and user interests.

Barnes and Wistow (1992) identify a typology of users which can be generalized to users who might participate in professional education. Their categories include distinctions between those who have exercised some degree of choice in seeking a service and those who are on the receiving end of a service against their will; those who require long term or continuing services and others who require short term episodic services; those who may be in competition with each other for scarce resources and others whose interests may be served by working collectively; those who are current users and others who are potential users of services; and finally, there is a distinction between users and citizens. Whether or not they have become users, all citizens are concerned with the provision of high quality services since they are an indicator of a civilized society, but these interests may conflict with their interests as tax payers.

Later in this chapter, I will explore the challenge for professional education of involving a range of different users, in particular addressing the difficult issues of representativeness and tokenism.

Different levels of user participation

In discussing involving users in professional education it is essential to recognize that user participation in practice takes place at many different levels, ranging from services to individuals to implementation of policy at a national level (Barnes and Wistow, 1992). For example, the White Paper, Caring for People (1989) emphasizes 'giving people a greater individual say in how they live their lives and the services to help them' (para. 1.8). The National Health Service and Community Care Act (1990) requires collective involvement of users in the planning process through the involvement of users and carers in the preparation of community care plans. Furthermore, there is the potential for involving users in 'standard setting, service specification and review procedures' which potentially engages users and carers in accountability procedures to a degree which has hitherto been virtually unknown (Barnes and Wistow, 1992: 9).

Barnes *et al.* (1990) identify seven different levels of involvement which can be generalized to fields other than community care, including the level of the individual practitioner and service user; groups of workers and users; management and planning a particular service; resource management; committee management and policy development; local authority and inter-agency management and policy development; and national policy development. As will be discussed later, involvement of users in professional education may include participation in the design, delivery or evaluation of specific courses, or it may be at the level of developing programme policy, programme management, or review.

How professionals, users and carers work together

Smith and his colleagues (1993) identified six community care projects which used imaginative and innovative approaches to the management and delivery of community care services and examined how professionals, users and carers worked together. They found that 'there is clearly a movement to shift power to consumers. The national policy is in place, the rhetoric has been developed and the creative thinking is going on' (Smith *et al.*, 1993: 209). They discuss 'equal opportunities' and the practical implications of working together and note five recurring issues which underpin successful user participation. These contain some important messages for involving users in professional education.

First, community care emphasizes professionals working alongside users, carers and communities to define their needs and deliver services. Power relations between these groups are unequal and innovative approaches are needed to assist participation and involvement between them. Secondly, the researchers noted that it can be difficult to move from addressing participation at the operational level, to the planning and strategic levels. Thirdly, there is the importance of acknowledging the differences in power of professionals to control the resources, set the agenda, define who is included and on what terms, and to devise models for working together. Fourthly, addressing equal opportunities means moving away from the culture that the professionals know best, towards the self-definition of user-represented groups. Fifthly, consideration of who the users are and issues of representation is important to addressing user participation. Users can be negatively defined by service provision or excluded from it. Finally, professional, managerial and organizational barriers to effectiveness and to achieving equality in service delivery were also identified, in addition to the barriers of avoidance and exclusion.

Hudson identifies two main difficulties that collaboration raises for the agency, both of which it will be seen are pertinent to a discussion of user participation in professional education:

> First it loses some of its freedom to act independently when it would prefer to maintain control over its domain and affairs. Second, it must invest scarce resources and energy in developing and maintaining relationships with other organizations, when the potential returns on investment are often unclear or intangible.

(Hudson, 1987: 175)

Hudson also identifies a number of factors which predispose agencies to work together, three of which are particularly relevant to professional education. The first is described as 'inter-organizational homogeneity', or a similarity in culture and values. The second is 'domain consensus', or agreement about roles and responsibilities. Third is organizational exchange, or the outcome of all parties gaining from working together. It is these three factors which provide a framework for discussion of user participation in professional education, although instead of organizational exchange as an outcome, I have chosen for the third factor to use instead Haspelagh and Jemison's (1991) notion of collaboration as being either value added or value capture.

Culture and values

Learning from service users challenges the whole notion of expertise, who holds it, and on what basis. If expertise is identified as being related only to propositional knowledge, this will exclude the contribution of the personal and process knowledge of the user. The perspective of the educator will remain the traditional 'best interests' one where the educator knows best what the students should learn and how they should learn it. Smith *et al.* (1993) refer to the professional culture which believes only it can define what is needed as opposed to wanted. Even if the educator acknowledges the value of the expertise of the user, there are other often more subtle differences in professional ideology and cultural beliefs which contribute to barriers to joint working with users:

> Much more damaging for joint working were the tribal beliefs of professional groups about 'non-professionals' . . . being non-professional relates to a package of negative characteristics such as unreliability, lack of accountability, failure to be representative, lacking competence and skills, and failure to monitor process and outcomes.
> (Smith *et al.*, 1993: 225)

Hopton (1994/1995) also suggests that the greatest obstacle to involving mental health users in the education and training of professionals is the occupational culture of mental health nursing wherein patients are thought of as the 'other' or as inferior persons. These are powerful stereotypes to overcome and deny the reality that many, if not all of us are service users of one kind or another at different points in our lives, and it is important in professional education to examine the mechanisms which distance our experiences from those of users.

For users to establish 'an equality of credibility' in the classroom (Beresford and Harding, 1993: 26) also requires educators to examine and be open to changing their attitudes. The negative characteristics associated with users are powerful inhibitors not only for the educator to overcome but also the students. In the interpersonal professions where the pervasive practice model tends to be the dependency model, educators and students are imbued with the philosophy that they must take responsibility for and act in the best interests of the patient or client. In my experience, students who would not hesitate to challenge a lecturer, are often reluctant to challenge or critically reflect on material presented by users. In discussing this with students, it is related to a belief about the vulnerability or weakness of the user and fear of harming him or her. Whereas it is appropriate to consider issues of safety for all guest presenters, to single out users as a particularly vulnerable group is discriminatory and very much reflects the dependency model. Fear of negative and discriminatory attitudes may also shape the attitude of the user to participating and this is an issue to be addressed in their training, as will be discussed later.

Who is included is a complicated question for the educator and raises complex issues of representation (Smith *et al.*, 1993). As discussed earlier there are many different categories of user and there is also an array of user groups who could be included. Some user groups are more organized or vocal than others, but the risk is then of excluding those users who are less organized and visible. For example, disability equality groups tend to be more organized than groups of older people or black users. Interestingly, whereas there is typically little questioning of the nature and legitimacy of the representativeness of educators or speakers from professional practice, the perceived 'failure' of users to be representative can be hotly debated by students and there may be intense discussion about accepting the views of lay people who do not meet some often unspecified criteria for representativeness (Smith *et al.*, 1993: 225).

Another issue which may also be hotly debated in conjunction with representativeness is that of tokenism. In his discussion of the contribution of mental health users to nursing education, Hopcroft suggests that given the conflict of ideology and occupational cultures between mental health professionals and the mental health users' movement it is not surprising that writers such as Beresford and Croft (1992) have observed that many user involvement schemes are tokenistic or only coopt users into trivial projects. If users' contributions to professional education are to avoid a similar accusation they must be integrated into a coherent framework which reflects user participation in relation to personal, process and propositional knowledge, rather than added on to an existing programme.

Roles and responsibilities

The culture and values of the organization will have a direct effect on the roles and responsibilities negotiated with users contributing to professional education. A national audit of user participation in professional education is likely to reveal *ad hoc* involvement at an operational level, led by individual educators who have given priority to this kind of participation. It is also important to involve users at planning and strategic levels (Smith *et al.*, 1993). Social work courses are required by CCETSW (1989) to be managed by partnerships of agencies and academic institutions and this presents an opportunity to involve user groups at the policy and management level which may not be required in other professional education courses. To what extent this opportunity is taken advantage of is difficult to assess, as data about the extent or nature of involvement of users in Diploma in Social Work Partnerships is not currently available.

Recognition of users as equals, rather than as people with needs to be met by professionals results in a different kind of working relationship. 'Collaboration involves power sharing and negotiating issues connected with different perceptions, values and interests so as to promote the collective ability to work together' (Beresford and Trevillion, 1995: 14). One crucial aspect of collaboration is clarity about differences in power (Smith *et al.*, 1993). Are the professional educators in control or are the users? In a course where users are not part of its conception and overall design, and where outcomes are specified by professional bodies, my experience of negotiating with users about their contribution suggests that the issue of ownership needs to be carefully managed. As with inviting any guest speakers, it is important that they are briefed with information about the context for their contribution, the purpose of their being invited to contribute, to whom they are presenting, what has gone before and what will come after.

The content and delivery of the actual contribution is then for the user to decide. The involvement of the users is in part to enable students to hear the voice of the user who will represent his or her experience in a particular way. The dilemma for the educator is to determine whether the experience can speak for itself, or whether it needs to be guided by a critique offered by a particular theory (Johnston and Usher, 1996). Yet introducing the latter dimension is another form of regulation and can be oppressive, silencing the voice of the user:

> The 'critical' can easily become a norm, final truth which is just as heavy in its regulation as any openly oppressive discourse – as for example, in the worst excesses of political correctness. This can have the effect of replacing one grand narrative with another and so replicating a culture of silence where some voices are privileged over others.
>
> (Johnston and Usher, 1996: 14)

By not regarding experience as something from which knowledge can be derived, but as knowledge in itself, this will make the voice of the user available. Inevitably, the experience of the user is constructed and reconstructed in the classroom, by both user and learner, but by valuing the experience as it is shared, it is not mediated by the educator.

The professional educator temporarily relinquishes power and control when a service user contributes in this way. Unquestionably, there are occasions when this feels risky as strong feelings may be generated by the anger and frustration of service users, particularly when their experience reflects examples of injustice and oppression. Students may in turn become angry and project this on to the educator who represents the profession. The facilitator skill of containment discussed in Chapter 6 is an important one in this context.

It is also important in relation to roles and responsibilities, to evaluate with students the contribution of the user. This represents good practice with all guest speakers as well as internal staff. This is likely to be written and conveyed later due to the reluctance of students to directly express any views to users (and staff) which might be construed as criticism.

In light of the importance of their contribution, it is reasonable to expect users to carry out their role carefully and responsibly. To contribute effectively service users must be trained to provide training. Increasingly, user groups such as the Wiltshire Users Network or Survivors Speak Out are providing such training. In the field of education and training concerned with rights, such as mental health work, 'it is not just a day off for consumers to vent their spleen, but a chance for people who may be subject to such restrictions on their rights to explore and discuss them fully and openly with people who may be imposing restrictions in the future' (Harrison and Beresford, 1994: 26). The purpose of training is not to dilute anger, but rather to explore issues such as skills in developing process knowledge to enable personal knowledge to be heard. Also, issues such as the importance of language can be addressed to avoid, for example, an incident I experienced where a service user talked about his 'coloured friends' offending students present, particularly black students, who experienced this terminology as racist. Training also provides support structures which are particularly important for users who may be inexperienced in the educator role. For example, user groups may follow the practice of requiring users to participate in pairs so that they can provide each other with support.

What are the terms and conditions for involvement of users in professional education? In carrying specific roles and responsibilities it is important for users to be included on the same terms as professionals whose services are being purchased by the course. For example, payment should be made at equivalent rates. Additional resources may be required. For example, some users require the services of paid carers to attend to their needs, others require payment for specific transport arrangements. Some disabled users require more time than non-disabled and this may have implications for starting times. If disabled users require paid assistance to get up in the morning, it is probably unrealistic to expect them to begin a session at 9 a.m. In relation to equal opportunities these are important issues to consider.

The other important aspect of terms and conditions is the accessibility of the institution. Institutions of higher education are often not accessible to disabled users. Low (1996) describes the problems for disabled students to negotiate a university campus, the absence of ramps and lifts, the dearth of disabled parking spaces or the scarcity of adapted toilets. Issues of access for deaf and visually impaired users (and students) have also been documented (James and Thomas, 1996; Taylor, 1996). Special arrangements may be made to enable disabled users to contribute to student learning, but it must be recognized that these may then further stigmatize users and underline their difference.

Increased value

It can be seen that if user participation is to be properly planned and integrated into the curriculum, it makes demands on the resources of the educator and the institution. If the potential returns on investment are unclear and intangible, this will inevitably influence the level of commitment. However much the individual educator may be committed to such a venture, like all educational innovations, it will be difficult to sustain if resources are not available to provide ongoing support. What is gained from the experience? Is there increased value as a result of the collaboration (Haspelagh and Jemison, 1991)? These questions require research before substantive answers can be provided. The following are my reflections based on my experience and feedback from both students and users who have participated in the process.

User participation enables students to learn first hand about the experience of users they will be working with in the future. Rather than learning about users from third parties, students learn from the users themselves about their experiences. This may include information about particular kinds of problems users experience, their experience with the professionals in relation to issues such as professional competence, confidentiality or the need for particular kinds of skills or attitudes, or their experience with institutions and government. The impact on the student of the sharing of personal knowledge in this way cannot be underestimated. The voice of the user is heard in a way which is not generally available in field practice where the purpose of the partnership is different. Perhaps most important it helps move students beyond the culture of viewing users as inadequate in some way, but rather to view them as people with strengths as well as rights.

In the process of determining roles and responsibilities, students also learn about the skills of working together with service users. If practitioners are to be equipped to collaborate with service users or even to have the will to do so, their education must address user participation in practice as well as theory. The participation of the service user in the classroom, and in the course and educational institution models some of the key features of participation in practice. This is an essential part of the repertoire of process knowledge for students to learn. By making as much of the process as explicit and transparent as possible, it becomes available for student learning.

User participation in education and training may also help empower users and enable them to develop more control over their lives as they are consulted about issues which affect them. Users feel they are often denied even the basic right to define their own experiences (Lindow, 1995). Training for participation in education and training is seen as one avenue to address the power relationship between service providers and users (SSI, 1994: 12).

Finally, trust is an important factor in successfully working together with service users. Earlier in this book I have referred to trust as an issue for both students and staff embarking on innovative approaches to learning. As

Nomthandazo Gwele, a nurse educator, from the University of Natal in South Africa said about an experiential learning programme for preparing health professionals:

> I have learned it is possible to trust that students do want to learn. That when you take away the threat of quizzes and endless tests and memory examinations, and focus on the appreciation of knowledge within the context of producing enquiring teacher practitioners, learning through the process of transformation of knowledge does take place.
>
> (1996: 25)

If staff and students can learn to trust the value of participation by service users in the process of learning in the classroom, this will enable increasing innovation in relation to user involvement and help sustain changes which are already taking place.

The capacity to innovate is crucial. It is the only way we can move forward in response to our changing world. The following statement by the General Medical Council about medical education and doctors could as well be written about any of the professions referred to in this book. We need professionals 'capable of adaptation to change, with minds that can encompass new ideas and developments and with attitudes to learning that inspire the continuation of the educational process throughout professional life' (1993: 4). Individuals operate within the context of organizations and the wider political, social and economic context, all of which play an interdependent role in introducing and sustaining change.

Appendix: Enquiry and Action Learning – The Structure

Enquiry and Action Learning (EAL) is an approach to teaching and learning implemented in 1990 by the Department of Social Work at Bristol University. This is a two-year full-time course leading to a professional qualification of the Diploma in Social Work awarded by the validating body, the Central Council for Education and Training in Social Work (CCETSW). A combined total of approximately 80 graduates and non-graduate students are admitted per annum and the course may lead to the academic award of either a Diploma or a Masters degree, depending on the route taken.

Within the framework of university and professional requirements, the structure of the course is designed where possible to integrate principles of self-directedness (Burgess, 1992). Lectures and seminars on discrete disciplines have been replaced as the primary mode of instruction by the 'study unit'. A study unit lasts on average two weeks and is built around 'problems', real-life situations drawn from practice. Topics for study units are determined by course planners with input from students about their needs. Each study unit focuses on a main topic, and also introduces a range of parallel or subsidiary issues. Students decide which aspects of the problem to work on according to their learning needs. They work in study groups of ten on a series of study units designed to meet the learning objectives specified by CCETSW (1989).

Study group membership remains constant for approximately one term and always reflects a mix of graduates and non-graduates. Membership for the first term is determined by course planners to ensure a balance of race and gender, and to ensure that students who come from groups oppressed in society are not isolated in a study group. Membership of groups in subsequent terms introduces an element of choice reflecting students' learning preferences and choice of specialism. Student wishes are taken into consideration on the infrequent occasion when a student does not wish to work with a particular student or staff member.

Where possible, students assume responsibility both individually and in groups for what they learn and how they learn. Each student group decides on and prioritizes the issue presented by the problem and the knowledge and skills required to work on it. The group then decides how to tackle the work in the time available. Students may select learning activities from suggestions provided or may design their own. In addition to dealing with learning tasks in relation to the problem at hand, groups reflect together on the process of learning and evaluate whether they have achieved their objectives. The central role played by the group in student learning, combined with the requirements of a professional course, have resulted in a course decision to require attendance at group meetings. A pattern of non-attendance will result in a meeting between the student and tutor.

Group meetings are chaired by the students with guidance from a facilitator. In the interests of encouraging student self-directedness, as well as economy of resources, the facilitator attends approximately half the group meetings. The role is a central one early in the course and becomes increasingly peripheral as the course progresses.

Study unit work is the core of the course. It is supplemented by one or two lectures a week on theoretical frameworks, one or two workshops a term on special topics, and a skills development programme. Students also undertake a block placement in an approved social work agency for each of the two years.

Resources are provided to support self-directed learning. Students are given information about written, video and computer resources to which they have access, although these are inevitably restricted by resource limitations. Students may choose to consult named consultants with expertise on aspects of the study unit topics. Consultants are drawn from the university and from practice.

Within a framework of requirements for assessed work, students have a wide range of choice about the focus of their assignments. The emphasis is on work which has a potential purpose beyond producing evidence for assessment. Students may therefore choose to submit briefing papers or presentations rather than the conventional academic essay. Control of summative assessment has remained with the staff but it is planned to introduce self and peer assessment as a central feature in the future.

References

Abercrombie, J. (1983) The application of some principles of group psychotherapy to higher education. In M. Pines (ed.) *The Evolution of Group Analysis*. London, Routledge and Kegan Paul.

Abrams, P. and Bulmer, M. (1984) Realities of neighbourhood care: the interactions between statutory, voluntary and informal social care, *Policy and Politics*, 12, 413–29.

Anderson, G., Boud, D. and Sampson, J. (1996) *Learning Contracts: A Practical Guide*. London, Kogan Page.

Areskog, N. (1995) Multi-professional education at the undergraduate level. In K. Soothill, L. Mackay and C. Webb (eds) *Interprofessional Relations in Health Care*. London, Edward Arnold.

Argyris, C. and Schön, D. A. (1991) Participatory action research and action science compared: a commentary. In W. F. Whyte (ed.) *Participatory Action Research*. Newbury Park, Sage.

Association of University Teachers (1995) Making demands: mature students and higher education, *AUT Bulletin*, January.

Baldwin, M. and Burgess, H. (1992) Enquiry and Action Learning in practice placements, *Social Work Education*, 11(3), 36–44.

Barnes, C. (1991) *Disabled People in Britain and Discrimination: A Case for Anti-Discrimination Legislation*. Calgary, Hurst.

Barnes, M., Prior, D. and Thomas, N. (1990) Social services. In N. Deakin and A. Wright (eds) *Consuming Public Services*. London, Routledge.

Barnes, M. and Wistow, G. (1992) Understanding user involvement. In M. Barnes and G. Wistow, *Researching User Involvement*. Leeds, Nuffield Institute.

Barnett, R. (1990) *The Idea of Higher Education*. Buckingham, SRHE and Open University Press.

Barnett, R. (ed.) (1992) *Learning to Effect*. Buckingham, SRHE and Open University Press.

Barnett, R. (1994) *The Limits of Competence: Knowledge, Higher Education and Society*. Buckingham, SRHE and Open University Press.

Barnett, R., Becher, R. and Cork, N. (1987) Models of professional preparation: pharmacy, nursing and teacher education, *Studies in Higher Education*, 12(1), 51–63.

Barr, H. and Waterton, S. (1996) *Interprofessional Education in Health and Social Care in the United Kingdom: Summary of a CAIPE Survey.* London, Centre for Advancement of Interprofessional Education.

Barrows, H. S. and Tamblyn, R. (1980) *Problem-Based Learning: An Approach to Medical Education.* New York, Springer.

Becher, T. (1989) *Academic Tribes and Territories.* Milton Keynes, Open University Press.

Becher, T. (1994) The significance of disciplinary differences, *Studies in Higher Education* 19(2), 151–61.

Belenky, M., Clinchy, B., Goldberger, N. and Tarule, J. (1986) *Women's Ways of Knowing: The Development of Self, Voice and Mind.* New York, Basic Books.

Beresford, P. (1994) Changing the Culture: involving service users in social work education. Paper 32.2. London, CCETSW.

Beresford, P. and Croft, S. (1993) *Citizen Involvement.* London, Macmillan.

Beresford, P. and Harding, T. (eds) (1993) *A Challenge to Change: Practical Experiences of Building User-Led Services.* London, National Institute of Social Work.

Beresford, P. and Trevillion, S. (1995) *Developing Skills for Community Care: A Collaborative Approach.* Aldershot, Arena.

Berger, R. (1992) Student retention: a critical phase in the academic careers of minority baccalaureate students, *Journal of Social Work Education*, 28, 85–97.

Bion, W. (1970) *Attention and Interpretation.* London, Tavistock.

Bines, H. (1992) Issues in course design. In H. Bines and D. Watson (eds) *Developing Professional Education.* Buckingham, SRHE and Open University Press.

Birch, W. (1988) *The Challenge to Higher Education.* Buckingham, SRHE and Open University Press.

Bird, J. (1996) *Black Students and Higher Education.* Buckingham, SRHE and Open University Press.

Black, P. N., Jefferies, D. and Kennedy Hartley, E. (1993) Personal history of psychosocial trauma in the early life of social work and business students, *Journal of Social Work Education*, 29, 171–80.

Blackburn, R. and Jarman, J. (1993) Changing inequalities in access to British universities, *Oxford Review of Education*, 19, 197–215.

Bligh, J. (1992) Independent learning among general practice trainees: an initial survey, *Medical Education*, 26, 497–502.

Blom-Cooper, L. (1985) *A Child in Trust.* London Borough of Brent, Brent Town Hall.

Blumberg, P. and Michael, J. (1991) The influence of content definition on self-directed learning. Paper presented at the Annual Meeting of the American Educational Research Association, Chicago.

Bogo, M. and Vayda, E. (1986) *The Practice of Field Instruction in Social Work: Theory and Process.* Toronto, University of Toronto Press.

Boud, D. (1986) Implementing student self-assessment, *Higher Education Research and Development Society of Australasia.* Sydney, University of New South Wales.

Boud, D. (1987) A facilitator's view of adult learning. In D. Boud and V. Griffin (eds) *Appreciating Adults Learning: From the Learner's Perspective.* London, Kogan Page.

Boud, D. (1988) Moving towards autonomy. In D. Boud (ed.) *Developing Student Autonomy in Learning,* (2nd edn). London, Kogan Page.

Boud, D. (1992) The use of self-assessment schedules in negotiated learning, *Studies in Higher Education*, 17(2), 185–200.

Boud, D. (1994) Assessment and learning: contradictory or complementary? In P. Knight (ed.) *Assessment for Better Learning*. London, Kogan Page.

Boud, D. (1996) *Enhancing Learning Through Self Assessment*. London, Kogan Page.

Boud, D. and Falchikov, N. (1989) Qualitative studies of student self-assessment in higher education: a critical analysis of the findings, *Higher Education*, 18, 529–49.

Boud, D. and Walker, D. (1990) Making the most of experience, *Studies in Continuing Education*, 12(2), 61–80.

Boud, D., Keogh, R. and Walker, D. (1993) *Using Experience for Learning*. Buckingham, SRHE and Open University Press.

Boud, D. and Knights, S. (1996) Course design for reflective practice. In N. Gould and I. Taylor (eds) *Reflective Learning for Social Work: Research, Theory and Practice*. Aldershot, Arena.

Boud, D. and Feletti, G. (1991) *The Challenge of Problem-Based Learning*. London, Kogan Page.

Broadfoot, P. (ed.) (1984) *Selection, Certification and Control: Social Issues in Educational Assessment*. London, Falmer.

Broadfoot, P. (1994) Editorial, *Assessment in Education*, 1, 3–9.

Brookfield, S. (1983) *Adult Learners, Adult Education and the Community*. Milton Keynes, Open University Press.

Brookfield, S. (1986) *Understanding and Facilitating Adult Learning*. San Francisco, Jossey-Bass.

Brookfield, S. (1993) Through the lens of learning: how the visceral experience of learning reframes teaching. In D. Boud, R. Cohen and D. Walker (eds) *Using Experience for Learning*. Buckingham, Open University Press.

Brown, A. (1992) *Groupwork* (3rd edn). Aldershot, Ashgate.

Brown A. and Bourne I. (1996) *The Social Work Supervisor*. Buckingham, Open University Press.

Brown, A. and Clough, R. (1989) *Groups and Groupings: Life and Work in Day and Residential Centres*. London and New York, Tavistock/Routledge.

Brown, S. and Knight, P. (1994) *Assessing Learners in Higher Education*. London, Kogan Page.

Brown, A. and Mistry, T. (1994) Groupwork with 'mixed membership' groups: issues of race and gender, Social Work With Groups, 17, 5–23.

Burgess, H. (1992) *Problem-Led Learning for Social Work: The Enquiry and Action Learning Approach*. London, Whiting and Birch.

Butler, L. (1993) The assessment of prior learning: relating experience, competence and knowledge. In J. Calder (ed.) *Disaffection and Diversity: Overcoming Barriers for Adult Learners*. London, Falmer.

Calderhead, J. and Gates, P. (1993) Introduction. In J. Calderhead and P. Gates (eds) *Conceptualising Reflection in Teacher Development*. London, Falmer Press.

Candy, P. (1987) Evolution, revolution or devolution: increasing learner control in the instructional setting. In D. Boud and V. R. Griffin (eds) *Appreciating Adults Learning: From the Learner's Perspective*. London, Kogan Page.

Candy, P. (1991) *Self-Direction for Life-Long Learning: A Comprehensive Guide to Theory and Practice*. San Francisco, Jossey-Bass.

Carpenter, J. and Hewstone, M. (1996) Shared learning for doctors and social workers: evaluation of a programme, *British Journal of Social Work*, 26, 239–57.

Central Council for Education and Training in Social Work (CCETSW) (1989) *Requirements and Regulations for the Diploma in Social Work*, Paper 30. London, CCETSW.

Central Council for Education and Training in Social Work (CCETSW) (1995) *Assuring Quality in the Diploma in Social Work – 1, Rules and Requirements for the Diploma in Social Work*. London, CCETSW.

Central Council for Education and Training in Social Work (CCETSW) (1996) *A Report for Social Work Educators: Developing shared learning with medical students and general practitioners*. London, CCETSW.

Challis, D., Fuller, S., Henwood, M., Klein R., Plowden, W. and Webb, A. (1988) *Joint Approaches to Social Policy, Rationality and Practice*. Cambridge, Cambridge University Press.

Chodorow, N. (1978) *The Reproduction of Mothering*. Berkeley, University of California Press.

Cleveland Report (1988) *Report of the Inquiry into Child Abuse in Cleveland* (Chair: Justice Butler-Sloss). London, HMSO.

Coles, C. (1991) Is problem-based learning the only way? In D. Boud and G. Feletti (eds) *The Challenge of Problem-Based Learning*. London, Kogan Page.

Corlett, S. (1991) Deaf students in higher education in the United Kingdom, *European Journal of Special Needs Education*, 6(3), 219–30.

Cowan, J. (1988) Struggling with self-assessment. In D. Boud (ed.) *Developing Student Autonomy in Learning* (2nd edn). London, Kogan Page.

Davies, M. (1984) Training: what we think of it now, *Social Work Today*, 24 January, 12–17.

Davis, L. and Proctor, E. (1989) *Race, Gender and Class: Guidelines for Individuals, Families and Groups*. Englewood-Cliffs, NJ, Prentice-Hall.

Dehar, M., Casswell, S. and Duigan, P. (1993) Formative and process evaluation of health promotion and disease prevention programs, *Evaluation Review*, 17, 204–20.

Department of Health (1989) *Caring for People: Community Care in the Next Decade and Beyond*. London, HMSO.

Department of Health (1991) *Care Management and Assessment: Practitioners Guide*. London, HMSO.

Dominelli, L. (1996) Deprofessionalising social work: anti-oppressive practice, competencies and postmodernism, *British Journal of Social Work*, 2, 153–76.

Dowling, S., Martin, R., Skidmore, P., Doyal, L., Cameron, A. and Lloyd, S. (1996) Nurses taking on junior doctors' work: a confusion of accountability, *British Medical Journal*, 312, 1211–14.

Egerton, M. and Halsey, A. H. (1993) Trends in social class and gender in access to higher education, *Oxford Review of Higher Education*, 19, 183–94.

Eisner, E. W. (1993) Reshaping assessment in education: some criteria in search of practice, *Journal of Curriculum Studies*, 3, 219–33.

Elliott-Cannon, C. and Harbinson, S. (1995) *Building a Partnership: Co-operation to Promote Shared Learning in the Field of Learning Disability*. London, ENB/CCETSW.

Ellis, R. (1992) An action-focus curriculum for interpersonal professions. In R. Barnett (ed.) *Learning to Effect*. Buckingham, SRHE and Open University Press.

Elton, L. (1987) *Teaching in Higher Education: Appraisal and Training*. London, Kogan Page.

Elton, L. (1988) Student motivation and achievement, *Studies in Higher Education*, 13, 215–21.

Engel, C. E. (1991) Not just a method but a way of learning. In D. Boud and G. Feletti (eds) *The Challenge of Problem-Based Learning*. London, Kogan Page.

Engel, C. E. (1992) Problem-based learning, *British Journal of Hospital Medicine*, 46, 325–9.

Engel, C. E. and Clarke, R. M. (1979) Medical education with a difference, *Programmed Learning and Educational Technology*, 16, 72.

Entwistle, N. J. (1983) Learning and teaching in universities: the challenge of the part-time adult student, in *Part-time First Degree in Universities, Conference Report*, 8 March, London, Goldsmiths College.

Entwistle, N. J. and Ramsden, P. (1983) *Understanding Student Learning*. Beckenham, Croom Helm.

Eraut, M. (1985) Knowledge creation and knowledge use in professional contexts, *Studies in Higher Education*, 10, 117–32.

Eraut, M. (1992) Developing the knowledge base: a process perspective on professional education. In R. Barnett (ed.) *Learning to Effect*. Buckingham, SRHE and Open University Press.

Eraut, M. (1994) *Developing Professional Knowledge and Competence*. London, Falmer.

Eraut, M., Alderton, J., Boylan, A. and Wraight, A. (1995) *Learning to Use Scientific Knowledge in Education and Practice Settings: An Evaluation of the Contribution of Behavioural and Social Sciences to Pre-Registration Nursing and Midwifery Programmes*. London, English National Board for Nursing, Midwifery and Health Visiting.

Erikson, E. H. (1968) *Identity, Youth and Crisis*. New York, Norton and Co.

Etheridge, D. and Mason, H. (1994) *The Visually Impaired: Curricular Access and Entitlement in Further Education*. London, David Fulton.

Falchikov, N. (1986) Product comparisons and process benefits of collaborative peer group and self assessments, *Assessment and Evaluation in Higher Education*, 11(2), 185–200.

Ferrier, B. M., McAuley, M. D. and Roberts, R. S. (1978) Selection of Medical Students at McMaster University, *Journal of Royal College of Physicians*, 12, 365–78.

Ferrier, B. and Woodward, C. (1987) Career choices of McMaster medical graduates and contemporary Canadian medical graduates, *Canadian Medical Association Journal*, 136, 39–44.

Fisher, M. (1994) Partnership practice and empowerment. In L. Guterriez and P. Nurius (eds) *Education and Research for Empowerment Practice*. Seattle, University of Washington.

Fransson, R. (1977) On qualitative differences in learning: IV – Effects of intrinsic motivation and extrinsic test anxiety on process and outcome, *British Journal of Educational Psychology*, 47, 244–57.

Freire, P. (1981) *Pedagogy of the Oppressed* (2nd edn). New York, Herder and Herder.

Freud, S. (1988) *My Three Mothers and Other Passions*. New York, New York University Press.

Fulton, O. and Ellwood, S. (1989) Admissions, access and institutional change. In O. Fulton (ed.) *Access and Institutional Change*. Buckingham, SRHE and Open University Press.

Gadamer, H-G. (1992) *Truth and Method* (J. Weinsheimer and D. G. Marshall trans.) (2nd edn). New York, Crossroads Publishing.

Garvin, C. and Reed, B. (eds) (1983) Groupwork with women/groupwork with men. Special issue of *Social Work with Groups*, 6.

General Medical Council (1993) *Tomorrow's Doctors: Recommendations on Undergraduate Medical Education*. London, Education Committee of the General Medical Council.

Gibbs, G. (1981) *Teaching Students to Learn: A Student Centred Approach*. Buckingham, Open University Press.

Gibbs, G. (1992) Improving the quality of student learning through course design. In R. Barnett (ed.) *Learning to Effect*. Buckingham, SRHE and Open University Press.

Gibbs, G. and Jenkins, A. (1992) *Teaching Large Classes in Higher Education*. London, Kogan Page.

Gilligan, C. (1982) *In a Different Voice: Psychological Theory and Women's Development*. Cambridge, Harvard University Press.

Gonczi, A. (1994) Competency based assessment in the professions in Australia, *Assessment in Education*, 1, 27–44.

Goodlad, S. (1984) Introduction to education for the professions. In S. Goodlad (ed.) *Education for the Professions. Quid Custodiet?* Guildford, SRHE and NFER-Nelson.

Gould, N. (1996) Introduction: social work education and the 'crisis of the professions'. In N. Gould and I. Taylor (eds) *Reflective Learning for Social Work: Research, Theory and Practice*. Aldershot, Arena.

Gould, N. and Harris, A. (1996) Student imagery in social work and teacher education: a comparative research approach, *British Journal of Social Work*, 26, 223–38.

Gould, N. and Taylor, I. (eds) (1996) *Reflective Learning for Social Work: Research, Theory and Practice*. Aldershot, Arena.

Griffiths Report (1987) *Community Care: An Agenda for Action*. London, HMSO.

Gwele, N. (1996) Experiential learning in action: A programme for preparing educators of health professionals. Conference paper presented at Reconstruction and Development: Experiential Learning in a Global Context, University of Cape Town.

Hallett, C. and Birchall, E. (1992) *Co-ordination and Child Protection: A Review of the Literature*. London, HMSO.

Halsey, A. H. (1993) Trends in access and equity in higher education: Britain in an international perspective, *Oxford Review of Education*, 19, 129–40.

Hammond, M. and Collins, R. (1991) *Self-Directed Learning: Critical Practice*. London, Kogan Page.

Harrison, C. and Beresford, P. (1994) Using Users, *Community Care*, 24 March.

Harrison, M. J. (1990) Access: the problem and the potential, *Higher Education Quarterly*, 44, 193–214.

Haspelagh, P. C. and Jemison, D. B. (1991) *Managing Acquisitions: Creating Value Through Corporate Renewal*. New York, Free Press.

Heron, J. (1988) Assessment revisited. In D. Boud (ed.) *Developing Student Autonomy in Learning*. London, Kogan Page.

Heron J. (1989) *The Facilitators' Handbook*. London, Kogan Page.

Hopton, J. (1994/1995) User involvement in the education of mental health nurses: an evaluation of possibilities, *Critical Social Policy*, 42, 47–60.

Houle, C. (1994) Overview of continuing professional education. In S. Goodlad (ed.) *Education for the Professions. Quid Custodiet?* Guildford, SRHE and NFER-Nelson.

Hounsell, D. (1987) Essay writing and the quality of feedback. In J. T. E. Richardson, M. E. Eysenck and D. W. Piper (eds) *Student Learning*. Buckingham, SRHE and Open University Press.

Hudson, B. (1987) Collaboration in social welfare: a framework for analysis, *Policy and Politics*, 15(3), 175–182.

Hugman, R. (1991) *Power in the Caring Professions*. London, Macmillan.

James, P. and Thomas, M. (1996) Deconstructing a disabling environment in social work education, *Social Work Education*, 15(1), 34–45.

Jaques, D. (1984) *Learning in Groups*. London, Croom Helm.

Jaques, D. (1992) *Learning in Groups*, 2nd edn. London, Croom Helm.

Jarvis, P. (1983) *Professional Education.* London, Croom Helm.

Jarvis, P. (1987) *Adult Learning in the Social Context.* London, Croom Helm.

Jarvis, P. (1993) *Adult Education and the State: Towards a Politics of Adult Education.* London, Routledge.

Johnson, K. (1988) Changing teacher's conceptions of teaching and learning. In J. Calderhead (ed.) *Teachers' Professional Learning.* Lewes, Falmer.

Johnston, R. and Usher, R. (1996) 'Adult learning and critical practices: towards a retheorisation of experience'. Conference paper presented at Reconstruction and Development: Experiential Learning in a Global Context, University of Cape Town.

Kelly, D. and Wykurz, G. (1996) 'Affecting change through an experiential approach to medical education'. Conference workshop presented at Reconstruction and Development: Experiential Learning in a Global Context, University of Cape Town.

Knowles, M. (1973) *The Adult Learner: A Neglected Species.* Houston, Gulf.

Knowles, M. (1980) *The Modern Practice of Adult Education: From Pedagogy to Andragogy.* Chicago, Follett.

Knowles, M. and associates (1984) *Andragogy in Action.* San Francisco, Jossey-Bass.

Leathard, A. (ed.) (1994) *Going Inter-Professional: Working Together for Health and Welfare.* London, Routledge.

Lindow, V. (1995) Power and rights: the psychiatric system survivor movement. In R. Jack (ed.) *Empowerment and Community Care.* London, Chapman Hall.

Low, J. (1996) Negotiating identities, negotiating environments: an interpretation of the experiences of students with disabilities, *Disability and Society,* 11, 235–48.

Lucas, S. and Ward, P. (1985) Mature students at Lancaster University, *Adult Education,* 58, 222–6.

Margetson, D. (1991) Why is problem-based learning a challenge? In D. Boud and G. Feletti (eds) *The Challenge of Problem-Based Learning.* London, Kogan Page.

Marton, F. and Saljo, R. (1976) On qualitative differences in learning, *British Journal of Educational Psychology,* 46, 4–11.

McAuley, R. G. and Woodward, C. W. (1984) Faculty perceptions of the McMaster M.D. progam, *Journal of Medical Education,* 59, 842–3.

McMaster University (1989/90) *Letter to applicants from Year 2 Students.* McMaster, Faculty of Health Science.

Merriam, S. B. and Caffarella, R. S. (1991) *Learning in Adulthood: A Comprehensive Guide.* San Francisco, Jossey-Bass.

Mezirow, J. (1983) A critical theory of adult learning and education. In M. Tight (ed.) *Adult Learning and Education: A Reader.* London, Croom Helm and Open University Press.

Mezirow, J. (1990) *Fostering Critical Reflection in Adulthood: A Guide to Transformative and Emancipatory Learning.* San Francisco, Jossey-Bass.

Miller, J. B. (1976) *Towards a New Psychology of Women* (2nd edn). Boston, Beacon Press.

Miller, C. M. L. and Parlett, M. (1974) *Up to the Mark: A Study of the Examination Game.* London, SRHE.

Millins, K. (1984) *Report on Access Courses.* London, Department of Education and Science.

Mills, A. J. and Molloy, S. T. (1989) Experiencing the experienced: the impact of non-standard entrants upon a programme of higher education, *Studies in Higher Education,* 14, 41–53.

Mirza, H. (1992) Young, Female and Black. London, Routledge.

Modood, T. (1993) The number of ethnic minority students in British Higher Education: some grounds for optimism, *Oxford Review of Education*, 19, 167–82.

Mullender, A. and Ward, D. (1991) *Self-Directed Groupwork: Users take Action for Empowerment.* London, Whiting and Birch.

Neufeld, V. R. and Barrows, H. S. (1974) The 'McMaster Philosophy': An approach to medical education, *Journal of Medical Education*, 49, 1040–50.

Neufeld, V. R. and Chong, J. P. (1984) Problem-based education in medicine. In S. Goodlad (ed.) *Education for the Professions.* Quid Custodiet? Guildford, SRHE and NFER-Nelson.

Øvretveit, J. (1993) *Co-ordinating Community Care: Mulitdisciplinary Teams and Care Management in Health and Social Services.* Buckingham, Open University Press.

Øvretveit, J. (1995) Team decision making, *Journal of Interprofessional Care*, 9(1), 41–52.

Palmer, A., Burns, S. and Bulman, C. (eds) (1994) *Reflective Practice in Nursing: The Growth of the Professional Practitioner.* London, Blackwell Scientific.

Papell, C. and Rothman, B. (1980) Relating the mainstream model of social work with groups to group psychotherapy and the structured group, *Social Work with Groups*, 3(2), 5–23.

Parker, J. C. and Rubin, I. J. (1966) *Process as Content: Curriculum Design and the Application of Knowledge.* Chicago, Rand McNally.

Parlett, M. and Hamilton, D. (1972) *Evaluation as Illumination: A New Approach to the Study of Innovatory Programmes.* University of Edinburgh, Centre for Research in Educational Sciences.

Parry, G. (1989) Marking and mediating the higher education boundary. In O. Fulton (ed.) *Access and Institutional Change.* Buckingham, SRHE and Open University Press.

Parton, N. (1994) The nature of social work under conditions of (post) modernity, *Social Work and Social Sciences Review*, 5, 93–112.

Patton, M. Q. (1986) *Utilisation-Focused Evaluation.* London, Sage.

Percy, K. (1985) Adult learners in higher education. In C. Titmus (ed.) *Widening the Field: Continuing Education in Higher Education.* Guildford, SRHE and NFER-Nelson.

Perry, W. (1970) *Forms of Intellectual and Ethical Development in College Years.* New York, Holt, Rinehart and Winston.

Pettman, J. J. (1991) Towards a (personal) politics of location, *Studies in Continuing Education*, 13(2), 153–66.

Phillips, R., Stalker, K. and Baron, S. (1995) *Barriers to Training for Disabled Social Work Students: A Study in the Tayforth Area.* Stirling, University of Stirling, Department of Applied Social Sciences.

Pietroni, M. (1995) The nature and aims of professional education for social workers: a postmodern perspective. In M. Yelloly and M. Henkel (eds), *Learning and Teaching in Social Work: Towards Reflective Practice.* London, Kingsley.

Pye, J. (1991) *Second Chances: Adults Returning to Education.* Oxford, Oxford University Press.

Ramsden, P. (1987) Improving teaching and learning in higher education: the case for a relational perspective, *Studies in Higher Education*, 12, 275–86.

Ramsden, P. (1992) *Learning to Teach in Higher Education.* London, Routledge.

Reitsma-Street, M. and Arnold, R. (1994) Community based action research in a multi-site prevention project: challenges and resolutions, *Canadian Journal of Mental Health*, 13, 229–40.

Rich, A. (1977) Conditions for work: the common world of women. In S. Ruddick and P. Daniels (eds) *Working It Out.* New York, Pantheon.

Rich, A. (1986) *Blood, Bread and Poetry: Selected Prose 1979–86.* New York, Norton.

Richardson, J. T. E. (1994) Mature students in higher education: a literature survey on approaches to studying, *Studies in Higher Education,* 19, 309–25.

Robertson, D. (1992) Courses, qualifications and the empowerment of learners. In *Higher Education, Expansion and Reform.* London, Institute of Public Policy Research.

Rogers, C. (1969) *Freedom to Learn: A View of What Education Might Become.* Columbus, Charles Merrill.

Rosen, V. (1993) Black students in higher education. In M. Thorpe, R. Edwards, and A. Hanson (eds) *Culture and Processes of Adult Learning.* London, Routledge and Open University Press.

Rossiter, A. (1996) Finding meaning for social work in transitional times: reflections on change. In N. Gould and I. Taylor (eds) *Reflective Learning for Social Work: Research, Theory and Practice.* Aldershot, Arena.

Rowntree, D. (1987) *Assessing Students: How Shall We Know Them?* (2nd edn). London, Harper and Row.

Russel, R., Gill, P., Coyne, A. and Woody, J. (1993) Dysfunction in the family of origin of MSW and other graduate students, *Journal of Social Work Education,* 29, 121–9.

Salzberger-Wittenberg, I., Henry, G. and Osborne, E. (1983) *The Emotional Experience of Teaching and Learning.* London, Routledge & Kegan Paul.

Schön, D. (1983) *The Reflective Practitioner.* London, Temple Smith.

Schön, D. A. (1987) *Educating the Reflective Practitioner: Towards a New Design for Teaching and Learning in the Professions.* San Francisco, Jossey-Bass.

Scriven, M. (1967) The methodology of evaluation. In R. W. Tyler *et al.* (eds) *Perspectives on Curriculum Change.* Chicago, Rand McNally.

Shardlow, S. and Doel, M. (1996) *Practice Learning and Teaching.* London, BASW Macmillan.

Smith, D. L. and Hatton, N. (1993) Reflection in teacher education: a study in progress, *Educational Research and Perspectives,* 20(1), 13–23.

Smith, R., Gaster, L., Harrison, L., Martin, L., Means, R. and Thistlethwaite, P. (1993) *Working Together for Better Community Care.* Bristol, School for Advanced Urban Studies.

Snyder, B. (1971) *The Hidden Curriculum.* New York, Alfred Knopf.

Social Services Inspectorate (SSI) (1994) *Users' Views on Training for Community Care.* London, SSI.

Soothill, K., Mackay, L. and Webb, C. (eds) (1995) *Interprofessional Relations in Health Care.* London, Edward Arnold.

Stefani, L. A. J. (1994) Self, peer and group assessment procedures. In I. Sneddon and J. Kremer (eds) *An Enterprising Curriculum: Teaching Innovations in Higher Education.* Belfast, HMSO.

Stephenson, J. (1988) The experience of independent study at North-East London Polytechnic. In D. Boud (ed.) *Developing Student Autonomy in Learning* (2nd edn). London, Kogan Page.

Tann, S. (1993) Eliciting student teachers' personal theories. In J. Calderhead and P. Gates (eds) *Conceptualising Reflection in Teacher Development.* London, Falmer.

Taylor, G. (1996) A sense of real achievement? The experience of deaf students in social work and youth and community work training, *Social Work Education,* 15(1), 46–74.

Taylor, I. (1993) A case for social work evaluation of social work education, *British Journal of Social Work*, 23, 123–38.

Taylor, I. and Burgess, H. (1995) Orientation to self-directed learning: paradox or paradigm? *Studies in Higher Education*, 1, 87–98.

Taylor, M. (1986) Learning for self-direction in the classroom: the pattern of a transition process, *Studies in Higher Education*, 11, 56–72.

Thompson, N. (1995) *Theory and Practice in Health and Social Welfare*. Buckingham, Open University Press.

Tickle, L. (1994) *The Induction of New Teachers: Reflective Professional Practice*. London, Cassell.

Tight, M. (1993) Access, not access courses: maintaining a broad vision. In R. Edwards, S. Sieminski and D. Zeldin (eds) *Adult Learners: Education and Training*. London, Routledge and Open University Press.

Usher, R. (1985) Beyond the anecdote: adult learning and the use of experience, *Studies in the Education of Adults*, 17(1), 59–74.

Usher, R. (1989) Qualifications, paradigms and experiential learning in higher education. In O. Fulton (ed.) *Access and Institutional Change*. Buckingham, SRHE and Open University Press.

Usher, R. (1993) Experiential learning or learning from experience? Does it make a difference? In D. Boud, R. Cohen and D. Walker (eds) *Using Experience for Learning*. Buckingham, SRHE and Open University Press.

Usher, R. and Bryant, I. (1987) Re-examining the theory-practice relationship in continuing professional education, *Studies in Higher Education*, 12, 201–12.

Usher, R. and Bryant, I. (1989) *Adult Education in Theory, Practice and Research: The Captive Triangle*. London, Routledge.

Wakeford, N. (1993) Beyond educating Rita: mature students and access courses, *Oxford Review of Education*, 19, 217–30.

Walby, S., Greenwell, J., Mackay, L. and Soothill, K. (1994) *Medicine and Nursing: Professions in a Changing Health Service*. London, Sage.

Watson, D. (1992) The changing shape of professional education. In H. Bines and D. Watson *Developing Professional Education*. Buckingham, SRHE and Open University Press.

Weil, S. (1986) Non-traditional learners within higher education institutions: discovery and disappointment, *Studies in Higher Education*, 11, 219–35.

Weil, S. (1988) From a language of observation to a language of experience: studying the perspectives of diverse adults in higher education, *Journal of Access Studies*, 3(1), 17–43.

Weil, S. (1989) Access: towards education or miseducation? Adults imagine the future. In O. Fulton (ed.) *Access and Institutional Change*. Buckingham, SRHE and Open University Press.

Weil, S. (1992) Creating capability for change in higher education. In R. Barnett (ed.) *Learning to Effect*. Buckingham, SRHE and Open University Press.

Weinstein, J. (1994) *Sewing the Seams for a Seamless Service: A Review of Developments in Interprofessional Education and Training*. London, CCETSW.

Weis, L. (1985) *Between Two Worlds: Black Students in an Urban Community College*. London, Routledge.

Woodley, A., Wagner, L., Slowey, M., Hamilton M. and Fulton, O. *et al.* (1987) *Choosing to Learn: Adults in Higher Education*. Buckingham, SRHE and Open University Press.

Woodward, C. A. (1989) The effects of the innovations in medical education at McMaster: a report on follow-up studies, *Meducs*, 2, 64–8.

Woodward, C. A. and Ferrier, B. M. (1982) Career development of McMaster Medical University medical graduates and its implications for Canadian medical manpower, *Canadian Medical Association Journal*, 15, 477–80.

Woodward, C. A. and Ferrier, B. M. (1983) The content of the medical curriculum at McMaster University: graduates evaluation of their preparation for postgraduate training, *Medical Education*, 17, 54–60.

Wright, P. (1991) Access or accessibility? *Journal of Access Studies*, 6(1), 6–15.

Young, M. (1971) *Knowledge and Control*. London, Macmillan.

World Health Organization (WHO) (1984) Glossary of Terms Used in '*Health for All*' *Series No. 1–8*. Geneva, World Health Organization.

Index

The Society for Research into Higher Education

The Society for Research into Higher Education exists to stimulate and coordinate research into all aspects of higher education. It aims to improve the quality of higher education through the encouragement of debate and publication on issues of policy, on the organization and management of higher education institutions, and on the curriculum and teaching methods.

The Society's income is derived from subscriptions, sales of its books and journals, conference fees and grants. It receives no subsidies, and is wholly independent. Its individual members include teachers, researchers, managers and students. Its corporate members are institutions of higher education, research institutes, professional, industrial and governmental bodies. Members are not only from the UK, but from elsewhere in Europe, from America, Canada and Australasia, and it regards its international work as among its most important activities.

Under the imprint *SRHE & Open University Press*, the Society is a specialist publisher of research, having over 70 titles in print. The Editorial Board of the Society's Imprint seeks authoritative research or study in the above fields. It offers competitive royalties, a highly recognizable format in both hardback and paperback and the worldwide reputation of the Open University Press.

The Society also publishes *Studies in Higher Education* (three times a year), which is mainly concerned with academic issues, *Higher Education Quarterly* (formerly *Universities Quarterly*), mainly concerned with policy issues, *Research into Higher Education Abstracts* (three times a year), and *SRHE News* (four times a year).

The Society holds a major annual conference in December, jointly with an institution of higher education. In 1994 the topic was 'The Student Experience' at the University of York. In 1995 it was 'The Changing University' at Heriot-Watt University in Edinburgh and in 1996, 'Working in Higher Education' at University of Wales, Cardiff. The 1997 Annual Conference is entitled 'Beyond the First Degree' at the University of Warwick.

The Society's committees, study groups and networks are run by the members. The networks at present include:

Access	Vocational Qualifications
Eastern European	Postgraduate
Funding	Quality
Mentoring	Student Development

Benefits to members

Individual

Individual members receive:

- *SRHE News*, the Society's publications list, conference details and other material included in mailings.
- Greatly reduced rates for *Studies in Higher Education* and *Higher Education Quarterly*.
- A 35 per cent discount on all SRHE & Open University Press publications.
- Free copies of the Proceedings – commissioned papers on the theme of the Annual conference.
- Free copies of *Research into Higher Education Abstracts*.
- Reduced rates for conferences.
- Extensive contacts and scope for facilitating initiatives.
- Reduced reciprocal memberships.
- Free copies of the *Register of Members' Research Interests*.

Corporate

Corporate members receive:

- All benefits of individual members, plus.
- Free copies of *Studies in Higher Education*.
- Unlimited copies of the Society's publications at reduced rates.
- Special rates for its members e.g. to the Annual Conference.
- The right to submit application for the Society's research grants.

Membership details: SRHE, 3 Devonshire Street, London
W1N 2BA, UK. Tel: 0171 637 2766. Fax: 0171 637 2781.
email: srhe@mailbox1.ulcc.ac.uk
World Wide Web: http://www.srhe.ac.uk./srhe/
Catalogue: SRHE & Open University Press, Celtic Court,
22 Ballmoor, Buckingham MK18 IXW. Tel: 01280 823388.
Fax: 01280 823233. email: enquiries@openup.co.uk

DEVELOPING PROFESSIONAL EDUCATION

Hazel Bines and David Watson

Institutions of higher education are currently having to react speedily and creatively to a range of demands connected with education for intending and already qualified professionals. In addition to traditional requirements for continuous professional development and updating, there is a growing awareness of skills needs, interprofessional cooperation, and innovative learning styles. This volume examines the context, development and management of a portfolio of professional courses. It draws on a number of practical case studies from one institution, Oxford Polytechnic, and emphasizes the necessity of a planned institutional framework including an overarching strategy for professional education. The overall design of the book identifies key issues and objectives and shows in practical ways how institutions can act to meet them. It should be of interest to those involved in the development and management of professional courses at both the course and departmental/institutional levels, as well as to others with a broad interest in issues of professional practice.

> I am sure it will prove of value to all parties involved in the vital task of developing professional education.
>
> (Sir Bryan Nicholson)

Contents

The changing shape of professional education – Issues in course design – Course delivery and assessment – Management issues – Interprofessionalism – The future: problems and prospects – Appendix – Index

192pp   0 335 09710 3 (Paperback)   0 335 09711 1 (Hardback)

USING EXPERIENCE FOR LEARNING

David Boud, Ruth Cohen and David Walker (eds)

This book is about the struggle to make sense of learning from experience. What are the key ideas that underpin learning from experience? How do we learn from experience? How does context and purpose influence learning? How does experience impact on individual and group learning? How can we help others to learn from their experience?

Using Experience for Learning reflects current interest in the importance of experience in informal and formal learning, whether it be applied for course credit, new forms of learning in the workplace, or acknowledging autonomous learning outside educational institutions. It also emphasizes the role of personal experience in learning: ideas are not separate from experience; relationships and personal interests impact on learning; and emotions have a vital part to play in intellectual learning. All the contributors write themselves into their chapters, giving an autobiographical account of how their experiences have influenced their learning and what has led them to their current views and practice.

Using Experience for Learning brings together a wide range of perspectives and conceptual frameworks with contributors from four continents, and is a valuable addition to the field of experiential learning.

Contents

Introduction: understanding learning from experience – Part 1: Introduction – Through the lens of learning: how the visceral experience of learning reframes teaching – Putting the heart back into learning – Activating internal processes in experiential learning – On becoming a maker of teachers: journey down a long hall of mirrors – Part 2: Introduction – Barriers to reflection on experience – Unlearning through experience – Experiential learning at a distance – Learning from experience in mathematics – Part 3: Introduction – How the T-Group changed my life: a sociological perspective on experiential group work – Living the learning: internalizing our model of group learning – Experiential learning and social transformation for a post-apartheid learning future – Experiential learning or learning from experience: does it make a difference? – Index.

Contributors

Lee Andresen, David Boud, Angela Brew, Stephen Brookfield, Ruth Cohen, Costas Criticos, Kathleen Dechant, Elizabeth Kasl, Victoria Marsick, John Mason, Nod Miller, John Mulligan, Denis Postle, Mary Thorpe, Robin Usher, David Walker.

208pp   0 335 19095 2 (Paperback)